Praise for *Screwnomics**

"A timely critique, and needed story. Masculinity's measure by money is not only ludicrous, it's getting downright dangerous."
—Nomi Prins, former managing director at Goldman Sachs and author of *All the Presidents' Bankers: The Hidden Alliances that Drive American Power* and *It Takes a Pillage: An Epic Tale of Power, Deceit, and Untold Trillions*

"*Screwnomics* tells it as it is—and shows that it does not have to be this way. We *can* build a more humane economy . . ."
—Riane Eisler, author of *The Real Wealth of Nations: Creating a Caring Economics* and *The Chalice and the Blade: Our History, Our Future*

"Important work—may there be many more women's voices in economics! And long may the existing work of women economists be acknowledged in this way."
—Jane Gleeson-White, author of *Double Entry: How the Merchants of Venice Created Modern Finance* and *Six Capitals: or Can Accountants Save the Planet?*

"A hopeful book that shows changes are not only possible but necessary, and are already happening where women have a say."
—Les Leopold, executive director of The Labor Institute and author of *Runaway Inequality*

"This smart and brave new book is not only educational and insightful but damn fun reading. In this #metoo time, it could not be more timely."
—Bronwyn Fryer, author and former senior editor at *Harvard Business Review*

"Banking in the public interest is only one of Diamond's topics, but its implications are huge—especially for small businesses, where women's numbers are growing."
—Ellen Brown, founder of the Public Banking Institute, fellow at the Democracy Collaborative, and author of *Web of Debt* and *The Public Banking Solution*

"We so much *need* this kind of book. I'm sending this to members of my old 1970s collective, Men Against Patriarchy; there will be rejoicing."
—George Lakey, author of *Viking Economics: How the Scandinavians Got it Right and How We Can Too*

"Everyone can learn something from *Screwnomics*. It takes apart our economic assumptions and practices, piece by painful piece, to show underlying bias and inequity. It also gives us tools . . . for learning conversations."
—Gwendolyn Hallsmith, author of *Creating Wealth: Growing Local Economies with Local Currencies* and *LASER: Local Action for Sustainable Economic Renewal*

"Rickey Gard Diamond's life experience provides clear guidance. . . . Required reading for achieving full gender equality and human rights!"
—Hazel Henderson, author of *Creating Alternative Futures: The End of Economics* and *Ethical Markets: Growing the Green Economy*

* *Screwnomics* is the unspoken but widely applied economic theory that women, including Mother Earth, should always work for less, or better, for free

Screwnomics*

How Our Economy Works

Against Women and Real Ways

to Make Lasting Change

Rickey Gard Diamond

Illustrations by Peaco Todd

*The economic theory that women should always work for less, or better, for free

SHE WRITES PRESS

Published April 3, 2018
Printed in the United States of America
Print ISBN: 978-1-63152-318-2
E-ISBN: 978-1-63152-319-9
Library of Congress Control Number: 2017958163

For information, address:
She Writes Press
1563 Solano Ave #546
Berkeley, CA 94707

Interior design by Tabitha Lahr

She Writes Press is a division of SparkPoint Studio, LLC.

For my grandchildren and yours,
and Gaia's too.

CONTENTS

PART III. HIS STORY OF WOMAN: *Females Are for Sex and Food—Or Else*

PART IV. HIS EMBODIED FICTIONS: *Collective Bodies of Nations, Corporations, and Labor Must Always Perform as Men at War*

PART V. BANKS AND BIG FIXES: *Systemic Financial Changes for Widespread Prosperity*

Introduction

The personal is political. The personal is economic.

Screwnomics is a book for women like you, who until now have wisely avoided a dismal subject. You'd like to know more about economics, if only to hold on to more money, but something has warned you off, like a frat house late at night: hazing, secret clubs with creepy names, hoarding private privileges, taking advantage, scoring girls.

Oh, it's true. My mother wouldn't like my title for this book, but it's better than what she called the *f-word*. In her day the economic frat house wasn't so corrupt as it is today—not so in-your-face f**k *you!*—or so fast and desperately dangerous. Still the sexual messaging behind money has long been consistent and routine.

Screwnomics isn't intended to help you manage your personal finances, but it will explain the larger assumptions of a system that makes managing impossible for so many. *Screwnomics* is my word for the unspoken but widely applied economic theory that women should always work for less, or better, for free. But why? Where did this come from?

Inside I translate economic history, terms, and definitions that especially disadvantage women, here and around the world. I introduce you to new, countering ideas and solutions that don't require a PhD, and may even inspire you to broach an economic subject with your friends.

As designed now, economic theory devalues family, love, young children, music and art, nature's splendiferous beauty, and the faithful devotions, the loyal commitments, that make any life worthwhile. A glut of fiscal verbiage can put you to sleep, or convince you it's too hard to comprehend or too boring. Yet its rules have made money the central story of our time. Our current economic ideas threaten to blot out any tale but that single one, as if money were all that mattered.

You know that isn't true. You may try to ignore money's constant murmur around you, but letting yourself doze off is as dangerous as sleeping with a huge python in the house. Only when a greater number of women understand economic secrets, muffled by slithery language, will we find the political will to transform them.

What sort of story can I tell to keep your attention? Over my lifetime, I've witnessed a vast drama of changing roles, expectations, and economic ideas, so along with the definitions, history, and experts unpacked in this book, I include shameful tales, insulting metaphors, and my family's dirty laundry. However different, all these elements carry a common thread of women confronting an ultra-masculine, ultra-rational mindset, the social construct of our time that I call *EconoMan*.

Screwnomics could be called economic porn because this book will show you how a growing number of us, whatever our gender, are being royally f***ed by EconoMan—but invisibly, mysteriously. We have lots of uncomfortable feelings about this and less time to think about it. Still stuck in an economic recovery unrecovered by most, we no longer believe in the American Dream, any more than we do in Superman flying to the rescue of "truth, justice, and the American way." If the economy were always part of the American way, then when exactly did it become the only way, with truth and justice fallen aside?

In the broadest sense, my premise is that economics, as a science analyzing mathematical market forces, has produced a systemic injustice and the justification for it. I am hardly alone in this assertion. I draw on economists and monetary thinkers whose work calls dominant fiscal assumptions into question—as did the Occupy Wall Street movement, claiming a voice for the 99 percent, and as did the Tea Party and Black Lives Matter and Standing Rock Water Protectors in recent elections. Perhaps now we can even talk of the female half of the 99 percent. We can look at the role of gender, that other most personal of subjects in the sorting-out process of the haves and have-nots.

In that sense within the world of money, the word *female* most often refers to being more motivated by love, nature, beauty, and family commitment than by ambition for power. That makes you girly—a negative—whatever your gender or sexual preference. In a similar sense, the word *political*, as I use it here, does not relate to party affiliation. I use it to mean the dynamics of power and authority, and who gets to decide how our collective power is defined and distributed, and for what end.

By now I've had the luxury of reporting, teaching, and thinking about the subject of women and the economy for over thirty years. But the history of women and money is much longer, and I include it in *Screwnomics* because it is not widely known, and it matters. Around the world, women and their children remain the poorest of the poor, the most vulnerable, and the least noteworthy to most economists. For example, Thomas Piketty's recent and much celebrated seven-hundred-plus-page work, *Capital in the Twenty-First Century*, which so expertly describes growing inequality, has exactly seven index listings for women or females.

Women are at the center of this book. I have interwoven my personal story with women's history and the economic principles I've learned about while working as a novelist, journalist, and professor. Generally we aren't encouraged to connect our personal stories with the effects of an economic and monetary system—everyone knows the economy isn't personal, right? But I know that, like me, you also have a money story. I hope you will find it easier to claim, reading mine.

"The personal is political," wrote feminist Carol Hanisch in a 1969 essay of the same name. Soon women everywhere were talking together, setting off a second wave of the women's movement that changed forever women's exclusion from education, commerce, and public policy. The glass ceiling, still in place however, turns out is actually made of green paper. Women need to talk together about who pasted this in place.

You will find in *Screwnomics* some big questions and big fixes, many of which were asked and proposed by women early on, but especially after the '70s, a period when a growing number of women were becoming scholars—historians, economists, and monetary thinkers. Big fixes I include, such as public banking, redesigned businesses, expanded accounting methods, and new currencies to name a few, give me hope that transformation will happen when more women discover what's going on, and how real change is possible.

At the end of each chapter, I share a question to ask yourself and others to confront money taboos. I call these *EconoGirlfriend Conversation Starters*, hoping that you'll talk to friends about the very real economics you experience day to day. Why? When you hear other women's perspectives, when you laugh, confide, and compare notes, light gets shed on a dense subject, and warring thoughts grow friendlier.

Visualizing and laughing at absurdities helps us women reframe our economic lives, so I've included cartoons throughout, my jokes coming to life through the illustrations by my delightful colleague, cartoonist Peaco Todd. (You may even want to take your conversations further and get my *Screwnomics* workbook: *Where Can I Get Some Change?* at www.Screwnomics.com to use in group discussions, or to forward your personal study with resources on a topic you care about.)

When speaking about these issues publicly, I have delighted in calling myself an amateur economist. My husband fears for my reputation using that word, *amateur*, concerned that I'm not leaning in to claim my expertise, which is in fact considerable given all my failures. But when I look at the Greek root, *ama* for love, I think it exactly what I most seek to claim.

Economics is Greek to most of us, its language skewed to avoid all subjective experience and feelings, especially loving ones. So to my mind, unswerving devotion and even the erotic, or *Eros*—a term modern psychologists use to mean the sum of all our instincts for self-preservation— is exactly the change in purpose our economy most needs to make it sexier and more inclusive.

Screwnomics may not help you to love economics, but ideally you may come to love some new possibility you see for your future, some real change that could make a difference where you live.

Up to now, the stars of the nation's preferred economic movie have been male, whether political cowboys like Franklin Delano Roosevelt and Ronald Reagan, or learned professors like Adam Smith and Alfred Marshall. However the economy has been defined, by whatever school of economic thought, we women have not owned it.

Not yet. So this book is for the bit players, you and me, who only keep the whole show going, making sure everyone eats and has clean socks.

©Peaco Todd & Rickey Gard Diamond, 2017

PART I

NO-WOMAN'S LAND

Economic Thinking for Men Only

Chapter 1: Talking Dirty about Dirty Secrets

The bargain of women's work comes cheap, while other prices inflate and go up.

Dressed in my business suit and new earrings, embarrassed and tentative, I take a seat in my local Michigan welfare office waiting room. It is 1979, and my shock at being here at all is met by a greater surprise in the eyes of other waiting faces, darker than mine and with eyes sadder than mine. I'm ashamed of how well off I must look, dressed in earrings and business suit, sticking out in the company of those darker mothers in T-shirts surrounded by young children—but also by how well I am treated by the all-white social workers. They rush me into a private meeting room, leaving those who have been waiting, waiting.

Race prejudice does play an important role in poverty, but I am not in the minority nation-wide, as I would later learn. The greatest numbers of poor in the United States are white like me and are often working single moms. Blacks and Hispanics are poor at more than twice the rate as white people, however, just as women are more likely to be poor than men. Unmarried women with children are among the poorest, women of color in that situation the most likely to be extremely poor. From 2000 to 2012, poverty grew from 33.3 million Americans to 48.8 million, and extreme poverty deepened, the latter a trend that began with welfare reform in 1996 and has deepened since, especially in city neighborhoods.

At the time, I didn't think monetary policy mattered to me or to those other moms in that office. I assumed my ignorance of the difference between macro- and microeconomics must mean that I shouldn't trouble my pretty little head. I was part of the economy but too busy working to think about something I mostly found intimidating.

I thought more about my own budget, scrawled out in pencil on a yellow pad, its numbers adding and subtracting but mostly subtracting. Despite working full-time, same as my ex-husband did, I couldn't make my budget work. I couldn't support my three children on my wages and child support of twenty-five dollars a week. I was scared and felt guilty. What was wrong with me?

Luckily for me, by the time I joined the company of the "low income," working women had begun to challenge economic divides. In 1982, for instance, I would learn that women as a group made fifty-nine cents on a man's dollar in the workplace. This helped explain my economic situation in a larger way than my personal failures. I began to see that some people's success was made harder, or even impossible. Eventually I would join others to make change, but that year I was on food stamps and welfare I only felt shame.

A Rising Standard

My hard initiation into the world of money made getting a college degree important. For women, but increasingly for everyone, college or specialized training is the only way out of financial dependency. I wouldn't have survived the demands of my work and school schedule on my tiny budget without my mother's grudging help with childcare and a gift of snow tires for that first post-divorce Christmas.

My mother herself had divorced not long after I was born in 1946. She quickly remarried and worked all her life, finally entering the middle class. With two incomes, she and my stepdad could move to the suburbs. They made real estate trade-ups and, reaching a level of comfort financially, had recently changed their politics.

Organized labor had set the job standard for my mom's generation. With only a high school education, she and my stepfather had won good wages, health insurance, overtime pay, weekends, paid vacations, and pensions. But now it seemed to them—and to my mother, especially—that unions demanded too much. Jimmy Hoffa and the Teamsters' ties with the Mafia left a bad taste in their mouth. She and my stepdad were voting for Ronald Reagan for president, not the union-endorsed Jimmy Carter.

People no longer knew what real work was, Mom often said. They'd gotten soft and expected an easy life. She cherished the notion that uppity college graduates often lacked common sense, and she liked the new Republican rhetoric about moochers and elitists too smart for their own good.

At the time, our rural southwest Michigan county, just up the coast of Lake Michigan from Chicago, was being sued by the NAACP in a class action suit for its practice of school segregation involving several municipalities. White flight from the once prosperous town of Benton Harbor where I was born had decimated jobs and property values in the 1960s and 1970s.

When I was young, my family had been part of that flight to a nearby town. We had seen our old neighborhoods and schools decay from neglect, poverty, and crime. My mother and stepfather believed this was the fault of the too lenient welfare programs and too lazy welfare families who didn't know how to work or take care of their things. What other choice did good white people like us have?

I had different and additional ideas, being more influenced by my Republican journalist father who bought me a copy of John F. Kennedy's *Profiles in Courage* for my sixteenth birthday, and who'd been moved by the speeches and marches of Martin Luther King, Jr. (Republicans and Democrats have changed since then.)

Before King was murdered in 1968, the civil rights leader said America had three deep, interwoven problems—race, poverty, and a growing militarism. He left out gender, but back then almost everyone did. Meanwhile, the Vietnam War that JFK had first financed was growling in the background.

Playing the Race Card

The country was divided in those days, as it is today, but party polarities would nearly reverse on race and the poor by the 1980s. Republicans came to play the race-hate card that had been played by the Dixie Democrats during the civil rights movement of the 1960s. The year I got food stamps, my newly Reagan-Republican mom posted a bumper sticker on her car that parodied the state's "water-wonderland" themed license plate. Michigan: The Welfare Wonderland, her car announced, whenever she pulled into her daughter's driveway.

I can't say whether she was consciously condemning me or perhaps was compensating, more ashamed than I was for my needing food stamps to feed my children, her grandchildren. I didn't have the courage to challenge her then; I didn't need another fight. My ex-married misery, my hope of starting again, was beside her economic point. In her view (and that of many Reagan idealists), marriage was a woman's one sure way to solvency, however lonely or abusive the relationship, whatever the color of her skin.

I was a woman of my generation, newly claiming liberation. I got my college degree, thanks to Pell grants and government-backed loans. I moved one thousand miles away to Vermont to earn a graduate degree while working in the War on Poverty there. The only African Americans I met were professors at the state university. Vermont's poor were as white as me and the long winter's snow.

Up until then, I had tended to ignore the scary language and numbers spoken by economists. I barely noticed that those who talked about what I didn't understand were nearly always men. I did see that millionaires and billionaires were nearly always men and those who ran the country were nearly always men, but it took me awhile to put all these men together.

Male Voice of Money

As the outspoken feminist Andrea Dworkin once put it, *Money speaks, but it speaks in a male voice.* I began to see it does matter very much that those who run our national economy and shape its fiscal policies serve a particular insider group of a particular class, of a particular race and gender. Three decades after my initial wake-up, economist Stephanie Seguino confirmed that the pattern I had first noticed in the political realm applied to economics as well. It is one of the dirty secrets this book is about. I had to invent a new word to more easily describe the ultra-masculine, ultra-rational mindset that has become a social construct of our times, the pale male voice of money and privilege: *EconoMan*.

With roots that go far back in history, EconoMan still celebrates king making with riches. During the day, his economic fraternity boys (and a few she-male impersonators) put on pressed and pleated suits of bloodless logic. But in their underwear and their attitudes, they still maintain a monkey boy relationship with "the female," competitively mounting whoever is smaller and less ruthless, dissing and name-calling each other *girly* or *pussy* or *bitch*—as if being female is a bad thing.

Economic secrets are most often out in the open, hidden right under our noses, when we don't speak the language. For that reason, I'll be introducing you to some of the language, not only through a glossary of common terms (see Appendix) but also in unpacked definitions set off with checkmarks, as below, throughout my chapters. These checked-off definitions go further than a glossary term might, looking at EconoMan language from a woman's point of view.

✓ ECONOMICS

The Greek historian Herodotus was the first man to define *oikonomia* about 2,400 years ago, in a time when the patriarch, the papa, had exclusive power to determine which infants born in his household to wives, slaves, and concubines would live or die. The Greek word, *oikos*, literally means dwelling or household, and *nomics* means management. In other words, if you keep a house or an apartment and eat now and then, you probably have already managed to become something of an economist.

✓ MACROECONOMICS

This is the Big Picture, concerned with the overall working of a national economy and its international relationships of public trade and development, as opposed to those of individual industries, firms, or households, the realm of *microeconomics*.

✓ MICROECONOMICS

This is the small stuff of daily life, its debits and credits, income and expenses in private businesses and households. Only cash flow, or the exchange of dollars, count here. All other trade-offs are invisible, except as something economists call opportunity costs, should you leave the job market or join it. Either way, you lose something. (We'll look more closely at these costs in Chapter 10.)

By the time I joined the War on Poverty in the 1980s, Lyndon Johnson's anti-poverty programs were under attack by our new president, Ronald Reagan. Every year, his proposed budget zeroed out funding to empower and organize the poor, substituting surplus cheese handouts for food stamps and legal aid, and installing a school lunch program that counted ketchup as a vegetable.

Vermont's anti-poverty agencies published a state newspaper, *The People's Voice*, and I became its editor, traveling Vermont to report on in detail the human impact of policy changes in a column for a central daily, *The Times Argus*. But I never broached Reagan's new ideas as economics, a realm that seemed over my head.

When George Herbert Walker Bush first ran against Reagan in the Republican primary, he called Reagan's ideas "voodoo economics." Yet political opinion on his ideas quickly reversed, and the real question is why. How did this transformation of public thought—veering from the need to have safety nets for the poor to cutting those nets and giving bigger tax cuts to the rich—happen so quickly, flying hand in hand with anti-government rhetoric?

Vermont's delegation resisted the change. We had Republican Senators Jim Jeffords and Robert Stafford, Democratic Senator Patrick Leahy, and Socialist Independent Representative Bernie Sanders in the House. They all worked together in Washington with a common assumption of the necessity of good government for the people's general welfare. I voted for candidates from both parties. All Vermonters needed some government help, if not food stamps for mothers then veteran's programs, protection of civil liberties in our courts, road repairs and bridges, and a functioning postal service and health care system.

In Michigan, I had voted for losing Democrats for president but also for Republican David Stockman as my state representative. He'd won, and by the time I moved to Vermont, Stockman had moved too, to Washington, DC, where he was put in charge of Reagan's ferocious OMB (Office of Management and Budget). Washington's tone of debate grew angrier, compromise becoming a bad word.

Beastly Rationale

Stockman's job in the early 1980s was "starving the beast," as he wrote later in his 1986 memoir, *The Triumph of Politics: Why the Reagan Revolution Failed*. The beast, to Reagan and Stockman, and the economists of their group, was the government. They wanted it smaller. Or so they said.

In reality, Reagan grew the beast, increasing overall government spending of a military kind and more than doubling the national debt. George W. Bush would later use a similar strategy to break down social safety nets, while again doubling the nation's debt. And Clinton? Did he really balance the national budget as he claimed? Or was it due to the tax raise imposed by his anti-voodoo Republican predecessor, George the First, who lost reelection because of it?

I didn't understand this tendency of politicians to talk constantly about the national debt and a hatred for taxes while freely spending and borrowing, but I began to ask questions and couldn't find simple answers. Who exactly owned that American debt? To whom did our nation pay interest? And how? Did the nation have a checkbook like mine? A credit card? A bank account it had to reconcile?

Screwnomics is about the answers I found, but for now, I'll just parrot Reagan's and Stockman's argument at the time, which is still popular today: shrinking government and cutting taxes is good for the economy. The economist who informed them, who would become a god by the 1990s, was a guy named Milton Friedman.

His ideas, which I'll unpack in greater detail in the next chapter, were popularly referred to as Reaganomics, or "trickle down" economics. The idea was that if the rich paid less tax, they would invest and create jobs, and money would trickle down to the middle and lower classes, lessening the need for government programs.

"There is no such thing as a free lunch," economist Friedman once famously said, forgetting his own reliance on government programs earlier in his life. During the Great Depression, fresh out of college, Friedman had gone to Washington to work in Franklin Delano Roosevelt's New Deal, a government program that bought him his lunch and his dinner, too. FDR's New Deal had put many young unemployed economists and plenty of others to work. Because of that working experience, Friedman won a faculty position at the University of Chicago in 1946, the same year I was born.

The university flourished during the thirty years that Friedman subsequently taught in Chicago, post-WWII, and this, too, was due to government programs. About two million American wage earners would newly reach the middle class by means of The Servicemen's Readjustment Act of 1944, better known as the GI Bill. Many veterans, including my dad and my stepdad, took advantage of this government program making education and housing affordable.

Private and public colleges would thrive from serving more diverse students, setting American higher education as a standard for the world. When I say "more diverse students," I mean men from farming stock, like my dad, and working class guys, like my stepdad, who got new opportunities. The GI Bill, though, remained a mostly white bill, even worsening discrimination in the south.

Government-backed housing loans enabled many more veterans to move to improved houses with indoor bathrooms, resulting in a housing boom. Later government highway funding also improved livelihoods, the benefits shared in lumberyards, on construction sites, at mortgage banks, and at factories that made the equipment, tools, and supplies used.

✓ COMMODITIES

This is the stuff any civilization needs for commerce, and it's a word most often used when buying and selling in large amounts. It may refer to manufactured goods, such as boards for houses or tires for cars, or to their raw materials, such as timber or rubber and steel. Commodities may be exported and imported in international trade. However, most of us are consumers of commodities in the micro-economy, not traders of commodities in the macro-economy.

Because the war had revealed badly nourished soldiers, by the 1950s and 1960s school lunches would set a higher standard for nutrition. Bipartisan support viewed lunches at school as an important farm price support. Food programs for the poor were also seen as good policy for farmers and the food industry, as well as for those who needed help—just as housing and educational support for veterans expanded whole segments of workers in the national economy.

Post-WWII's new wave of educated men may also have increased public reliance on experts, those university men at legal firms, public relations offices, and brain trusts of foundations, to whom Congress and the new media of television looked for some guidance on how to make sense of an increasingly complex world.

Home Economics

The GI bill was as masculine as GI Joe. Most women enjoyed its achievements vicariously, cleaning those new houses, laundering work clothes, or typing their men's dissertations while putting their own education on hold to have babies and raise families. Even when the American Dream remained personally out of reach for them, women remained the real, if devalued, economic experts. Held back from higher education and most careers, women managed their part of the micro-economy.

All that needed to happen to plummet a woman into poverty was for her man—father or husband—to lose a job, get sick, die, or disappear. Meanwhile, family household expenses like gas and food kept increasing, and inflation, which shrank the dollar's ability to purchase goods, was in the news.

The word *inflation* makes little sense when thinking about your money's value. Your inflated money is worth less. You need more money to pay for the same stuff your mother used to buy with fewer dollars. More accurately, prices (not money) is the inflated thing, but even that understanding is too simple for the complex set of monetary relationships we'll get to later. For now, the word inflation is a good example of EconoMan's secrets kept under our noses. You may hear and fear the word without understanding what is actually going on. Long-winded explanations from Econo-Man discourage your curiosity.

> ## ✓ INFLATION
>
> In the fourteenth century, *inflation* meant a gathering of "wind" in the body, or flatulence. It could also mean puffing up with pride. By the nineteenth century, it referred to an increase in the amount of money in circulation, supposedly controlled by the government. Too many dollars could cause devaluation.
>
> Few in the twentieth century understood that our largest privately-owned banks control the amount of dollars circulating through the US Federal Reserve, a system you'll learn more about in Chapter 16. As part of that control, the banking system literally creates money out of air. A rude person might say the Fed farts money at will.

In fact, there are different theories of inflation, all of which sound scientific. Some economists admit to educated guesses but typically only to describe their opposition. In other words,

EconoMan's terms are contested and depend on a point of view. Arguments are really about which group is in power, or seeking to become so.

For now, let's just say that you and I are not in power—that's one thing we know—and prices for commodities, for the stuff we need, keep on inflating faster than the rest of the economy, especially our wages. The question is why? What is behind this bad case of perpetual, inflationary gas? Read on in pursuit of this mystery.

Quick Rehash

- People of color and women are poor at higher rates than the US population as a whole, but the majority of the poor are white and are working, whatever their color.
- Economic knowledge has been created and dominated by men of a particular insider group of a particular class, of a particular race and gender.
- There is a class system within economics: the micro and the macro, the big and the little, and we all know which one is on top and over most of our heads.

EconoGirlfriend Conversation Starter

Here is the first of questions I'm suggesting you ask your girlfriends when you're out for a walk, or having a cup of coffee or glass of wine:

Have you ever worried about becoming poorer in future? What would that look like for you?

Get used to being worth less, girls. We'll be worth a high school man when we get our BAs. Go for an MA? More education = a wider pay gap with male peers. And it's worse if you're my color.

But we elected a black president!

She's talking GENDER & race, Suki-pie.

Want to understand macroeconomics? Who cleans the toilets at your house?

©Peaco Todd & Rickey Gard Diamond, 2017

My ex never even put the lid down. So... worldwide? That's macroeconomics?

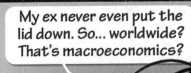

PEACO

Chapter 2: **No Girly Stuff Allowed**

Economics is hard! Competition is stiff!
EconoMan tells us about himself and his manly economic world.

This chapter touches on one man's ideas about inflation, but in a way, this entire book is about the practical problem of prices expanding while wage dollars and savings shrink over time. It isn't physics and it isn't natural, but it is inevitable without change. It's made complicated so you will give up trying to understand—but don't.

Keep on reading to unmask economic sexism where you might not expect it and, more importantly, to find sensible fiscal solutions. It gets easier once you hear more women's personal stories, and can decode EconoMan's language. Getting back to my own story . . .

By the time Ronald Reagan was reelected president in 1984, as I've already said, I had witnessed a transformation in how our government viewed the economy. Reagan's favorite economist, Milton Friedman, had promoted "trickle down" prosperity for all, theorizing that cutting taxes on the rich would soon eliminate the need for government safety nets by growing the economy. It sounded good. What had been called "voodoo" became the greatest thing since sliced bread.

I later learned this economic pivot had actually begun in 1976 when Friedman was catapulted into fame as the winner of Sweden's Nobel Prize in Economics. That award is living proof that EconoMan really does count on most of us not paying close attention.

Economics was never included in Alfred Nobel's recognition for noteworthy endeavors established in 1895. In 1969, the Swedish Central Bank (*Sveriges Riksbank*) created its own separate award, the Memorial Prize in Economic Sciences, in memory of Alfred Nobel, timed rather cunningly to blur its difference from the older, original awards for chemistry, physics, literature, and peace. Until recently, when the Nobel family protested, the press had routinely left out this detail, apparently considering the banking world's conflict of interest in elevating the field of economics irrelevant.

Two years before Friedman, British economist Frederick Hayek had won the same almost-Nobel prize. He and Friedman sought to link economics to a physics of natural forces, describing its parts with complex mathematics. The award they both received helped pose their prescriptions as something loftier than power and politics, and in terms less disputable, more like gravity and momentum.

In other words, they promoted the lying notion that a class of privileged men did not create these ways of thinking or at all benefit from them—rather, they were only describing inevitable, natural laws. You know, like the natural law that says a woman without a man should live in poverty.

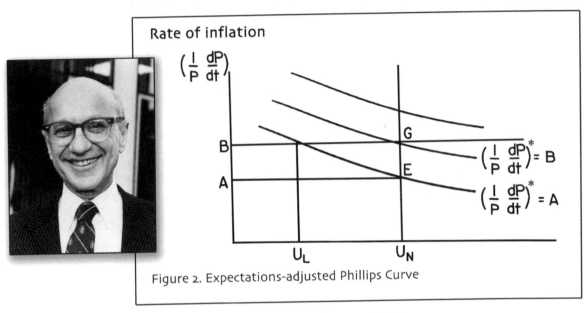

Figure 2. Expectations-adjusted Phillips Curve

Economist Milton Freedom and "adjusted expectations" from his 1976 Nobel lecture.

Adjusted Expectations

Okay, take a deep breath. You may be tempted to turn away from this reading now, having looked at Friedman's picture and seen his scary math diagram, and perhaps sensing in me a dangerously feminist tone. You would prefer I be nicer, as everyone knows Milton Friedman is an important expert.

Stay with me though, don't run, because his influence, first tested in Chile, is coming home to roost in the United States. It affects you quite personally if you are among the 99 percent of Americans who have been told to adjust your expectations to lower-paying jobs, fewer benefits, weaker safety nets, and less democracy.

Friedman's mathematical diagram is intended to illustrate labor's relationship to inflation with "expectations-adjusted," the subject of Friedman's almost-Nobel lecture. His data had come from his research while advising General Augusto Pinochet, whose military had just overthrown the democratically elected president, Salvadore Allende.

General Pinochet, made dictator with the aid of our CIA (Central Intelligence Agency), enriched himself and terrorized his country for seventeen years, and eventually was indicted for imprisoning and torturing thirty thousand Chileans for political reasons. In 1990, the Chilean people prepared to bring him to trial, and the general fled the country.

"Adjusted expectations" was the problem that American labor also faced when Friedman gave his 1976 Nobel lecture, as wages kept failing to keep up with higher prices. Americans began to be told they couldn't afford social programs, either. Yet Friedman's presentation looks like something you might find in a physics text.

Here is a quote from his lecture, which emphatically denies political leanings to his theories: "Ideological war has raged . . . yet the drastic change that occurred in economic theory has not been a result of ideological warfare. . . . It has responded almost entirely to the force of events: brute experience proved far more potent than the strongest of political or ideological preferences."

Notice Friedman's figures of speech: *war* has *raged*, ideological *warfare*, *force* of events, *brute* experience, *more potent* than *the strongest*. Now look again at Friedman's picture, and let's compare notes, girlfriend to girlfriend. If you ran into this guy at a bar and heard him talking this way, would you think that maybe he's worried about the *size* of his ideas?

Men Explaining Badly

I am going to call this way of talking *EconoMansplaining*, inspired by Rebecca Solnit's famous 2008 essay, "Men Explain Things to Me." Solnit describes her encounter with another male expert at a party. He advised her to read an important new book, one that just happened to be hers.

She had just won an award for it, but in this encounter the man poses at being sure he knows more about its contents than she does—despite Rebecca's friend Sallie telling him in another female voice he ignored, "That's her book." Sallie tries three or four times to tell him her friend Rebecca is the author. But he sees only "a young ingénue," Solnit writes, and it is his habit to explain the world to her, "with that smug look I know so well in a man holding forth, eyes fixed on the fuzzy far horizon of his own authority."

Solnit makes the link between "the social misery of small encounters" like this one, with men accustomed to being experts, and the routine crushing of young women into unquestioning silence. She writes, "It trains us in self-doubt and self-limitation just as it exercises men's unsupported overconfidence."

Young readers of Solnit's essay soon named what they too had experienced *mansplaining*. Nearly every woman has had such an encounter, and many men have as well: it is a tone and way of talking, by someone who is not listening to what you say, interrupting to make sure you understand that the way you experience the world is trivial and unimportant—never mind *your* perspective, which is obviously skewed by your tits, or the color of your skin, or by your being a dyke or some kind of girly man.

Your experience, your questions, your arguments, your inability to see things his way, only occurs because you are not so smart as he is, and surely not so very certain.

Mansplaining blurs the relationships of power, evading responsibility. Just so, Friedman's economics, supposedly concerned only with numbers and natural forces, counseled many government leaders to adopt what he called "shock treatments." Canadian journalist Naomi Klein traces the rise of Friedman's vicious economic ideas in her 2007 book, *The Shock Doctrine: The Rise of Disaster Capitalism*. When the people are traumatized and without government help, Friedman taught, then sweeping economic changes can be imposed.

In 1975, Chilean graduates of Chicago University invited Friedman to lecture. In interviews and a cabinet-level conversation with General Pinochet about dealing with inflation, Friedman recommended these actions in rapid succession: end social programs, sell off public assets, and free foreign investment. The metaphor he used? "You don't cut a dog's tail off in pieces. You chop it off."

Friedman was still advising heads of state in 2005 when he counseled President George W. Bush after Katrina's devastation in New Orleans. With public resistance crushed, he told W., it was the perfect time to replace public housing with private condos, and public school systems with vouchers for privately owned education.

EconoMan's Assumptions

Friedman is merely the latest EconoMansplainer in a male-dominated field of expertise. As Solnit points out, the institutions created by male experts have routinely left women out. She calls feminism the work of "making women's voices credible and audible," and reminds us in her essay that US courts have only recently upheld "a woman's right to the property of her truth."

She refers to a woman's right to make private decisions about her own body, won in 1973, though still in question in many states, and a woman's exclusion from basic rights. The last state to exclude women jurors, Louisiana, lost its US Supreme Court case in 1975. Harvard did not admit women until 1977. Yes, you read those dates right.

It is easy to lose sight of just how much legal ground had to be pioneered by our foremothers the past 150 years for economic reasons. Lilly Ledbetter's 2007 fair wage Supreme Court case was merely the latest injustice. If three women had sat on the court then, as they do now, the verdict might have been fairer, but Ledbetter lost. Women judges on that court remain a pioneering phenomenon.

Not that long ago, women were all but invisible legally under English Common Law. In the late eighteenth century, a married woman could not own property. She could not keep wages earned, enter into a contract, or own a bank account because she and her husband were one. He was the one. If her husband died, she was entitled to one-third of his estate but could only sell it with her son's permission or, lacking that, with the permission of the most closely related family penis.

Women's legal existence in marriage was the real subject of First Lady Abigail Adam's famous letter to husband John, in which she wrote, "Don't forget the ladies." Running their estate's business while he helped foment an American revolution was no doubt made harder for her by her legal nonexistence. In many parts of the world, Solnit points out, a woman's testimony still has no legal standing. A woman in some Middle Eastern countries must have the proof of a male witness to counter her rapist's denial in court, since her truth, her account alone, does not count.

Fisticuff Talk

Violence is the last word in mansplaining. Solnit grew up in a violent home and a violent neighborhood, and notes that husbands or ex-husbands kill three women in the United States every day. Domestic violence is one of the main causes of death for pregnant women. Symbolic violence matters, too, Solnit says, like those catcalls that tell women the streets are not hers.

Sexual threats routinely belittle women gamers online, and off-subject sexual comments plague female scientists on the Brainscoop channel on YouTube. Women sportscasters put up with tweets that are much more than mean. The *New York Times* reported in 2013 on the persistent problems at Harvard Business School:

> *Year after year, women who had arrived with the same test scores and grades as men fell behind. Attracting and retaining female professors was a losing battle; from 2006 to 2007, a third of the female junior faculty left. . . . Many Wall Street-hardened women confided that Harvard was worse than any trading floor. . . . Some male students, many with finance backgrounds, commandeered classroom discussions and hazed female students and younger faculty members, and openly ruminated on whom they would "kill, sleep with or marry" (in cruder terms). Alcohol-soaked social events could be worse.*

No mansplainer poses at being more certain than EconoMansplainer, whether in training, or at parties, or at work on Wall Street, or in the top ranks of the biggest corporations traded in the stock market there. Faking other people out with unwavering confidence, skimming facts, is an essential part of his performance.

Economic Inequality Insured

One repeated and reliable EconoMan message is so casual and universal that we hardly notice its silent, dismissive shrug that communicates "women are less than." Paying women less than men for the same work—regardless of the occupation, female- or male-dominated—gets dismissed as the result of her choices. The wage gap leads to media questions—not of experts, who own things, of course, but of her: Why are you women so lacking in confidence? Why don't you just lean in?

Those of you with lady parts: your suspicions about this economy's intentions toward you reveal you are indeed paying attention. Whether we women are business owners, salaried managers, or weekly wage earners, our monetary share of each economic sector tends to be much smaller, and often we are barely squeaking by.

This matters. Why? Because only when you have more than enough money, a surplus, can you increase your money without a direct relationship to time spent in the real world. You can then rent out that surplus to others as investment. Most often, however, time-bound women workers can only add or subtract, and mostly we subtract. Surplus dollars are a dream for many. Income, Investment, and Interest—what I call the Three Big I's—reveal women's built-in disadvantage.

✓ INCOME

This refers to money regularly earned, generally in two ways, by renting out your time or by renting out your money. *Wages* are earned by the hour and can only be calculated by adding or subtracting, because we only have twenty-four hours in a day. Higher paid managerial positions are paid *salary*, calculated annually not hourly, which helps camouflage inequalities. Both wages and salary are returns for renting out time but can be dramatically different. Most Americans depend on wages or salaries for income, but the highest paid salaries continue to be male, while most minimum-wage workers are women.

✓ INVESTMENT

About half of Americans reportedly earn income from surplus cash rented out as an *investment*, most often through pensions or 401(k) plans. No one tracks what percentage of this second kind of income returns to women, but it is widely admitted that women are under-pensioned, and that testosterone fuels Wall Street investments. Because of wage and salary inequality, men are more likely than women to have surplus cash. Only investments can geometrically multiply income without relationship to hours in a day.

✓ INTEREST

The rental fee for rented money is called *interest*. Surplus cash can "earn" interest, also called returns, on loans (via *bonds*) or investment in business (via *stocks*). This income can be thought of as tenant payments to the money landlord for money's temporary use. Whenever an investor risks investing in a bond or a stock that might not pay the expected rent, the rent charge goes up. Thus stocks generally "earn" more than bonds because they are generally riskier. The promise of higher returns helps tempt investors to take risks.

Do you assume these terms have little to do with you? Here's how the Three Big I's help insure that women's economic inequality continues: In virtually every field, a woman can expect to earn less over her lifetime than her male counterpart, regardless of education. Over a forty-seven-year work life, reports the Wage Project of the National Committee on Pay Equity, this gap amounts to an estimated loss in wages of $700,000 for high school graduates, $1.2 million for college grads, and $2 million for a grad school professional.

That's a huge potential loss for a great many families who, lacking surplus money, are virtually locked out of opportunities to invest and multiply their money or capital. They can only add or subtract hours rented out, or add and subtract expenses in their budget.

Stealing the Language

For too long, women have left the economy to experts who have awarded themselves honors for sometimes doubtful achievements—and who generally rake in big wads of dough for their trouble. More of us need to pay closer attention. Clearly the Chileans who crossed an ocean in 1976 to protest Mr. Friedman's almost-Nobel event in Sweden saw the connection between Friedman's ruthless economic ideas and dictator Pinochet's murders.

Mansplaining has so exclusively shaped economic thought that I have had to make a special effort to avoid some word like *battle*, to describe economic conflicts. Terms of violence and war shape our daily figures of speech. We *attack* our problems and wage *war* on drugs, on poverty, on cancer, on terror. We can't let down our *guard*, we *shoot* down opponents, we *combat* ignorance, we *fight* for our rights. Even the nonword *nonviolence* reveals a lack and a dangerous habit of mind.

The purpose of language is to communicate, but words also shape how we think about things. For instance, the words *mankind, policeman, chairman, spokesman,* and *clergyman* helped to define whole realms as exclusively male until the 1970s when women pointed out our sex's presence and contributions. Similarly, war words for the economy exclude more friendly ways of thinking.

In a *Dateline NBC* interview just four months after Wall Street's 2008 crash, billionaire Warren Buffett, one of Wall Street's godlike investors, called the financial meltdown "an economic Pearl Harbor." CNBC's Becky Quick reminded him of this in May of 2009, asking him for an update.

Stuck in that old male habit of mind, Buffett rattled his sword, saying we could have "lost the war. And there was a strike at the heart of the American system, the financial system. . . . We got past that. Some of the right decisions were made then, so I give people great credit. . . . The war isn't over, though."

Okay, so metaphors help explain what's going on—but who exactly was Buffett's invader in 2008? Weren't our own biggest banks scamming international investors and American mortgagers alike? So who was warring with whom exactly?

Wall Street may love war. Victors get rich and, like Buffett, become king of the mountain, but winners need losers, just as kings require subjects. Americans gave up kings in a declaration written in 1776. The heart of the American system is democracy, not "the financial system" that Buffett here cites.

New Metaphors Needed

For most of its history, economics has been a man-to-man conversation among the upper class. The stories that most matter to women (and most men)—about our families, our devotion, our courage—are never considered legitimately economic by EconoMan.

Just as the legal language of male experts of the past pretended that women had no legitimate independence or voice, EconoMansplaining discounts living female contributions and the genetic exchanges that make all life possible. The un-monetized work of homes, churches, communities, oceans, and compost piles is widely accepted as irrelevant to Wall Street global bankers, multinational corporations, and Washington economists.

Speaking in code to each other, these players test which man is smartest, coolest, on top, and winning in an overblown, masculine war game. They discount our massive unpaid work at home, calling it "informal," not the foundational economy it is. Likewise, they minimize any environmental damage done, calling it an "externality," not a knife to the living webs of life we depend upon. (We'll examine externalities in Chapter 16.)

✓ THE INFORMAL ECONOMY

Economists call the labor exchanges done for free at home, in cashless trade, or in cash-only transactions the *informal economy*. Women, especially mothers, are the majority of all such workers, working in private, unaccounted for, and unseen. They make far less money than *formal* workers, who by definition receive a company paycheck and benefits, and pay taxes as publicly visible workers. Today a new class of professional contract workers is emerging, often educated, but without job security or benefits. Economist Guy Standing has named them the *precariat*.

We women rarely organize ourselves into death-dealing armies. We, perhaps more easily than men, can avoid "fighting" for what we want, and create new economic language and similes. Our figures of speech could describe the useful give-and-take exchanges of our everyday lives, cooking up and tucking in nonviolent images as vivid as Wall Street's booms, busts, and crashes.

We could grow and enlarge what we personally see and desire. We could describe a million possibilities for getting to yes, and for developing and birthing a new prosperity that doesn't have to cost our humanity or our happiness. I'm betting women could even whistle up some economic dogs whose tails wag and don't need chopping.

Smarter economic policy making is, I'm afraid, another case of women's needing to become the princes we had hoped would rescue us. We will have to reimagine a future and aspire to it together. Unlike Rapunzel, trapped in her tower, it will be up to us to climb down on the hair of our own thoughts and experience.

Women need to make economics sexy. This would first require an acknowledgement of our biological underpinnings and mortal fate, made bearable by all those juicy genetic exchanges along the way—the bumblebees', the apple trees', the dark, wet world of mammal wombs, the tragic relationship between air and fire, its production of ash.

EconoMan wants none of that girly kind of stuff, but please, Mr. Buffett, give me metaphors of children and trees and rivers for any financial system you expect me to buy. Without those, the eco-economy of our biological lives becomes as hard for me to see, as for a fish to see water.

✓ ECOLOGY & ECONOMY

An even newer science than economics, *ecology* shares the same Greek root, *oikos*, which means house or dwelling. Ecology studies relationships among organisms in a particular home environment. Economy began by studying human homes and their interactions. Relationships and homes are familiar female territory, so claim your expertise in both realms.

You may already recognize that an economy must always dwell within an ecology. You may already notice that it matters whether you value only your own private dwelling or can see your home's connection to a larger, shared environment—a community, a nation, a planet. No one becomes a healthy individual alone, or enjoys what EconoMan appears to seek, a freedom from interconnected, mortal life.

A living metaphor for women's economic situation today would find us swimming in whirlpools of experts' circular language. Our swimming together might increase our safety, as could tracking the eco-ocean's currents, sensing what exactly made those ripples ahead: A river mouth's exit? A predator with teeth?

Which leads me to another great, white EconoMansplainer you should know about and will meet in the next chapter, John Maynard Keynes.

Quick Rehash

- In 1969, the study of economics had been slyly elevated to Nobel status by the creation of a bank's memorial prize.
- The US government changed its economic direction in 1980 with Reaganomics, influenced by newly famous economist Milton Friedman.
- EconoMansplaining can blur power's use of force and violence.

EconoGirlfriend Conversation Starter

Have you ever experienced EconoMansplaining? What was it like?

Chapter 3: Two Kinds of Men

Economists come from a long line of fishy thinking about females,
but gentlemen Keynesians are kinder.

My mother used to tell me there were two kinds of men—those with honorable intentions toward a woman, the *gentlemen*, and others who were cads, as she called them. Today we'd call the cad a *player*. He's charmingly seductive—but it's not about *you*, girl. He's after a conquest.

My mom's analysis was rooted in traditional notions. A woman needed a male breadwinner back then. Your choices were not postmodern but dualistic and simple, between a good man and a bad one. A sexual double standard for men underlined the danger lying within your own vagina, a part of your anatomy upheld by tradition as a treasured commodity, something a girl must present untarnished to the man she would marry.

In those days, becoming a bride was every girl's business enterprise. You might not have stopped to think about it, but these old ideas are rooted in measures of woman as property, whether daughter or wife. A bride is "given" to a groom by her father. The meaning of giving the bride away, largely an affectionate gesture now, wouldn't become clear to me until women historians began to uncover women's collective story, examined more closely in Part III.

Until the early 1970s, the phrase *women's history* was really an oxymoron. History was about kings and generals, not women. Economic history largely remains so.

Concrete Differences

In the 1960s, I already tended to discount my mother's assumption that men were a girl's only path to adult life. As a teenager, I had read Simone de Beauvoir's groundbreaking book *The Second*

Sex, first published in the United States in 1953, though I read it more than a decade later. In it, de Beauvoir says, "The most sympathetic of men never fully comprehend woman's concrete situation."

De Beauvoir's observation seemed truer to me than my mother's. Good and bad were abstract ideas, and what Mom meant and what I meant when it came to good men usually didn't match. De Beauvoir's "concrete situation," however, pointed to a tangible, touchable, living reality. We had a vagina and womb with all the responsibilities and conflicting expectations for becoming Madonna and Whore when women are neither, and both, and so much more.

Our vulnerabilities were much worse in de Beauvoir's day before the pill, but they remain concrete and tangible whenever male violence, rape, and its threat are discounted. Wherever men exclusively define the world, women remain the second sex. Men then have no need to stretch their imagination and attempt to comprehend her. But when women enter the economy, creating their own values, men try harder to extend their thoughts into the foreign land of women—and not only to claim her with a flagpole of ownership.

Women's values, when respected, make for a richer world. Today, my second husband gives workshops on violence prevention in schools. Our friends and children are thinking and talking openly about skin color, sexuality, gender, and male and female roles at home and at work, and our gay family members have come out of the closet. All our relationships seem deepened by expanding social territories.

Yet the power of a woman's money remains unsettling for her to assert. That powerful men are worried about women's looming potential for reshaping business as usual is proven by the recent spate of woman-controlling state laws in the United States. In 2013 alone, the Guttmacher Institute reported that 694 new state provisions blocked women's access to sex education, birth control, and abortion.

Our still mostly male legislative bodies seek to enforce an outgrown classification of woman as womb without moral agency, intelligence, or essential citizen rights to life, liberty, and the pursuit of her happiness. Made a bridal property of the government, her womb can still be given away and with it her economic independence.

In 2012, Erin Gloria Ryan filed a story with Jezebel.com titled, "The Ten Scariest Places to Have Ladyparts in America," linking that year's legislative "transvaginal probes" with poverty, infant mortality, rape, domestic violence, and abortion restrictions, complete with a map.

I had sensed from a young age that our female anatomy put both my mom and me inside a near-invisible sexual fence—though I didn't yet know enough to describe its electric charge in economic terms. Still, for purposes of explaining trends in twentieth-century economic thought, my mother's formula for categorizing men works pretty well. For we have met both the gentleman and the cad in our recent economic history.

My Lord Baron

You've been introduced to the cad in Chapter 2. But the gentleman, Englishman John Maynard Keynes, Baron of Tilton, actually came first and was well known during my mother's lifetime.

Keynes challenged the merchant economists of his day and decades later was himself overthrown by Friedman and Hayek, whose ideas still dominate.

Written about widely, Keynes's career, distinguished by the Great Depression, was framed by two World Wars, the second one predicted by him. His then new ideas of government intervention in economics so influenced his field that a whole Keynesian school of thought evolved.

He excelled at mathematics, says biographer Robert Skidelsky and many others, but it was language and vivid metaphors that delivered Keynes's surprising concepts to his male colleagues. Keynes had an elite education, and hung out with avant-garde intellectuals and artists who called themselves the Bloomsbury Group. Innovators, interested in Freud's new field of psychology, they included the writer Virginia Woolf and other famous figures.

As a young man in his thirties, Keynes had already risen to a British treasury post. He had a wry sense of humor. In a later book, *Essays in Persuasion*, Keynes wrote about his profession: "If economists managed to get themselves thought of as humble, competent people on a level with dentists that would be splendid." He enjoyed history and the arts, had many homosexual affairs, and later in life married a Russian ballerina, having fallen "very much in love," says another biographer, D. E. Moggridge. Keynes adored the theater and ballet.

A thoroughgoing capitalist, he became a savvy and wealthy trader. He argued that in times of economic downturn, it was wiser for the government to protect the interests of working-class renters over his own upper-class landlord friends. He wrote that in downturns for business, government spending could be aimed at putting people to work. This would keep the economy healthy.

Eliminating jobs and decent wages inevitably backfired, reducing demand for business products and services, he said. By contrast, good wages helped free demand, and wider demand supported good prices for the products of business. In downturns, government's purchases, incentives, and tax credits could help.

> ## ✓ SUPPLY & DEMAND
>
> The moving dynamic between the supply of a product and consumers' demand for that product, like a teeter-totter in theory, are said to eventually balance out in a fair market price. But this assumes suppliers and consumers in our global-sized markets are equal, though they seldom are. Nor is balance the goal of most suppliers or shoppers. All look for bargains, or getting the most for the least.

Big Bulls

How does supply and demand work to affect prices? Say you grow a new food, called corn. Because it is new and rare, corn demands a high price, and only the rich can afford to eat it. Over time, the market grows *bullish*, meaning optimistic. Others grow corn, hoping for rich buyers, too, but as supply grows, the bulls must compete with each other and so drop their prices to sell it. Soon corn becomes so abundant, it is as cheap as chicken feed, putting the teeter-totter of supply and demand in balance with everyone well fed. At least in theory.

> ## ✓ AGGREGATE SUPPLY & AGGREGATE DEMAND
>
> The Latin word *aggregate* refers to a flock or a herd, the kind of agricultural wealth that Herodotus first named *oikonomia*. In macroeconomics, aggregate *demand* is the total amount of all the goods and services that a national flock of consumer chickens needs. On the other side of the teeter-totter balance, aggregate *supply* shows the total amount of goods and services a nation's herd of businesses can supply us.

Keynes believed the Great Depression was in part caused by oversupply—more chicken feed than we clucks could buy. Overproduction, or the making of more products than could be purchased, depresses prices. For today's free-market traders, the answer to oversupply is a global economy and expanded international trade.

In the best of all possible worlds, world aggregate demand would exactly meet and be fairly exchanged with world aggregate supply. Then, everyone could take a vacation. Of course, the two never do quite balance, given the bulls on one end of the teeter-totter scales and we chicks on the other.

Man of Empathy

Keynes resigned his treasury position after participating in the Paris Peace Conference in 1919 because his own Britain, in alliance with the United States and France, imposed overly harsh economic penalties on Germany after the First World War. He worried that German citizens would be traumatized by war debts that he could see were impossible to repay. Not only that, but Germany's resulting inability to import goods without money to purchase needed supplies would affect not just Germany but its international suppliers, he argued.

Keynes's first book, *The Economic Consequences of the Peace,* published after he returned home from Paris and resigned, is now viewed as an accurate predictor of what eventually happened in Germany. His economic language, graceful and clear, his literary influences obvious, revealed humanity and compassion. In it, he protested "that year by year, Germany must be kept impoverished and her children starved and crippled." He even warned of German revolution as a reaction to the economic vengeance he saw the Allies imposing.

Post-WWI, a new German democracy, the Weimar Republic, replaced Kaiser Wilhelm's royal family rule. (Wilhelm was cousin to England's King George and Russia's Czar Nicolas.) As Keynes had feared, however, their new republic collapsed in just fourteen years, handicapped by war debts.

The Nazis rose to power precisely when Germany's currency, the mark, became so inflated it was worthless. (We'll return to how this can happen in Part V.) Stories of Germans buying bread with a wheelbarrow full of marks in the 1920s were followed by Hitler's trumpeting the superiority of the Aryan race in the 1930s and 1940s, while scapegoating Jewish Germans for economic hardship.

Keynes's later masterpiece, *The General Theory of Employment, Interest and Money*, published in 1936 after WWI and the Great Depression, contrasted with earlier economic works. In it, he confronted the tensions of a British-dominated world empire and money power. He argued that supply and demand were not always naturally kept in balance, which had been the popular creed of the upper class until then.

While far from being a Marxist or socialist, Keynes did recognize that the wealthy owners of the means of production did not always perfectly and fairly meet the interests of the laboring classes. The government, too, had an important role to play in the economy, he argued, by regulating fairness and by spending in downturns to increase aggregate demand.

Man to Man Talk

To understand the EconoMan conversation that Keynes expanded, we need to touch on earlier ideas about productivity. In 1776, Adam Smith had written the first modern economic tome, *The Wealth of Nations*. In it, he illustrated the efficiency of a pin factory with its new division of labor, each worker specializing in a job that was part of the pin production process. No longer would each worker craft each pin from beginning to end. Instead, production could be more efficiently organized, specialized, and increased.

By 1900 and Keynes's era, however, that principle of specialization had been magnified hugely into nation-sized industries of steel, meat, coal, and oil, to name a few. The size and complexity of assembly-line production and its chain of distribution required so much money that only the very richest could afford them. As a result, a few men controlled materials, suppliers, distributors, and prices, their supply lines crushing smaller competition.

That lack of competition is called *monopoly*. The game you have played by that name pictures the famous mustachioed Wall Street banker, J.P. Morgan, on the Chance Card. It reveals the unbeatable advantage of those who own red hotels on Park Avenue and all four railways. Real monopolies actually work that way.

Early in the twentieth century, muckraker journalist Ida Tarbell exposed the methods of oil tycoon John D. Rockefeller in her 1904 book, *The History of the Standard Oil Company*. She opens it with a gardening quote from him, just as descriptive for growing a monopoly: "The American Beauty Rose can be produced in its splendor and fragrance only by sacrificing the early buds which grow up around it."

The sacrifices, she showed, were never Rockefeller's own. Crushing smaller opponents resulted in his blooming fortune, and made him America's very first billionaire.

Rockefeller and his oil monopoly conspired with railroad moguls Cornelius Vanderbilt and

Henry Flagler, steel giant Andrew Carnegie, and financiers Jay Gould and J.P. Morgan to create what is now called the Gilded Age. Together they controlled prices the rest of the world paid.

Describing their willing collusion in his book *Economix: How and Why Our Economy Works (and Doesn't Work)*, Michael Goodwin also quotes Rockefeller: "What a blessing it was that the idea of cooperation, with railroads, with telegraph lines, with steel companies, with oil companies came in and prevailed to take the place of the chaotic conditions."

He reports that George Peters, then a partner with J.P. Morgan, defended Morgan's organization of the steel industry as no different or worse than the way a governmental US Department of Steel might operate. What was the difference, he wondered. The difference had to do with democracy. Private money and secret deals among a tiny minority ruled the lives of most and increasingly corrupted governments elected to represent the majority.

As Goodwin points out, once Morgan and Rockefeller had invested money in steel production, they couldn't risk interruptions in the supply of raw materials or demand for steel. Any pause cost them money, so demand had to be created to meet their enormous supply. That context of concentrated money power, so huge it became difficult to distinguish from national interests, resulted in national contracts and international trade. Any conflicts also won them huge profits from military exploits.

War Works

Women excluded from such institutionalized power may more readily have perceived its corrupting effects. They objected to their "concrete situation," living with men's wars. Well before Keynes's first book, Jane Addams of Hull House fame had joined other suffragist founders of the Women's Peace Party to speak out for disarmament.

They helped form the Women's International League for Peace and Freedom in 1915, meeting at The Hague in the Netherlands. By then, Austria had already attacked Serbia; and Russia, Belgium, and France were arming themselves. American anarchist Emma Goldman went further, speaking out against economic collusion between government and big business in Europe's first war already underway.

Goldman was deported, the United States joined WWI in 1917, and war profiteering became a dirty label. Yet it remained hard to sort out the fat cats from the patriotic. Financially strapped Germans, post-WWI, misplaced their hopes in Hitler's authoritarian alliance with big corporate business. The Nazi party's presenting goal was a German economic comeback, which included ingenious weapons making. Similarly, Hitler's ally in Italy, Mussolini, answered his nation's humiliating war debts with an economic comeback. He disliked the word *fascist*, preferring *corporatist*, a term he called "truer."

Corporate allegiance directly enriched Nazi and Fascist leaders who ultimately enforced and directed terror, enriching men at the top in politics and in business. Dehumanizing Jews and any dissidents or misfits justified confiscation of their property—as well as their forced slave labor for corporations during WWII.

When Hitler began his blitzkrieg attack on London in 1940, having already invaded and occupied France, our gentleman Keynes would ingeniously borrow ideas from the American New Deal and American economist Simon Kuznets (whom we'll meet again in Part IV). Keynes gathered data on the shape, size, and sorts of private enterprises in England to create a new aggregate picture. His resulting financial plan for funding England's war against Germany's new weapons won out, in alliance with the Brit's former colony and its even more frightening nuclear arsenal.

Enter the Players

Our own country's economic prosperity followed US war production to meet Allied demand for armaments. Rosie the Riveter's lower wages had been a patriotic bargain for industrial expansion. When soldiers came home in 1945, women were sent back to homemaking and brand-new appliances that retooled industries now supplied. The hard times of the Depression and the war seemed behind us.

The same year I was born, 1946, Milton Friedman landed his first teaching job at the University of Chicago, and Lord John Maynard Keynes died of a heart attack at sixty-three, exhausted by his work "restoring economic structure to a world twice shattered by war," as the *New York Times* put it.

Keynes's recommended policy of government spending in times of business slumps worked so well that most leading economists remained Keynesians a generation after his death. Male veterans and union members won blue collar breadwinner pay, increasing consumer demand which was further boosted by a new generation of gray-suited ad men. The future looked mass-produced, technological, and golden.

Professor Friedman remained an outlier. Throughout the 1950s and 1960s, Keynesian economics dominated nations that opposed Marxist ones—Russia, China, Korea, and then North Vietnam. The Cold War had begun, and by 1961, President Dwight Eisenhower was warning of the dangers of a military-industrial complex that threatened democracy.

It was the same mammoth institutional wealth, big business colluding with government to profit from war, that Emma Goldman and Jane Addams had talked about fifty years earlier.

The last of the Keynesian gentleman to be widely read and travel in the inner circle of Washington's national power was John Kenneth Galbraith. He supported women's reentry into the work world in the 1960s, and late in life he was awarded the Medal of Honor by President Bill Clinton in 2000. By then, however, Keynesians had been largely displaced.

As happens in an academic world shaped by male intellectual warfare, by the late 1970s Milton Friedman's school of thinking had won out. His quotable one-liners would soon enthrall Americans who were after that one thing again, conquests and winning. And no, it was never about *you*, girl.

Some economists, such as Paul Krugman and Joseph Stiglitz, remind the public of Keynesian principles, such as the importance of government spending during downturns, but these gentlemen remain well outside the White House and the US Treasury's circle of power. Few but they question profits made from American wars and weaponry, seeing the costs to our "concrete situation." In 2015, Stiglitz told journalist Amy Goodman that our taxpayers' bill for conquests in Iraq and Afghanistan will run from $5 to $7 trillion.

Cads, the other sort of man my mother warned me about, dominate now, as you'll see in the next chapter. We'd more likely call this EconoMan a *player* today, but that term hides the intent of his charm, his slithery whispers.

Quick Rehash

- The Gilded Age gave us our first billionaire and industries so large that their interests became conflated with US national interests.
- Women, more generally excluded from power, called for an end to war profiteering even before WWI. Imagine if men had listened.
- Keynesian economics held that governments and businesses were better off cooperating rather than warring. Unlike tycoons, they argued that the economy prospered from policies favoring renters over landlords, consumers over suppliers, and the many over the few.

EconoGirlfriend Conversation Starter

What in your life is in high demand? What in your life is in short supply? Are they connected?

Chapter 4: Played by the Players

*Neoliberals go by many names, but they all use
the same old rich tricks to make a score.*

He's two-faced, my mom would say about any man she didn't trust, and frankly, that was most of them. Like the word *cad*, it's an old-fashioned expression I haven't heard used for decades. A two-faced cad might smile to your face and say nice things, but behind your back, he would ruin you.

I'm afraid the expression fits those men who inherited the economics of Keynes. They upended his key principles, changing the course of the American middle class with smiling lies that sounded good but ultimately undid us.

Every Man for Himself

After Keynes's death, the University of Chicago became a center for radical economics, and Milton Friedman became its most public economic thinker. Naomi Klein describes in *The Shock Doctrine* how Friedman's students called themselves the Chicago Boys, taking pride in an elite and exclusive fraternity. The other label they gave themselves, *neoliberal*, sounded like an invitation to a fun toga party.

You'd be right to be wary, though, the reason I say they were two-faced. The term neoliberal didn't mean what people generally thought. How would you translate the term?

Neo means new, original, and fresh, and is always considered a smart thing, an improvement. *Liberal*, to most people, usually means, well, free. Kind of leftie. In favor of social programs and a government safety net—that sort of thing. For instance, Lord Baron Keynes, our artful economic gentleman, was a member of England's Liberal Party, and he was hardly ashamed of it.

The dictionary defines liberal this way: "Not limited to, or by, established authoritarian attitudes, or dogma—to be free from bigotry." Liberal is a word with a proud, long history. If women had not liberalized the United States, no woman would now be voting, much less running for office or working for money, except as maids, schoolmarms, or prostitutes.

So who wouldn't want to be a neoliberal?

I didn't understand at first that economic liberalism is not at all like social and political liberalism. In fact, it is the opposite. Neoliberalism reintroduced an older classical notion that money matters are best left to those with money. Let rich guys trade freely and liberally, so that supply can always neatly and perfectly meet demand and balance out—an idea that Keynes had challenged.

Neoliberals found government the enemy of the economy, not its ally, as Keynes's gentleman era had taught. This was the neo part. The invisible hand of the market, left free of regulation, would naturally balance supply and demand, they asserted.

There was no more pussyfooting or elegant your-lordship either—it was all numbers and hard science now, nothing personal. You remember Friedman's math diagram from Chapter 1 and his wish to describe economic forces in the realm of physics. In the academic world where I worked for over twenty years, hard science is considered more purely rational (translate: *masculine*) than is social science, that field measuring human interconnections considered softer (translate: *feminine*). The supposedly purest science of all, the most ingenious and high-minded, is physics with mathematical tools.

One of the first things I noticed about this new economic stance was its removing itself from the taint of any pushing or shoving for advantage in the concrete situation of downsizing and payroll cuts that seemed to accompany its approach. Numerical graphs obliterated subjective human experience on the ground. Financial feelings like Keynes's empathy for defeated Germans disappeared as economics grew manlier.

Up on Masculine Mountain

If Friedman's neoliberal economics removed itself from social and political mores by becoming more detached and theoretical, it is interesting to think about why. Why did economists no longer want to be held responsible for the fate of innocent children and victims of too-great war debt, as did gentleman homo and ballerina lover Keynes?

I believe we women may have frightened them. The work world widely experienced by women during WWII in the 1940s shrank drastically during the 1950s when women were urged to return to homemaking as their single vocation. By the 1960s, though, a reinvigorated women's movement had gained entry into colleges where smart, young women soon put their heads together to raise consciousness.

Women began to recognize the college degrees they earned included nothing of women's history, women's art, or women's literature. It was rare to see a woman professor. Women soon flung signs for equality from the Statue of Liberty. We marched, we yelled, growing sassy and irreverent.

Feminist activist Jo Freeman writes on her website about WITCH, a kind of economic guerilla theater, fast and fun. Young women pulled hats and capes out of their bags, painted their faces white, and chanted rhymes ending in a hex before vanishing. In a film about this era, *She's Beautiful When She's Angry*, political activist Alice Wolfson described students who were challenging "the white man's canon" with their chant, "Knowledge is power/ through which you control/ our minds, our bodies, and our souls. HEX!"

The WITCH acronym changed, depending on the demonstration. Women's International Terrorist Conspiracy from Hell became, on Mother's Day, Women Interested in Toppling Consumer Holidays. When protesting at the phone company, WITCH stood for Women Incensed by Telephone Company Harassment. Women hexed bars in New York and the presidential inauguration in Washington, DC, and, writes Freeman, "Chicago women zapped everything."

At the University of Chicago in 1969, the same year that Friedman made the cover of *Time* magazine, eight undergraduate students in witch garb hexed the chairman of the sociology department for the firing of a popular woman professor.

It was then, in the context of women's growing dissatisfaction—and that of the civil rights movement, Black Power, the American Indian Movement, and the success of anti-war street protests against the Vietnam War—that Friedman's school sought the enhancement of their field, setting it higher atop the academic, masculine mountain. Out of reach of any politics, this school's purist, numbered abstractions refrained from the touchy-feely realm of theater, literature, history, and the arts, places where gentleman Keynes had hung out.

This hypermasculine stance ignored living women and their concrete situation, a nuanced one, full of smells and tastes, colors and voices of emotion. An insistence on pure reason inevitably results in objectifying whatever or whoever is more emotive and expressive, calling weak what is actually more fully human. With that first lie, it then becomes easier to deny any tangible opposing truth, and to claim women and any "lesser" men as subjects or rungs on a ladder to be mounted on the way up.

Neoliberalism's insistence on a physics of natural economic forces is similar to the natural order of the races promoted by antebellum churches to justify America's slave trade. It is like the common misuse of Darwin's natural "survival of the fittest" to endorse the economic violence of the Gilded Age, and like science's head measurements of indigenous people to rationalize their "improvements" as we tapped out their resources. All these stories of what's natural help to increase the riches of the already rich.

What Comes Naturally

Here's an example of Friedman's hard-numbers approach to what is only "natural" for women. I'll paraphrase his clear and much-repeated argument that any government efforts to promote "equal pay for equal work" ultimately hurt the very women who believe it only fair. You can watch a video and hear him for yourself, as he repeated this story many times.

Rules imposed on the free market would remove what Friedman calls "the cost of prejudice" for business owners. Say there is one business employer who dislikes working with women, and one who prefers them. Doesn't matter, Friedman says, because economic laws, certain as gravity, will prevail.

The employer who dislikes women will still practice his prejudice and avoid hiring them, asserts Friedman—all the more so if she costs just as much as the man he prefers. Without government rules, she would have the "advantage," his word, of offering to work for less and so be more likely to be hired, even by a sexist employer.

If she does the work of her job competitively and for lower pay, then the competing employer who hired her will have a clear advantage over the employer who pays more for his male-only employees. The competing business can then undersell the business that pays top dollar for his guys, and thus will soon be put out of business by "the cost of his prejudice."

Voilà! It's free market magic. The bias of sexism and racism is easily eliminated.

You see how this works for us, girls? Sell yourself cheap, Friedman advises, align with power and then enable those in power to grow more powerful. This has long been a way of getting ahead. It is the essence of being a player, but it is hardly new or radical.

Nothing Neo Under the Sun

You may be wondering what classical economics is, and why neoliberals renewed it, given the Great Depression. To understand better, we have to go back even further in time to the era just before the United States became a nation. I'll be summing up two centuries of economic thought here in a few pages, so keep in mind I'm generalizing a great deal and will give it all short shrift. But in bare outline, *classical economics* describes the first modern economists of the eighteenth century. Yes, I know it's confusing—usually "classical" doesn't also mean *modern*.

Adam Smith, who published *The Wealth of Nations* in 1776, was part of a small circle of upper-class men who knew each other well. The early scholarly association of Smith, David Ricardo, Thomas Malthus, and a French group that called themselves *physiocrats* was a little like the Chicago Boys, an exclusive club. Each man had a personal interest in the money to be made by knowing men who made money.

A key idea introduced by Smith was that markets regulate themselves via the famous "invisible hand" of self-interest. Efficiency from inner self-interest was a new idea in a time when most looked to the outer guidance of the invisible hand of God, which directed nations and families. Kings in those days were believed to rule by divine right, and in a similar way, Smith believed a nation's efficient division of labor would sort itself out.

Laissez-faire economics is a slightly older French term for the same classical notion that the economy, left to itself, will always seek and find equilibrium, with supply and demand meeting in a natural balance. Voltaire, the French philosopher of the Enlightenment, wrote the first critique of this idea in 1758, two decades before Adam Smith wrote his book.

Voltaire's novel *Candide* tells a story of disillusionment as a young man hears his mentor, Pangloss, praise "the best of all possible worlds" while working for kings and nobles, very well-paid for his trouble. Candide, the young man, notices it is a comfy world for the royalty who employ Pangloss as comfortably, but not so much for their poor subjects.

Laissez-faire literally means "let things take their natural course." When referring to markets and money, such an easy, loose attitude is similar to the free market of today, both terms promoting the existing order that enabled the rich to become rich. In this view, much preferred by kings and tycoons, becoming rich is the highest calling, the best that anyone can ever hope to attain, and clear proof of superiority.

The Least Sympathetic of Men

Where were women in classical EconoMan theories? Good question. The original classic, our Greek Herodotus who coined *oikonomia,* had praised the busy "queen bee" of the patriarch's hive. He credited her for creating much of the agricultural wealth that became the patriarch's property. However, women were mostly omitted from modern classical EconoMan explanations of the world, much as they were from more modern Keynesian ones, and those of Friedman's club.

In *The Wealth of Nations*, Adam Smith said enlightened society was evolving, but a woman had no need of education. Her training was provided by her guardians, "either to improve the natural attractions of their person, or to form their mind to reserve, to modesty, to chastity, and to economy; to render them likely to become mistresses of a family, and to behave properly when they have become such." Smith never married. As we learn from Katrine Marçal's delightful book, *Who Cooked Adam Smith's Dinner?*, for most of his life, Smith lived with his mother.

Women's single, classical career path as a bride and breeder did have an economic downside, pointed out by Smith's friend of that same eighteenth century, the minister and economist Thomas Malthus. Malthus was the first to see that human reproduction increases geometrically, doubling every few decades, while food produced on arable land increases at a simpler arithmetical rate, merely adding or subtracting.

Crops cannot double every few decades as people can, he wrote, and so food shortages and starvation must therefore result. He blamed the poor's overbreeding for the inevitable result of war, disease, and starvation. For him, charity was a bad idea, only resulting in more people starving in the future. (Neoliberal politicians appear to have inherited his ideas.)

Later economists like John Stuart Mill and Alfred Marshall expressed an awareness of female injustices but thought it unwise to upset the social order. That had already happened alarmingly. Upstart colonies in North America had sparked it, refusing loyalty to King George in 1776. Their electing a short-term leader they called a president, not a king, had shocked economic club members, born to their high-placed positions. France's 1789 revolution had rolled royal heads of the upper classes.

By 1851, Harriet Taylor Mill seemed readier to question the usual norms, writing in an essay, "When, however, we ask why the existence of one-half the species should be merely ancillary to that of the other—why each woman should be a mere appendage to a man, allowed to have no interests of her own, that there may be nothing to compete in her mind with his interests and his pleasure, the only reason that can be given is that men like it."

In fairness to Harriet's economist husband, John Stuart Mill, he credited his wife and publicly supported women, though money never came up in his 1869 book, *The Subjection of Women*. More basic, he defended woman's ability to think and make moral decisions, which his male reviewers called "strange," "indecent," "ignoble," and "mischievous."

Mill also first coined the term "unearned income" to refer to increased values of property, such as land or stock, without effort or expenditure by its owner. Fearing monopolies and too much money power, Mill first proposed this unearned income be taxed, a then radical notion.

Today, unearned income has been proudly renamed *capital gains*. It is taxed—but at a much lower rate than your time-earned wages or salary. Economist Michael Hudson, in his book *Killing the Host: How Financial Parasites and Debt Bondage Destroy the Global Economy*, says such income is really "economic overhead." He credits classical economists for understanding its economic cost for most people.

✓ PROPERTY & ASSETS

Any property owned by a person, corporation, or nation is an asset. Your income and what you purchase with it—stocks, bonds, real estate, and material goods—are all assets. Assets have value, a form of wealth, and can be used to meet debts or bestow as a legacy in your will.

The term *net assets* mean the value of your property minus any debt still owed on it, as with a mortgage balance owed to a bank or a car not yet paid off. The net value minus debts is referred to as *equity*, your share of an asset. In 2016, the top 1 percent in the United States owned 41.8 percent of all US assets and property.

Classic Horsepucky

Classic economic ideas were first critiqued by German philosopher Karl Marx and his coauthor Friedrich Engels in 1848. They clarified and challenged the unequal relationship between labor and capital in their pamphlet, *The Communist Manifesto*. Wage earners were not equal to capitalist asset owners, they essentially said, and that made any free market balance of supply and demand impossible. Its teeter-totter was hopelessly weighted toward those with bagsful of money, the owners of the means of production.

The middle class, really the pivot of the nineteenth-century socio-economic teeter-totter, were named the *bourgeoisie* by Marx. They copied the wealthy and, much like Pangloss, served power while tending to disown their closer neighbors—the poor clucks that Marx named the *proletariat*.

Marx and Engels advocated "socialist" modes of production, or forms of collective ownership. Eventually, these ideas led to arguments for state ownership, but more often, trade unions, some of them socialist, sought to win more public accountability through limits and taxes on private property and its fortunes, and laws protecting laborers.

Being men, Marx and Engels hoped for a violent revolution by the proletariat, the working class. This did happen in Russia in 1917, Czar Nicholas and his family being murdered by revolutionaries who themselves were quickly murdered by Vladimir Lenin's even more violent communist regime.

The threat of bloodshed in Marxist ideas probably did make rich men in power in Europe and the United States more inclined to negotiate labor reforms. They developed more inclusive economic policies with the help of the less-dangerous trade unions. Keynes is a good example of this greater openness to interests beyond the usual classic, well-born economic club. Marxist ideas probably made later Keynesian ideas thinkable, although Keynes intended to preserve England's money power, not overthrow it.

Marx and Engels did consider women in their tomes, but thought household labor in the industrial age a peculiar leftover to be outgrown. Lucky for him, Marx had married his childhood sweetheart, Jenny Von Westphalen, a noblewoman of independent fortune. She supported Marx and his writing while living in exile, birthing seven children, and tolerating their devoted house-keeper's bearing Marx a son.

Challenge to Male Norms

Whatever the realm of modern EconoMansplaining, whether classical or Marxist, Keynesian or neoliberal, women's concrete situation was never central to the discussion. Women worked, chose to be single, and even contributed articles to economic journals, but women's inherent interest in the economy was mostly overlooked. That doesn't mean some women didn't try to challenge male norms.

Four early twentieth-century women in particular gained public attention for their eloquent critiques of economics and the rule of a wealthy male echelon. In the United States, Charlotte Perkins Gilman published *Women and Economics* in 1898, drawing on the insights of Darwin's evolution. Widely recognized, she established a magazine called the *Forerunner* in which she urged women toward economic independence. Her sci-fi novel, *Herland*, imagined a future world with women in power, one where hot daily dinners were delivered door-to-door.

The already mentioned Emma Goldman, a Russian immigrant, became known as "the most dangerous woman in America." Over a thirty-year career, she spoke up for working people and against the collusion between government, big business, and war making. She was deported in 1919 for urging young American men to resist WWI's draft call. She famously told her radical male friends, "If I can't dance, I don't want to be part of your revolution."

Meanwhile in Germany, a young Marxist-socialist named Rosa Luxemburg published *The Accumulation of Capital* in 1913, a critique of big money and its economists. She suspected that if economists couldn't say what they meant in simple, clear terms, then either there was something to be gained from mystifying what they were doing, or they themselves did not really understand what they claimed to.

Around the same time in England, Eleanor Rathbone, born to a wealthy family, was part of the earliest women's rights movement. She argued for the economic needs of mothers in her 1924 book, *The Disinherited Family*. Mothers performed a nation's most essential work at home for no pay while at the mercy of circumstance, she argued. Her research of women during WWI, the same war Emma Goldman protested, finally resulted in Parliament's passage of the Family Allowance Act in 1945, but only after a second world war. A stipend was paid directly to all English mothers with more than one child.

The Family Allowance Act is still in place there and in Canada. It influenced European countries like Germany and France. Payment no longer is universal, means-tested now, but it remains an amazing feat. More amazing is how well kept a secret this is from most American women. Had you ever heard of a mother's allowance before?

None of these four women is widely known, but all were bright spotlights in an otherwise largely unexplored economic dark continent. Still, without women's broader economic education and sustained organizing to embrace women's economic values, such exceptional women would remain exceptions.

Discounted Differences

Friedman wasn't alone in his pity for wrongheaded women. In the later twentieth century, women served as examples for economic scolding. Countless articles and ads set impossible standards, while women were charged with managing prices determined in a macroeconomic arena where she had no control.

Keynes once used women as a metaphor in a famous beauty contest that appears in his masterpiece, *The General Theory of Employment, Interest and Money*. It describes the pack behavior of men with macro-money—though Keynes didn't call it pack behavior, I just did. It helps explain price fluctuations in the microeconomic world where most women live.

✓ CONSUMER MARKETS

Economists call those who regularly shop for supplies in the micro-economy *consumers*, and they are the endpoint for a chain of supply. Consumers shop at retail stores like a Piggly-Wiggly grocery or an Ace Hardware store. Those whose products appear in those markets are called *vendors*, who sell at a lower *wholesale price*. Stores then resell products to consumers at a marked-up *retail price*. Whether buying wholesale or retail, microeconomic shoppers always look for bargains, meaning the best supply in exchange for their dollars' demand. Sometimes consumers, vendors, and stores have multiple choices, sometimes few. Time and geography limit bargain hunting. Those with less time and access often pay more.

✓ STOCK & COMMODITIES MARKETS

Economists call those who regularly shop for commodities or stocks in the macro-economy *traders*. Like consumers, traders are looking for bargains, but unlike consumers whose purchases are private, traders' purchases and prices are watched by other traders out in public. Also, unlike consumers, traders turn around and trade what they just bought. By 1870, ticker tapes telegraphed stock prices, speeding up trades, increasing transactions. Today's computerized tickers do the same but faster, resulting in the average time for a stock to be held by a trader as just twenty-three seconds.

Keynes's beauty contest metaphor reveals this important difference between markets—consumer ones and the macroeconomic markets. To understand, he urged his macro-male readers to imagine a newspaper contest with pictures of one hundred women. The prize goes to those who choose the six most popular.

Keynes calls "naïve" the fellow who simply chooses the six he likes best. He writes, "It is not a case of choosing those faces that, to the best of one's judgment, are really the prettiest, nor even those that average opinion genuinely thinks the prettiest. We have reached the third degree where we devote our intelligences to anticipating what average opinion expects the average opinion to be. And there are some, I believe, who practice the fourth, fifth, and higher degrees." Those higher degrees of guesswork gentleman Keynes called "sophisticated."

Are you wondering why this is considered higher? Are you disappointed in Keynes? Remember economics has never been about real women and surely not about what women want. Rather, it is about winning. And if, like me, you find women being compared to a market commodity on auction rather offensive—well, it's best to take that quite personally.

Neoliberalism Updated for Today

We'll look closer at how women are changing an all-male cast in the economic story in the rest of this book, but Keynes's demise and the post-WWII appearance of neoliberals bears a bit further explaining. Both Friedrich Hayek and Ludwig von Mises, influential European economists, developed neoliberalism in response to Lenin and Stalin, those Russian communist tyrants who'd overtaken socialism and Marxism. They had some reason to hope that the private fortunes of gentlemen would do better than what Stalin's Soviet state-owned economy had delivered, which was brutality and Ukrainian starvation.

At first, mid-twentieth-century neoliberals sought a strong nation-state with ample public money coupled with a strong market and private money. Both public and private money sources could have lived together in harmony, but by the time Milton Friedman influenced American economics, neoliberalism had reverted to the laissez-faire economics of royalty, a moneyed self-interest that waged wars to obliterate enemies.

Today's twenty-first-century neoliberals blow a lot of smoke. They are also known as libertarians, free market economists, free trade economists, the Austrian School, the Chicago School, trickle-down economists, monetarists, and supply-siders. When trading in international weapons, they become neo-cons, which sounds the opposite of neoliberals but isn't.

So how can you recognize this elite but slippery fraternity? The words *public* and *private* are clues. Neoliberal kingmakers call private money "good" and public money "bad"—that is, unless public money is paid to them through government contracts and bonds, transforming our shared taxes into their private fortunes. The surest method for this reliable conversion is making and trading weapons systems with huge price tags.

Neoliberals prefer their own private interests to any shared public ones, except for the protection of private property maintained by police and a military. To this way of thinking, public lands, public water sources, and shared natural resources like mineral rights are of no use unless mined by private interests for private profits—and surely not for shared public dividends. That would make us socialists!

Therefore, any fees paid by private companies to the public for its mineral rights or grazing rights are tokens only, and the profits are kept private. To this mindset, private, for-profit military and security forces like Blackwater are much preferred over a public payroll for the military. Private package delivery is better than your town's post office, privately owned prisons and hospitals better than your publicly owned ones, parking meters better managed by private corporations than by cities, and private insurance like Cigna better than public insurance like Medicare.

Why? Because, neoliberals argue, everyone knows for-profits are far more efficient than public nonprofits, despite ample evidence to the contrary (still ahead). Neoliberals, whatever they call themselves, claim that wealth and the profit motive left unfettered will create "the best of all possible worlds."

We saw this in Friedman's illustration of women making an employer "pay" for his prejudice: *That'll teach that bad employer. I'll work for less! Take that!*

Brand Names Go Generic

As my mom and I learned, you surely will *not* recognize neoliberals by their political party. We both met its two-faced power in campaigns that sounded good but betrayed us economically. The Chicago Boys rose to power with Republican Reagan. By the time Republican George W. was in charge, Congress had managed to cut our public revenue and raise our public expenses twice, until the federal budget looked as bad as the one I took to the welfare office. Republicans left us flat broke in the wake of a huge bank bailout in 2008. The resulting Great Recession has now gone on for nearly a decade.

Democrat Bill Clinton's administration, in between those of Reagan and Bush II, prided itself on balancing the country's budget, yet Clinton opened the gates of global trade with NAFTA (North American Free Trade Agreement) and loosened banking regulation in shocking ways you'll see in coming chapters. I'd like to believe that the Dems' Bill Clinton and Barack Obama mistook neoliberal ideas as I did early on, without understanding. More likely, seeing a continuity of advisors, it comes down to gentlemen's agreements and big campaign donations.

For the past thirty years, presidents and a Congress of both parties have agreed to shrink social safety nets, another neoliberal doctrine—first evident in Chile, but coming home under Clinton's welfare reform and a war on drugs that built prison populations. Both Dems and Republicans agreed that removing government oversight of markets and finance—creating the wealthy man's playground—should be celebrated as "deregulation," "modernization," and "globalization."

President Obama, a Dem, sought a fast track for the Trans-Pacific trade agreement and rollbacks in some 2008 Dodd-Frank financial reforms. Now Republican President Donald Trump talks of eliminating Dodd-Frank. He wants to rebuild public roads through private contracts, earning tolls and fees, instead of using public financing as Eisenhower had for the first highways.

All the presidents of our time and a Congress of both parties have equated public interests with private ones. However, in our current arrangement, only the private fortunes of a few are growing, while the shared fortunes of a majority and our public endeavors diminish. Neoliberals consistently refuse taxes on the wealthy, especially any intended to support women and social safety net programs, which they refer to as "nanny government."

Put Down the Laundry

EconoMan may call us girls naïve, or see us as commodities in a contest men judge, but in truth, women keep the economy going. Without the informal economy and the micro-economy, there can be no macro-economy and no international trade. When you stop and really look, it isn't that hard to see through an entrenched habit of deceit and obfuscation that poses as sophistication of the most powerful players.

Pretending everyone is equal, today's EconoMan is all for free markets, as if liberty ruled the movement of your money and mine and not the necessity of our needs—and as if tall piles of money didn't privilege the few who can multiply their surplus gains with an electronic blip of their stocks or bonds or currency.

Public income for government comes from taxes, tariffs, and fees. Private income derives from paychecks, profits, and investments. When the wealthiest private fortunes get enormous tax cuts, the publicly shared government must cut budgets or go into debt. Government's budget problem is made worse when Congress repeatedly funds huge war expenses and weapons purchases, and then bails out our largest banks.

The money that we-the-people have to borrow for our shared national debt just "naturally" comes from the richest who, just as "naturally," have newly tax-freed surplus money to loan us. The past thirty years of tax cuts and ballooning government budgets has created a vicious cycle for most of us and a merry-go-round for the wealthiest.

On Park Avenue, ensconced in a red hotel, it perhaps looks as if the invisible hand of the market has ordained this. It must feel a little Godlike. This was the philosophy of Voltaire's Pangloss. This was the thinking of the Social Darwinists of the Gilded Age. And that is our present, self-satisfied, neoliberal leadership saturating both major political parties in the United States today.

Both my mom with her Republican and I with my Democrat were dealing with a two-faced, lying power. That this money power is mostly male and pale remains rude to point out, but you will see this more clearly—and more horribly—in Part II. You've heard about Wall Street's 2008 meltdown before but probably not of the handful of women involved. Their lessons are warning us still. Will we listen?

Quick Rehash

- *Neoliberal* sounds new and inclusive, when in fact it's the same old story of what's supposedly natural—the rich getting richer and the poor getting poorer.
- The 240-year-old male conversation called modern economics has not concerned itself with women's concrete situation, though some women have persisted in reminding them.
- Both major political parties in today's US politics have failed to challenge neoliberalism's grip on economic policy and its rhetoric of the so-called free market.

EconoGirlfriend Conversation Starter

If you had been invited, which you weren't, to join in the conversation of male economic ideas, which school of thought might you have most enjoyed? Or most hated? Why?

PART II

HIS LATEST BIG BUST, 2008

EconoMan Keeps Profits But Shares Costs

Chapter 5: Learning Consequences the Hard Way

Whoever makes the money makes the rules—nice or not.

My mother had little patience with girls like me who had to learn the hard way. She'd tell me to clean up my mess, and I'd "forget," my nose stuck in some book. Then, with my room still a wreck, I'd miss going out for ice cream. Or when I called her pot roast too stringy and got hungry later on, she'd say, Too bad dessert's all gone. Now help me fold the laundry. It was really a test to see whether I wanted to complain some more.

My mother taught me the cost of consequence. She taught me family values. We all made choices and had to live with them, and those choices went into a shared family soup pot. For an edible life we all could swallow, choices sometimes had to simmer for a while. Sometimes we'd chill overnight. And sometimes we'd chuck it and start over. Try a new recipe, maybe new rules, new agreements.

About one thing there was never any question. Those who made the money in your family, they made the rules. Your time was not your own. First came church, school, chores, and then fun. Fun must include larger gatherings of cousins and uncles, neighbors, friends, stories and gossip—a bigger soup pot with more ingredients to boil out meanings.

We kids learned to discern wise choices from a hodgepodge of opinions and metaphors, looking for meaning behind common figures of speech. Keeping a *stiff upper lip* and a *shoulder to the wheel* got approving nods, but certain relatives and neighbors *flew off the handle*, or couldn't *bury the axe*, or *flew the coop*, or went *two sheets to the wind*.

You still had to help relatives and neighbors who made stupid choices and got into trouble. Maybe not *you*, not every time, but somebody had to, maybe many working together, boiling and simmering, chilling and trying new recipes out. That was just life. Everybody screwed up, and made stupid, bad choices at times, but everyone had to eat. Everyone needed help when they got sick, or no longer were spring chickens.

When we kids got old enough to get a job—picking strawberries or babysitting or waiting tables—everybody wanted to know what you did with your first bit of money. Did you make wise choices or stupid ones? This was always up for debate, the consequences weighed.

Choices and Rules

As I got older, I began to notice something, though. No choices worked well without trust, and choices definitely worked better for some than for others. Sometimes grown-up choices weren't between good and bad, but between bad and horrible. Was it good to spend my savings to travel one thousand miles to have my first baby with my newly drafted husband, headed for Vietnam? Or was it better to stay close to Mom and everything I knew for this passage, while helping her face some scary breast surgery?

Good was not even an option sometimes. The guys in charge made choices for you, and they could make choices you didn't want. Racism and sexism worked like that. The war in Vietnam did. Doctors did. Imposed choices could be thrust down your throat too fast and forcefully to be refused, however much your head dissociated to keep you alive.

To preserve societal order, what was then called the Establishment enforced our choices with laws colored by money and property. Money told you who made the rules. Bosses signed your paycheck or collected your taxes. Sometimes they opened doors. Or they didn't. They could slam them shut too, fair or not, and then doors would get slammed back at home where soup pots held our smaller, leftover choices.

> ### ✓ CAPITAL
>
> This word's Latin root, *caput*, literally means "head." Capital came to mean "first," "chief," or "principal" when gold crowns were displayed atop royalty's noggin. Capital crime in the Middle Ages held vivid significance when public beheadings asserted the king's power. Today's capital demands growing profits—money still the crowning achievement.

I was lucky. My husband survived Vietnam, my mom's surgery went well, and my baby was born healthy. But the country was changing. It got tougher to make a living, and people questioned the status quo by the 1980s. I blamed the bosses. Mom trusted hers, though doors at her company were slamming. On other people.

Her company got sold and downsized, merging with another. She survived and even advanced, but she grew more fearful, never blaming the bosses, quicker to fault other workers, the unions. Mom said people could work harder and shouldn't expect it to be easy. She retired and repeated what Fox News said, and what politicians of both parties were saying by the 1980s. Big government was the problem.

Relative Comfort

In her widowhood, Mom bought a little white cottage, paying for it in cash by downsizing her home. Her flower gardens were so beautiful, people drove by just to see them. Inside, her bookshelves held her albums of family photos and mementos. They were taken out and pored over, prompting memories and stories for the kids to make meaning.

✓ MORTGAGE

This French word literally means "dead-pledge" for a property bound to the creditor until the debtor has paid in full. Only when the pledge is dead is the debtor no longer at risk. Although many Americans pride themselves on owning a home, in truth, the bank owns it until the debt is paid in full. Failure to pay as agreed can result in the bank's foreclosure, or repossession of the property. Foreclosure forfeits the borrower's equity in the property, equity being the payments you'd already made.

✓ COMPOUND INTEREST

Bank mortgages double the cost of housing. We rent the bank's money, paying *compound interest*, meaning interest on the principal (the borrowed amount), plus interest on the interest owed. The typical American purchaser of a $150,000 home with a thirty-year mortgage at 7 percent interest compounded annually will pay $358,971 in total. It isn't until year twenty-two of a thirty-year mortgage that payments toward the principal equal payments on the interest. The bank always gets its interest paid upfront, and that's every time you move and every time you refinance.

Money had been hard won by Mom, important to her dignity. She had scrimped and saved to leave her children and grandchildren a small legacy. She died in late November of 2008, just as the economy collapsed. She never saw her own door slammed, but after her death, her home-sweet-home equity lost $30,000 in value, vanished in a huge banking failure and the resulting devalued real estate market.

I guess I'm glad she never lived to see that. Losing $30,000 would have *really* upset her. Which is not the same as saying she would have changed her political allegiance or ideas. She had arrived in the middle class and was not about to become any less conservative. She had lived conservatively in her widowhood, never spending more than she had, always saving for the future, for a rainy day, for us kids. She believed this was the way government should operate, too.

Frankly, I agree with her. But to be politically conservative no longer means what it did. Despite both political parties supposedly growing more "conservative," the mood of the country more "conservative," I cannot expect my great-grandchildren to be better off, no matter how thrifty they are, no matter how hard they work. Our choices have consequences, but money's rules have changed and gotten harder to understand.

Sounds Good

Something like my mom's ideals—expecting that American jobs, education, and opportunity will be there for those who work hard—is always the rhetoric of politicians. Our shared American values and figures of speech are well known. Yet despite promises, our economy's soup is looking thin, like somebody gobbled up the good parts.

My mom worried about the little guy—the small grocer, the independent pharmacist, the hardware guy in business for himself—swallowed up by larger national chain stores impossible to compete against. Big box retail was less than his wholesale, she'd say, so she knew the little guy was being squashed. She refused to buy anything made in China.

And yet she never saw herself as one of the little guys. She was, in fact, among the littlest. She would hate my saying that, but she had been an employee, not an owner. She was a woman, not a man, a bargain for bosses. That put her in a majority she never claimed. She retired to live as if near poverty, with her only sizeable wealth her housing asset.

That asset separated her from many more women even less well off who lacked that security. African American or Hispanic homeowners in her neighborhood were a tiny minority, distrusted and viewed by her as threats to her property value. Until their houses were paid in full like hers, they all were at risk. Like my mom, they too had to pay rising property taxes and rising prices for keeping a middle-class life.

Mom joined them, shopping at Wal-Mart for groceries, prescriptions, and appliances. She had to, she told me. Like many far worse off, she lived in fear that what little she had would be taken from her. Wal-Mart's old greeter at the door told her this was possible, speaking in code of his own loss, of his warning about retirement: Have a nice day!

✓ **CREDIT**

A credit is a plus. You add any income, like your paycheck, on the left side of your checkbook account. The Latin root of credit is *credo*, meaning "to trust or believe." If your trust is misplaced, a check might "bounce." Mutual trust and credit are essential to healthy economic exchanges.

✓ **DEBIT**

A debit is a minus. You place it on the right-hand side of your checkbook and subtract it. To become a debtor and buy on credit, you usually need proof of your ability to repay. Today bank servicers track your credit rating, a number gauging your reliability. If you break trust, your credit rating goes down, and your interest rate for loans goes up.

Trust Essentials

Our trust in the fair exchanges of our checkbooks' credits and debits keeps the economy cooking. Surveys regularly ask us consumers about our "confidence," measuring what we believe about our future. If most of us feel worried, businesses know consumer demand will lessen. If we're feeling rosier about prospects, we might risk buying a car or a home.

Without trust, economic exchanges slow down or even come to a halt. Political rhetoric and the media's language plays an important role in how we feel. Advertising matters, too. Its business is putting us in the mood to buy whether we can afford it or not.

In earlier America, when a depression or panic happened, a more diverse media with many more distinct audiences explained varied theories about the details of capitalism, labor, and conflicts over distribution of concrete resources. Muckrakers like Ida Tarbell and Upton Sinclair dug into big money's control of oil, meat, and weapons. During the 1890s Gilded Age, presidential candidates debated monetary policy and bankers' gold versus more plentiful silver.

In the post-Depression 1930s, after the stock market crashed, both political parties talked openly about working class exploitation. The greed of specific upper-class men in very real and specific situations was challenged. Franklin Delano Roosevelt referred to these men as royalty, and he knew how royalists thought. He had grown up one of them.

Royalty and capitalism have a long intertwined history. Since our country was founded, repeated calls for more widespread economic democracy have challenged the exclusive right of the rich and their hired bosses to make all the rules. Nevertheless Americans have generally aspired to be like these rich men. We're encouraged to admire them by institutions and publications they own.

A countering education in economics was part of the mission of the little guys who organized into trade unions and political groups. Some openly challenged rich capital bosses and the rules they created with strikes affecting whole industries and states. But only the wealthiest capitalists can unhinge a national economy as happened in 1929 and again in 2008.

Misplaced Trust

Compare those Wall Street crashes to, let's say, the air traffic controller strike of 1981 that so alarmed Reagan and brought his government to the rescue. Reagan sided with the EconoMan elephant in the room—the corporate airlines and their financers' big money—not the union little guy's peanuts. That trend has continued.

While conservative politicians and media of our time despise unions of little guys, corporations of big guys are accepted and honored as affiliates, fellows, and partners in public/private alliances today. We forget that elephants can be trusted to eat peanuts whenever they can.

ALEC, the American Legislative Exchange Council sponsored by wealthy men, has wined and dined state legislators friendly to their interests since 1973. The National Association of State Treasurers (NAST) likewise has proudly sponsored moneyed affiliations with Wells Fargo, J.P. Morgan, and other mega-financial firms since 1986, actually sitting the chair of its affiliation board on its own nonprofit board. Big money's influence has been normalized.

It isn't the first time. The wealthiest men of the nineteenth century created Wall Street's biggest investment banks, like Lehman Brothers, Bears & Stern, J.P. Morgan, and the Rockefeller's Chase Manhattan Bank. They elected their rich friends. They financed the trading of elephant-sized assets, and by the 1920s, their stock market that owned those assets was boiling hot.

Most Americans couldn't afford to invest in stock, but with so much money to be made, more people than ever before bought stock or bonds *on margin*. This was an expression meaning they borrowed money from the same brokers who sold them the securities.

✓ SECURITIES

The term *security* literally means something that is safe and stable. A financial security used to come with a certificate to prove legal ownership of publicly traded stocks or bonds. Today's owner evidence more likely comes in a computer file, the easier to trade (buy and sell) at a faster rate. For its owner, securities represent a hope for profit, getting more in the future than was originally paid in. Buying stock "on margin" means you borrowed money from your broker to do it.

In 1929, when stock prices began to go down, brokers issued "margin calls," meaning they demanded payment for their loans. Stock sales resulted, but when too many sellers cash in stocks in too big a hurry, it bursts what financiers like to call "bubbles," a nice way of describing Wall Street's overconfidence, inflationary flatulence, and greed.

The word *cabbage* is slang for money, which is fitting since too much cabbage in your soup pot produces gassy bubbles. Wall Street's cabbage boiled for most of the 1920s, but when its bubble burst in 1929, the stink affected everyone. By 1933, the whole country had a bad case of economic indigestion and the bank runs.

Worried Americans better understood their vulnerable odds in 1929. In the days after the stock market crashed, depositors went straight for their savings, fearing that bank-owning elephants would grab all their peanuts. Whenever everyone goes all at once, it's called a *bank run*, similar to the stock market's panic.

Banks typically don't keep money in a vault, as you might have thought. They only had a little in reserve (why is found in Chapter 16). The history provided by the FDIC (Federal Deposit Insurance Corporation) on its website shows that after the 1929 stock market crash, 1,350 banks closed their doors. The panic spread. In 1931, 2,293 banks failed. By 1933, forty-eight states had failed banks and the President's Economic Council reported that nine million savings accounts had been wiped out, $140 billion dollars simply vanished—a little like my mother's real estate value in 2008.

Newly elected President Franklin Delano Roosevelt and a majority in Congress were thoroughgoing capitalists like gentleman economist Keynes. They were all about rediscovering trust and security to refire America's economic stove. It was the only way capitalism could survive.

In 1933, FDR and his Congress put Wall Street's really big cabbage in a separate pot for those with stronger elephant stomachs. The Glass-Steagall Act, among other things, said Wall Street investment banks could trade away, chasing overpriced bubbles, but they weren't to issue insurance. Only regulated insurance companies could do that. Nor would the government insure their elephant-sized trades. That would take way too much cabbage.

Tummy Soothers

On the other hand, the peanut-sized deposits of Main Street's local banks would be covered by government-backed insurance, namely the newly created FDIC. Banks paid premiums to FDIC to protect their depositors' peanut-sized cabbage.

That increased trust. With new bank guarantees, Americans began to take their money out from under their mattresses. Post-crash, however, even rich men were worried about security, hoarding their gold, so that same year, 1933, FDR ordered all gold coin, gold bullion, and gold certificates turned into the Federal Reserve, the central banking system of the United States, to be redeemed for its current market price.

Government profits from rising prices of gold were then used to extend credit to the little guys. The resulting increase in the money supply helped spur recovery and helped to stabilize trading. FDR and Congress then created the Securities Exchange Commission (SEC) to help wealthier Americans. Its new job was to regulate stock and other securities, keeping public stock markets honest.

The Great Depression dragged on. Elders were going to the poor farm, so FDR began to talk about old-age security. In 1935, FDR and Congress passed the Social Security Act. Just as Main Street bankers were required to buy FDIC insurance, so would the little guy who used those banks now purchase a government-backed insurance that would deliver an old-age pension.

By now we know this is one anti-poverty program that unquestionably has worked, particularly for women. The National Organization for Women (NOW) reports that 57 percent of Social Security recipients age sixty-two and up are women, and 68 percent of those over eighty-five are women.

Labels Matter

If we call something an "old-age security law" and a purchased "insurance plan," as Eleanor and Franklin Roosevelt referred to Social Security when introducing it, then we feel inspired to pull ourselves up and contribute to what we want for ourselves in old age. But call that same thing an "entitlement," as politicians have lately, and as Americans we want to get rid of it. Entitlements are not fair. We know that.

Technically speaking, Social Security benefits are entitlements, meaning you have to legally qualify to receive them. But the connotation of the word *entitlement* is now being used to reshape public opinion. Highly trained brains that might themselves be called "entitled" work for elephant-sized fortunes that already own the most and want to change more rules.

Hired EconoMansplainers at think tanks like the Brookings Institute, Cato Institute, and the Heritage Foundation influence academic economists and politicians of both parties who are often wined and dined together in luxurious company.

✓ THE WASHINGTON CONSENSUS

Economist John Williamson first coined this term in 1989 to name a set of specific economic policy prescriptions that became a standard package imposed on developing countries by Washington, DC-based institutions. Regardless of which US party was in power, neoliberal economic medicine was the same for both, aiming to open up a nation's trade and assets to global investors (translate: billionaires) and give market forces free reign while cutting government social safety nets, newly named as unnecessary cost.

These same free-market austerity policies have lately affected developed nations like Ireland, Iceland, and Greece. Europeans pushed back, as have the Latin American countries first victimized. In the United States, Occupy Wall Street and the Tea Party both express the people's growing suspicion of being sold down river.

Today's Washington calls Social Security for your grandma an entitlement, which supposedly we cannot afford any longer—although an America much poorer than we are now first undertook these programs. Did I mention that most of those advocating cuts in Social Security (as well as in Medicare, Medicaid, the Affordable Care Act, and other social programs) tend to be pale, wealthy males?

Eleanor and FDR listened to the same kind of alarm bells from the same moneyed group. Dire predictions came from mansion-filled neighborhoods: Social Security would be the ruin of the country! The opposite happened.

With their new pensions, elders could maintain themselves and continue to buy groceries and use services. Take a Keynesian break for a moment. Consider the aggregate demand that our old-age pensions represent. Even as our population ages, and we try to recover from 2008, Social Security helps maintain our nation's aggregate demand for what businesses supply. Its loss on Main Street would be as disastrous for the butcher and baker, as it would be for your grandma.

Wrong Fix

Identifying Social Security as an American crisis of entitlement is an invented distraction from the corruption of big money bosses, where the real problems lie. Sorry Mom, but I do have the facts to back me up.

For those who now fear that baby boomers' numbers will tap out Social Security, one simple change would secure our young people's retirement. In 2017 the Social Security Agency by law could only tax incomes up to $127,200. Annual incomes greater than that go untaxed. Did you know that?

If this cap on the tax were gradually lifted, Social Security would continue to pay out full benefits to all Americans. Currently about 84 percent of all US earnings are taxed, and if this were increased to include just 90 percent of US earnings, any financing gap would be met.

The political parties of the pro-capitalist 1930s would have assured that this happened. And quickly. Four other financial solutions exist, as well—yet none of them are taken up, says the Social Security Administration. Why not? Why the continuous dire warnings about Social Security's demise?

If we can be convinced that the government is forcing us to pay for something that won't benefit us, we'll object and try to get rid of it.

Social Security is a safe public investment earning modest returns, shared by all of us. Neoliberal EconoMan would prefer pension money go into privately owned financial markets, where we're told it would make more profit. Their proof is found in the top 10 percent of Americans who are rolling in private dough even after the crash of 2008. But 2008 did happen, and 90 percent of us live in little guy neighborhoods still affected by its damage.

Here is one social security fix we never hear talked about. A small increase in the capital gains tax on those Americans whose billions come from our economic overhead, not from their hours on a job, could easily fund everyone's pension. But the unearned income that John Stuart Mill first named in the nineteenth century rarely comes up for debate in a Congress far more preoccupied with *our* peanut entitlements.

In Vermont, we have a saying: "If it ain't broke, don't fix it." Most of Social Security is working just fine. One little pump on the tire, and we're back on the road. But politicians and EconoMansplainers in Washington, DC, have a vested interest in avoiding simple solutions. As Upton Sinclair once put it, "It is difficult to get a man to understand something when his salary depends on his not understanding it."

Bullish on Bull

Like my mom, a lot of Americans still trust their bosses. Donald Trump's following shows how many Americans still rely on what the richest guys tell us. The richest guys sign paychecks, right? A rich guy's measure is the loot he's made, his money numbers kept like a scorecard. He who makes the money makes the rules in a nation, as well as in a family.

But the bigger the soup pot of choices, the more trust is required for keeping it all cooking. The more carefully we have to craft agreements and rules, and listen to figures of speech to sort out meanings. Who really does make our nation's wealth? Is money its truest and only measure? What is earned, and what is lucky? What is stupid to spend national budget money on, and what is a wise investment?

We all live with our choices. But the decisions made for us by the men with big money in the macro-economy—slamming some doors, opening others—those consequences could use women's closer scrutiny.

When the stock market is doing well, and prices are rising, insiders call it a *bull market*; the traders are *bullish*, the news tells us. My mother used the word *bull* when she doubted what salesmen were telling her. It's what they don't tell you, she'd say, getting out her glasses. Then she'd read the fine print on the contract.

I like to think that were she alive, Mom would be getting out her glasses about now, looking closer at choices and consequence. Since 2008 too many of us have forgotten the Great Depression's lesson that security has to be shared, or trust will vanish.

More of us "little guy" women should have paid closer attention to EconoMan's bullishness during the decades leading up to Wall Street's second big meltdown, as you'll see in coming chapters. But back then, if my mother or I had ever heard of the Commodity Futures Trading Commission (CFTC), we wouldn't have understood its name or anticipated its importance. Was it *our* Futures being talked about?

Yes, as a matter of fact. Too bad we had to learn that the hard way.

Quick Rehash

- Those who make the money make the rules, but the rules and moneymaking have changed fundamentally since the Great Depression.
- Economic ideas that influence rule changes are shaped by language that women rarely create or influence, but can decode, understand, and even change.

EconoGirlfriend Conversation Starter

What would real security look like to you? Would more money deliver it? If so, how much do you need?

Chapter 6: Women's Work Is Never Done

*In the late 1980s, Mrs. Gramm turns up the heat on our economy's cabbage,
while Professor Warren notices bankruptcies rising.*

I don't remember my Grandma Elsie or her sisters ever talking about what must have been thrilling when they were just girls. Women winning the vote in 1920 meant that they finally had some say in who got elected. My grandma and my mom never missed a vote, and made sure I took elections as seriously as they did.

Women have gained influence in politics since then, but if the 2008 drama revealed anything, it was how exceptional women remained to the upper echelons of money. It matters. When our democracy first started, only white property-owning men could vote, a small clique of the very richest.

I'm proud that over time women of different political allegiances and ethnicities expanded our national notions of who exactly has inalienable rights under God. They helped more closely define what exactly the government's job "to promote the general welfare" means. Even before women could vote, they worked to establish public schools, libraries, clinics, and hospitals that generally included those commonly left out.

The Buck Stops Here

That impulse for inclusion, often denigrated as soft and feminine as you'll see in coming chapters, does not apply to women's typical relationship to money. Women tend to be conservative and risk-averse investors of their money, apparently aware that a bull market can be exactly that—*bull*. The stock market goes down, as well as up.

✓ BEAR MARKETS & BULL MARKETS

Early Californians combined bullfighting with bearbaiting for paid amusement. Images of bears and bulls were eventually applied to Wall Street, describing different forms of attack: a bear swipes its paws downward, while a bull thrusts its horns upward. Just so, a bear market pushes prices down. A bull market raises prices up.

These symbols frame Wall Street trading as a deadly fight, though traders are rarely the ones in danger. A bull market occurs when confident investors outbid one another, driving prices up and creating overvalued bubbles. A bear market's falling prices become a problem when fear sets off a panic and everyone sells, driving prices down.

My mom and grandma were anything but soft when it came to money, and their votes reflected that. Far from tax-and-spenders, they viewed failing to educate the community's kids as more costly in the long run—as was failing to admit you would inevitably age or have someone you love get sick. "Be prepared" is the Girl Scout motto, and so the women of my family thought it sensible when Congress passed the Federal Insurance Contributions Act (FICA) in 1935. It's the same FICA that is on your annual W2 tax forms.

Since its passage, both employers and employees have paid into the Social Security Trust Fund through the FICA payroll tax to provide for our inevitable aging and our possible disability. Despite reports that Americans could no longer afford "entitlements," my Republican mom never volunteered to surrender her benefits. I haven't heard of any politicians giving up theirs, either.

The Social Security Trust Fund invests our money entirely in US Treasury Securities. In 2014, those investments returned about $99 billion.

✓ US TREASURY SECURITIES

Widely considered as the world's safest investment, US Treasury Securities are essentially loans to the government. Such a loan may be called a *bond*, a word related to *bondage* or *chain*, but may also be called a *T-bill*. The interchanged terms can be confusing, originally related to who *owns* a debt and who *owes* it. Municipalities, states, and corporations can also issue bonds, and these longer-term loans are generally considered safer than stocks.

The US Treasury first issued T-bills to raise money for WWI but now regularly auctions many types, widely traded around the world in financial markets. About a third are held by Social Security and other public trust funds.

Imagine if old ladies, including my mom, had followed the 2005 advice of President George W. Bush and his team of EconoMansplainers, and taken Social Security's public funds to the privately owned banks and brokers of Wall Street. Political salesmen promised higher returns, but higher returns always come with greater risks. And unlike the gains promised, EconoMan losses do not trickle down. They pour, they gush, they drown those below them.

It is astonishing to me that so-called "conservatives," like House Speaker Paul Ryan, still argue for privatizing future generations' pensions even after the 2008 meltdown that CNN *Money* reported caused $1.7 trillion in household net worth to vanish—my mom's $30,000 a tiny drop in that ocean. In 2017 US Senator Sherrod Brown (D-OH) reported to the Senate Committee on Banking, Housing, and Urban Affairs that five million American homes had been foreclosed, and nine million workers had lost jobs that would never be replaced.

Even after six years of economic "recovery," a 2014 Federal Reserve study found 47 percent of Americans surveyed said they wouldn't be able to handle a $400 emergency expense out of savings. When I was a working single mom, in trouble and needing new tires, my mom helped me out with just about that amount—$400. Would she have been able to assist me had she lived past 2008?

Risky Business

All financial contracts or products are essentially ways of buying time and taking a risk. You buy an auto on time payments, and the interest-rent you pay enables you to move into your car sooner instead of waiting to save up needed money. The automaker takes a risk on your paying on time. You risk your credit rating and your car, should you become ill or lose a job.

Mostly this works out. The trouble comes when too many people are taking too many risks, going further out into the future with larger amounts of borrowed money for doubtful endeavors. This happened in the 1920s. Leading up to the Great Depression, global investors who'd lost money on a financial product turned around and sold it to the unsuspecting. This trick is exactly what happened again in the run-up to 2008.

It took awhile to undo all that FDR had put in place to protect us, but eventually we got sold Wall Street's bad cabbage. It grew so gassy, it produced *bubbles*, that polite name for Wall Street's inflated flatulence.

Like Reaganomics' transformation from voodoo economics, the move to free up cabbage markets in the 1990s was considered brilliant in mainstream media. But as with Milton Friedman's ideas, it took longer-term salesmanship behind the scenes for it to become widely accepted. In 1978, two neoliberal economist professors, Wendy and Phil Gramm, went to Washington. Democrat Phil was elected a Texan representative to the US House. Both Gramms believed in a single answer to the nation's poverty, its vanishing farms, and its Rustbelt: grow the economy's numbers and wait for the trickle.

David Stockman, the Republican I voted for back in Michigan, was also in Washington by 1980, managing Reagan's beast-killing federal budget at the OMB. He considered Phil a good spy. By 1984, Gramm had swapped parties and become a Republican senator. As a ranking member in the US Senate Banking Committee, he would spearhead the long, inside effort to undo and repeal FDR's Glass-Steagall Act.

Meanwhile, Wendy did her part to free up the cabbage when she was appointed head of the Commodities Futures Trading Commission (CFTC) in 1988, a backwater bureaucracy few knew about. With the help of elephant-sized bankers, she would transform the commission's role on Wall

Street, creating corporate America's unprecedented profits —unsupported by concrete reality as it turned out, and sometimes found criminal.

Trickled On

Internet fortunes on Wall Street boomed while the Gramms served in Washington. The microchip and precision laser manufacturing replaced millions of workers. Wall Street corporate mergers eliminated more middle-management jobs. Productivity increased. Jobs and wages did not. The resulting big capital "earnings" endorsed neoliberal ideas in the media. The Federal Reserve lowered interest rates, which boosted Wall Street's leveraged deals, and encouraged Americans on Main Street to risk more debt for mortgages, autos, and a relatively new phenomenon—credit cards.

> ## ✓ CREDIT CARDS
>
> You're already approved—for debt. In the 1980s, nationally chartered banks, the big ones, began flooding our mailboxes with offers of *unsecured credit*. No *collateral* was needed. Collateral is something of value a debtor surrenders should she not repay as promised. If you purchase a house or car and not pay, your home or car will be repossessed. The earliest credit cards had required a monthly balance be paid. But newer credit cards offered "freer" terms.

Credit becomes a debit when used. And Americans used new credit hawked to them in their mailboxes' daily offers of zero-percent interest. In the fine print were the compounded rates, the fees and penalties you might pay, and post-introductory interest rates that a highway robber could admire. Accepting credit cards on Main Street cost small businesses new fees, too.

As middle-class debt increased, unscrupulous mortgage boondoggles hit the streets, with flyers put on parked cars, mortgage deals and refinancing deals feverishly sold to us. No one but a small group of academics, including then Harvard law professor Elizabeth Warren and her daughter Amelia Warren Tyagi, noticed our rising bankruptcy rates. Their 2003 book, *The Two-Income Trap*, describes this period of credit expansion and its dire result.

In 1967, American credit card debt was $1.7 billion. By 2008, it would increase a thousand times to $1,005 billion—more than a trillion bucks, reported the Federal Reserve. They said consumers reduced debts after the 2008 crash. Yet by 2010, the website *Investopedia* reported average household credit card debt remained $7,394. Worse, the rate of interest averaged between 17 and 20 percent.

That $7,394 credit card average was money badly needed by the middle class to replace stagnant wages. I had credit card debt, too, which my mother had advised me to pay off every month to avoid any fees. When I needed a personal computer for my work, I worried I had nobody to blame but myself for having to rent the bank's money. Warren's book gave me another larger, systemic view of the 1980s and 1990s.

Mrs. Gramm's Washington

Milton Friedman's theories were important for forging a new economic cookstove in the 1980s, but Wall Street bankers with an agenda lit the stove in the 1990s. Nomi Prins explains in her 2014 book, *All the Presidents' Bankers*, how high-level politicians of both parties were being sold on the idea that America was hobbled by FDR's old-fashioned Glass-Steagall, with its separate pots.

Thomas LaBrecque, CEO of Chase, representing the American Bankers Association, and Robert Downey of Goldman Sachs, representing the Securities Industry Association, told Congress that separating Main Street's deposits and loans from Wall Street's new and exciting financial tools only kept us little guys from earning far more than our measly peanuts. Regulator Wendy Gramm was newly approving Glass-Steagall exceptions and expansions at her commission.

Commodities futures contracts had first been used to protect farmers from market manipulation, and by the 1970s, the CFTC began to regulate agricultural commodities markets and currencies traded around the globe. Futures made it easier to manage the time lag between planting and harvesting, and to pay with whatever international currency might be needed.

If you've ever signed a contract for cable service, locking you into a set rate, you already know how futures work—sort of. It locks two parties to a fixed price, even if the price goes up for others later on.

✓ FUTURES

Unlike your private cable TV contract, futures are bought and sold in a public market. Such contracts protect, or *hedge*, the risk of higher prices. A commodity seller who owes delivery is called the *short position* and the purchaser holds the *long position*. Say Farmer Short enters a contract with the Long Cannery for four hundred bushels of carrots delivered in three months for $1,200, or $3/bushel. The next day, because everyone is planting carrots, expanding the supply, the market says carrots are worth $2/bushel. Because of his futures contract, Farmer Short just gained $400 while Long Cannery lost $400. But unlike the stock market, where gains and losses aren't realized until the shareholder sells the stock, the futures market is calculated in the accounts of buyers and sellers and—this is important—adjusted daily. These are positions only, not payment. Only when carrots are delivered and cash settles the contract is the deal closed.

It's hard at first to see the fluidity and movement of futures trades. The daily accounting of positions, without money changing hands, makes futures a very speculative market. Many Wall Street players take long and short positions that are essentially bets. Until either party decides to close out the contract, real money isn't exchanged. Positions can quickly be changed, adjusting guesses.

Position trades and their predictions affect prices consumers will pay. Today the biggest macro-players use too-fast-to-fail software programs called *quants* that use algorithms for "high-frequency trading" in futures. High-frequency trading might make a fraction of a penny per trade, but software now makes it possible to do ten thousand trades in a second. There is no evidence that nutty speeds of trading profit any but a few.

Settlement of a futures contract and purchase of an actual commodity is done in the cash market. In a global economy, currency values change at the same crazy, breakneck speed, so more futures positions hedge, or seek to protect or insure, currency values and exchanges.

Pressure Cooker

Wendy Gramm reigned at CFTC from 1988 to 1993, with her agency regulating futures trading in oil, gold, cotton—the country's most valuable resources. She was intensely lobbied by the biggest players, such as commodity producers like Koch Industries, and investment banks like J.P. Morgan. She "liberally" interpreted Glass-Steagall to allow trades in previously ineligible securities and new financial products.

Increasingly complex contracts locked prices in while allowing third parties to protect against default. Such contracts only moved risk to third parties, like insurer AIG (American International Group), but Wall Street was selling the idea of an end to credit risk. Easy credit helped leverage this illusion.

New futures contracts combined cabbage, an asset worth money, with what was newly called *derivatives*. I'm going to describe derivatives as radicchios to help you better picture them. Radicchio is often chopped up in salad mixes at the store, but fresh-picked, it's a little red cabbage that will fit in your hand. A relative of the big cabbage (an asset worth money), a derivative radicchio is the promise of the cabbage's future price. And remember, it's red, the color of debt.

You or I might call these little red cabbages bets or guesses, or perhaps insurance by another name. Cabbage assets and radicchio derivatives were sold together, prepackaged as if for salad or soup. Radicchios became very trendy on Wall Street in the late 1980s, in demand by sophisticated or "qualified" investors, meaning they were elephant-sized with at least a net $1 million in assets.

✔ **DERIVATIVES**

Derivatives insure a price in the future. Prices of assets normally fluctuate, depending on what traders are willing to pay. Commodities, stocks, bonds, currencies, and even interest rates may generate derivative contracts, since all have fluctuating prices. From the late 1980s on, this kind of private insurance grew more complex and less connected to real-world value in a fast-moving betting game. What is most important to know is that derivatives were often *highly leveraged*, a fancy phrase for borrowing big money. You'll remember what happened in 1929 when buying stocks on margin hid the risk of too many bets and IOUs.

Generally, radicchios weren't sold to you and me, nor to most women. At least not in a way we would recognize. Your pension plan, if you were lucky enough to have one, might buy some, or your town or city or university might, and maybe your bank, if they were sophisticated enough and qualified.

Over time more radicchio derivatives appeared with catchier, chic names like *credit default swaps*, or *risk transfer agreements*. These could bet either way on prices, up or down. They were also called OTCs, meaning they were sold over the counter, not in public markets, kept secret for high-end investors.

They really ought to have been called UTCs for under the counter, but whatever their names, they all remained those odd little red cabbages. With so much money to be made, leveraging to buy and sell them seemed smart.

In 1992, Wendy Gramm moved to exempt Enron's new "energy swap derivatives" from government oversight, apparently overlooking Enron's campaign contributions to her husband. A year after that exemption, she took a position on the audit committee of the board of Enron, handsomely compensated, retiring from the CFTC to do so.

Her last act before stepping down in 1993 was to largely exempt all OTCs from Glass-Steagall restrictions. She'd been widely known for her belief in what the biggest Wall Street players called *self-regulation,* meaning government should butt out. With this last remnant of public regulation gone, Wendy butted out herself.

My Personal Perspective

Like many women back in the 1980s and early 1990s, I knew nothing about Wall Street and Glass-Steagall, or what the Gramms and investment bankers were up to. My only connection to the economy came from my paycheck, my bank accounts, my mortgage, and later when I remarried, my husband's small business. I fantasized I was a business owner, meaning that I had signed my name to my husband's business loan. My good credit rating earned post-poverty had some value.

If you remember, entrepreneurism and home ownership were booming by the 1990s. Couples were "flipping" houses, selling remodels at a profit to those without the time. Women were starting businesses, too. In fact, most of the middle class by then had gone online and on call, 24/7. Computers were in our homes and in our phones. The World Wide Web made even small businesses global ones, whether they wanted it or not.

My husband had designed one of the earliest websites selling hard-to-find world music for the educational market. New CDs and DVDs were as exciting as websites. When our business outgrew our little house, we learned we could easily buy a larger one and rent out our first—credit was that easy. The world seemed our oyster.

Tax cuts for owners, including little ones like us, would enliven America, said everyone who was anyone. Open the world for American business, finance it with tax cuts, and, no worries, the story went, government's tax base from all of that new business growth would increase, and the Gross Domestic Product (GDP) would grow. It looked like a win-win for private enterprise and public governance. How could Americans fault two good things in one package?

Magic Growth

Meanwhile, college faculty jobs like mine at Vermont College, with relatively good pay and benefits, got harder to come by. More women were being allowed into the academy but most often as adjuncts on short-term contracts, often teaching online. Face-to-face college had become much too expensive—and who had time anymore?

Not students. Many of these were adults who needed to upgrade their skills to find scarcer jobs. I tried not to think about the debt my students were racking up. Faculty pay wasn't as good as when men were exclusively professors. But the university's health care plan and pension were generous, all of my contributions matched by the institution. Until they stopped. Until their health care plan changed and cost more.

I kept my unmatched pension plan. It took money out of my wages before I ever saw it. I filed reports away without close study, only grateful there were people on Wall Street who were actually interested in something called "growth" and those boring columns of numbers, which always got bigger as if by magic.

This was simply how investments worked: whether bonds or stocks or real estate, owning such things made you money. So I'd arrived, I believed. I was part of it. Yet prices kept going up too. And what did I own, exactly?

I'd begun to notice that everyone in business, including the biz called higher education, had a mania for growth, to make more, to sell more, to expand more. No matter how large an entity—whether a vendor supplier, a retail seller, or a wholesale distributor—all companies, institutions, and owners seemed in a great hurry to deliver more and more, faster and faster, in order to get bigger and bigger. Why was that?

It wasn't just greed. We had bills to pay, and some had interest due. But I didn't yet put that together with the Federal Reserve, which I didn't understand, or the Gross Domestic Product, the GDP—whatever *that* was. It also needed to grow, everyone said. I didn't know why.

Bigger Picture Needed

In fact, I was barely asking questions then, too busy running away from the poverty I hoped never to revisit. Pension or not, job or not, I remained only a few paychecks away from disaster. I knew that from my earlier work with the poor. An illness, a disability, a job loss, a divorce—how quickly most any woman can go broke.

My husband's music business was a sole proprietorship, the most common type, easiest to start. Despite that "sole" word, as his spouse I was as equally liable for his business debts as I was for our personal ones. Like most wives, I discovered the law's "equality" in the debt department the hard way. Like 65 percent of small businesses, according to the Small Business Administration, his startup was supplemented by easy plastic credit, sent in the mail, already approved. As a business owner, my debts were bigger than ever.

Had wages and benefits kept pace with production in the decades I'm describing, more Americans might have managed savings that would have "earned" us interest, instead of costing us interest. We might not have needed credit cards then. But without higher wages, credit was often needed for emergencies.

These were more likely now that most households require two wage earners to support them. As Elizabeth Warren and Amelia Tyagi found in writing *The Two-Income Trap: Why Middle-Class Parents Are Going Broke*, families who got into trouble had often counted on two incomes to move into better neighborhoods with good schools. Bigger mortgages, increased transportation costs for two workers, their kids' education, and health care costs had pushed more families out on a debt limb.

In my mom's time, only three of ten women aged twenty-five to fifty worked for pay; today seven of ten from that age group earn paychecks, and an unprecedented number are mothers of toddlers and infants. Women and their families benefit from their jobs, but also live complicated lives, as I'd already seen from my mom's example. Warren and Tyagi said it: needing two earners in the family to keep the household afloat really only doubled your possibilities for something going wrong. About half of all US bankruptcies were triggered by medical costs, they found.

> ## ✓ BANKRUPTCY
>
> Since 1500, bankruptcy law has allowed persons to declare in court an inability to pay debts. Forgiven or renegotiated debts reduced creditors' taxes, and debtors could get a fresh start. A harsh 2006 law dramatically reduced US bankruptcies by making it more costly and difficult. Discharging student debt became impossible in most cases. So what is happening to the most hard-pressed Americans today? Without ample bankruptcy data of the sort Warren and Tyagi examined, we literally cannot know.

We Were Sold

Education as a well-paid work field became less promising, as accounting became less promising, as the music business and the news business went online, all things digitized. Wherever more software entered, concrete livings got harder to earn. Media talk got meaner. My struggles were not exceptional.

Neither were the Gramms' self-serving maneuvers. It is not as if they were alone. Believing greed was good, that greed was necessary, seemed a mantra in the air—and really, we didn't know the half of it.

If the middle class felt squeezed, at least property values were going up by the late 1990s. You had to sell to get your money. Or, you did until banks and finance companies developed new products called *equity loans* or *reverse mortgages* to add to your refinance efforts. In my grandma's post-Depression days, these had been called second mortgages, a source of shame. Now these were advertised as another route to new freedom.

None of the credit cards in our mailboxes were ever called debt cards. None of my students considered their futures indentured and owned. None of the housing refinance deals were called liar loans—except on Wall Street.

We wouldn't hear about that until after the 2008 crash, although a female successor to Wendy Gramm, Brooksley Born, did try to warn us. Her story of the late 1990s, facing off with EconoMan's fraternity, is even more shocking and instructive than the Gramms', as you'll read in the next chapter.

Quick Rehash

- All financial contracts or products are essentially ways of buying time and taking a risk.
- Credit cards and futures derivatives with fancy names came from the same elephant-sized banks on Wall Street that ultimately delivered the 2008 meltdown.
- Elephant-sized productivity and the GDP in the 1980s and 1990s went up, but wage peanuts went down.

EconoGirlfriend Conversation Starter

Have you ever filed for or considered bankruptcy? Do you know anyone who has? If not, is this because you and your friends are financially secure, or because bankruptcy carries a stigma?

Chapter 7: A Watched Pot Never Boils

In the late 1990s, Brooksley Born tries to turn down the heat on our economic pressure cooker, but instead Washington's bullies run her out of town.

I wonder if Wendy Gramm's successor, Brooksley Born, saw something like I did growing up in the 1960s with a working mom. Hers at least kept school hours, working as a teacher. Mine juggled a nine-to-five job year-round while also responsible for kids, meals, and family appearances. Mom managed the laundry, the housekeeping, the gardening, and the shopping, and was always the first one up. She'd fall asleep in front of the television after popping us all popcorn.

My stepdad was pretty good about sharing household chores as, years later, social scientist Arlie Hochschild and economist Elaine McCrate found was true for many working class families. A woman's ability to enlist her man's help at home was related to the portion she contributed to the family budget. Hochschild wrote about couples in *The Second Shift*, finding domestic duties were shared least in upper-class families, where purchased domestic services were more common.

My folks hadn't enough money to hire any help (except me, when I was old enough). But as was true for all the working women in *The Second Shift* whatever their status, Mom remained the real family-home manager. My stepdad and we kids would help, but only at Mom's direction. Did Brooksley see this, too?

All in the Family

Something a bit like this dynamic was happening in Washington by the time Born went there in 1996 to head the CFTC (Commodities Futures Trading Commission). Few politicians had the time or know-how to write actual financial legislation, or create economic policy without help from Wall Street experts. Just as my mom used all our hands to make our home run smoothly, upper-class Wall Street made Washington function. Lobbyists were called "advisors." They contributed to campaigns and cranked out think-tank conferences and position papers.

Nomi Prins describes a long history of the influence of Wall Street in *All the Presidents' Bankers*, but she notes the milestone of the mid-1990s, writing: "Times had truly changed. No longer were family ties and inbred relationships the key to internal ascension at the nation's biggest banks; a tough predatory, more sociopathic nature was required and rewarded. Mental combat, voracious killer instincts, and acquisitions of other banks (with their share of citizens' deposits) propelled the banking elite to the top of their field. Huge compensations followed." Keep reading to see how huge.

The savings and loan crisis of the Reagan–Bush I era had reset bank assets at bargain basement prices. Growing bigger was seen as the key to winning Wall Street's undeclared war with Europe's banks for global dominance, explains Prins. The biggest banks had long held sway in Republican politics, but by the time Arkansas Governor Bill Clinton ran for president in 1992, Wall Street was backing "conservative" Dems. Both parties were feeling the love.

By 1996, the two-party Washington Consensus that included the Republican Gramms and the Democratic Clintons was on full display, informed and well managed by neoliberal free market think tanks and big-moneyed power. Despite what the new president, Bill Clinton, said in public about ending Wall Street's greed, he welcomed their funding and their insider advice.

Clinton's Treasury Secretary Robert Rubin, for instance, had been co-chairman of the Wall Street investment bank Goldman Sachs, serving there for twenty-six years. Rubin appointed his longtime friend Larry Summers as deputy secretary. Summers had been born to a family of economists influential on Wall Street. Summers helped mentor equally well-born Timothy Geithner, another Treasury deputy secretary, later promoted to Treasury secretary by Barack Obama. Geithner first worked for Henry Kissinger, Nixon's presidential advisor, and next directed policy at the IMF (International Monetary Fund).

Before becoming Clinton's head of the SEC (Securities and Exchange Commission), Arthur Levitt had been on Wall Street for sixteen years, serving as chairman of the American Stock Exchange before becoming its regulator. Another Goldman Sachs co-chair, Hank Paulson, would be named Treasury secretary under George W. At Treasury's critical 2008 meetings about Wall Street's meltdown, Tim Geithner sat at Paulson's elbow as head of the New York Federal Reserve.

This all-male money fraternity is rooted in Ivy League schools and powerful associations, while appearing to be far above partisan politics. Alan Greenspan, Geithner's boss, head of the US Federal Reserve in Washington, DC, for nineteen years, was another kindred economic soul. (The Fed is discussed further in Chapter 16.) Greenspan had not only admired the novels of Ayn Rand but had been part of her personal circle in Chicago. Rand's ideas about superior men who owe nothing to society still influence Washington politics today.

There was little to distinguish Republican Greenspan and the Gramms from Democrats Summers, Rubin, and Geithner in their economic approach. They all promoted a free market which, by the late 1990s, had become the only game in town.

Winner Take All

All these big money bosses in government, as well as the private world of banking, took a special interest in lady lawyer Brooksley Born. In 1996, Born was appointed by Bill Clinton to head the CFTC—the same regulating agency that Wendy Gramm had left a few years earlier. Hers remained a small operation, compared to the elephant-sized government regulators like the SEC, the Federal Reserve, and the Treasury, all headed by the highest-status, government money guys.

With Glass-Steagall and regulation loosening, Wall Street paychecks had exploded, accompanying the new trend of merging companies while eliminating jobs. This brought with it that merciless ambition that Prins writes about in *All the President's Bankers*, reporting that "Jamie" Dimon, who eventually would head the biggest merged bank, JPMorgan Chase, personally banked $36.8 million in 1997.

Dimon worked in those days with "Sandy" Weill, who through his acquisition deals had headed American Express and then Smith Barney, and then the investment arm of Citigroup, created from merging Smith Barney with Salomon Brothers, which were both Wall Street banks. Sandy Weill had doubled his earnings from a measly $26.9 million in salary in 1996 to $49.9 million in salary, bonus, and stock options in 1997, ultimately banking $220.2 million from his stock options. (Learn more about stock options in Chapter 14.)

Writes Prins, "These astronomical sums were not even on the same planet as those achieved by bankers in the middle of the 20th century. The level of public responsibility that bankers felt or exuded—which was already nearly nonexistent by the late 1990s—declined in inverse proportion to the rise in their compensations." By then EconoMan's fast-moving game-boy culture was playing dare-double-dare you, taking jackass risks.

Enter Cassandra, Warning

The unregulated derivatives market dominated by the largest banks, including Dimon and Weill's newly huge Citigroup, had also more than doubled in size by 1997—estimated at $28 trillion. No one really knew all the details, since these radicchio OTC (over-the-counter) contracts were not visible on a public exchange in a public market.

Born, who had been among the first women to enter Stanford Law School and had graduated valedictorian, had little regard for daredevil trading. Rick Schmitt, formerly with the *Los Angeles Times* and the *Wall Street Journal*, describes her in *Stanford Magazine* showing up at CFTC hearings with an elegant air, looking like a younger Queen Elizabeth, purse on one arm. Yet Brooksley later told *Frontline* she had trouble sleeping in those days.

To better understand why, take the next few moments to think about numbers and what our growing US inequality really amounts to. A million here, a billion there, we know it starts to add up, but *million*, *billion*, and *trillion* are words that sound very similar. They really are worlds apart. It's easier to see their stupendous differences when translated into time.

✓ MILLIONS, BILLIONS, TRILLIONS

A *million* is one thousand thousands. Imagine a stack of one thousand, thousand dollar bills. Better yet, count each single dollar as one second in time. One million seconds gives you 12 days.

A *billion* is a thousand millions. So how does it compare to a million? A billion seconds gives you 31 *years*.

A *trillion*? That's a thousand billions—and it adds up to 31,688 years!

We really ought to differentiate these very unequal numbers with syllables mimicking their multipliers. A thousand thousands would thus become a *mi-million*, a thousand mi-millions would become a *bah-da-BOOM-ba-billion*, and a thousand bah-da-BOOM-ba-billions would be expressed as *tralala-lala-la-LAH-tra-trillion*. These words would sound so ridiculous that *Forbes Magazine*'s Richest List would soon stop drawing serious attention.

But instead, even after the crash, CNN *Money* reported the United States still had 6.7 million mi-millionaires, many of them multi-mi-millionaires. In 2009, *Forbes* worried that many had lost billions, but the United States still had 371 bah-da-BOOM-ba-billionaires.

Billionaires bounce back. Our richest bah-da-BOOM-ba-billionaire, one guy named Bill Gates with $46 billion in 2008, had more than 14 centuries' worth (1,426 years) all for himself. By 2017, *Forbes* counted a record-breaking 2,043 billionaires in the world, 233 more than the year before—and Gates in his retirement had nearly doubled his fortune to $86 billion. Each billion seconds is 11,574 days, so he now has the equivalent of 2,725 years.

Meanwhile, the median American household income in 2008 was $57,211 or the equivalent of just under 16 hours. By 2012, median household income had fallen to $51,371 or less than 14 hours and 27 minutes. It began to rise, but the latest US Census numbers from 2015 were still short of the 2008 median by $1,436, or about 24 minutes. No wonder most people are hustling more than ever. Half of all Americans make less than the median, and the female half of that half had the least of all in assets, income, *and* time.

Sleepless in Washington

Brooksley Born had spanned these different money worlds, traveling from her mother's public school teacher's home to the hallowed halls of moneyed realms. She and her staff believed it was the CFTC's job to worry about what might go wrong with estimated Futures *exposures* in the trillions.

Exposures are another name for risks, or what happens when a contract comes due, and you come up short—caught with your pants down so to speak, exposed.

Professor Wendy Gramm had been untroubled. Like my mom, I think she trusted the smartest bosses in the room. OTCs were her ideal free market, but Brooksley Born knew the game better and suffered insomnia. So much gassy cabbage—and those borrowed red radicchios, worse yet. Who knew who'd eaten how much debt, or whose bubble would burst first?

Unlike Gramm, Born had experience with financial power plays. As a partner at the Washington, DC, law firm Arnold & Porter, she had specialized in derivatives law for nineteen years. Prices and markets could be manipulated, she knew, having represented the London Commodities Exchange in its rulemaking. She had headed a major Swiss bank case that stemmed from the Hunt brothers' Dallas attempt to rig the silver market in the 1980s. (That's another EconoMan bust—as was the savings & loan scandal and the Black Monday crash of the 1980s. See Endnotes in Appendix.)

Brooksley Born later told *Frontline* reporters: "We had no regulation. No federal or state public official had any idea what was going on in those contracts, so enormous leverage was permitted, enormous borrowing. There was also little or no capital being put up as collateral for the transactions."

There was no reporting to anybody. A few regulators at Arthur Levitt's SEC were beginning to wonder, according to Schmitt and *Frontline*, prompted by frightened investors. Procter & Gamble, a client of Bankers Trust, had sued over some of their OTC derivative deals, charging fraud and racketeering. Orange County, California, blamed its 1994 bankruptcy on OTC derivative trading losses involving Merrill Lynch. That had shocked the market but not enough.

About a dozen of the largest Wall Street banks wrote the lion's share of OTC derivative contracts sold around the world. Bankers like Jamie Dimon and Sandy Weill had found these a cash cow for bank profits, and Born and her staff thought these banks might be taking advantage of Gramm's regulatory exemption.

Team Pile-On

Born and her agency circulated a draft "concept release," really more a series of questions, to other regulators and trade associations about what troubled the CFTC. She had every reason to believe powerful government colleagues would be her allies and help her gather information.

Instead, Brooksley's modest proposal got lambasted. Greenspan at the Fed, Rubin and Summers at Treasury, and Levitt at the SEC, all in step with EconoMan's Washington Consensus, went nuts. The CFTC proposal was "viciously attacked" at meetings and conferences with reports of "foot-stomping and the pounding of tables," Rick Schmitt wrote, and major papers confirmed the mood. Just talking about government regulation would send global markets into a tailspin, EconoMan predicted in many loud male voices.

That Brooksley was female had nothing to do with this, of course. Post–2008 Crash, Treasurer Robert Rubin told the *Washington Post*, "My recollection was . . . this was done in a more strident way." Yes, he called Brooksley Born's behavior "strident." And he wasn't alone. Other federal regulators found her "hard to work with." Oh my.

EconoMan failed to notice how badly his numbers matched up with concrete situations. By June of 2008, the OTC derivatives market would be more than $680 trillion of notational value—or more than ten times the gross national product of all the countries in the world, Born pointed out in a 2009 speech. (This amount would add up to 21,547,840 *years*, translated into time.)

Brooksley's real problem at the CFTC was that she didn't back down. At a Treasury Department meeting of top regulators late in April 1998, Born confided to reporter Schmitt that Treasury Secretary Rubin tried to stop her, saying the CFTC had no legal jurisdiction. "I told him . . . that I had never heard anyone assert that . . . and I would be happy to see the legal analysis he was basing his position on." She added, "He didn't have one because it was not a legitimate legal position."

Greenspan and Levitt also opposed her, while Greenspan had already shown his cards at their first luncheon together, she told *Frontline*. Greenspan had said, "I guess you and I will never agree about fraud."

"What's not to agree about?" she asked.

"You will always think there should be a law against fraud. But I don't think there is a need . . ."

This summed up the general attitude at that April Treasury meeting, she said. "It was as though the other financial regulators were saying, 'We don't want to know.'"

Doubling Down

Brooksley nevertheless put her proposal out for public comment two weeks later in mid-May. Within hours, her co-regulators Rubin, Greenspan, and Levitt issued a joint statement calling for Congress to stop Born and the CFTC from doing their job. No government regulators had ever done such a thing before.

In her testimony before the US House Committee on Banking and Financial Services on July 24, 1998, Born warned that these markets were not so private as everyone kept claiming. Their lack of transparency could hurt the wider public. "Many of us have interests in the corporations, mutual funds, pension funds, insurance companies, municipalities, and other entities trading in these instruments."

In September 1998, the fates supplied Brooksley with proof. Long Term Capital Management (LTCM), a hedge fund founded by two Nobel Prize genius economists, had tripled its assets in just three years, using algorithms and super-fast trading software for derivatives they had claimed would never fail. Why? Because they were, you know, geniuses. Then suddenly LTCM went bust, shocking Wall Street.

It was no surprise for Brooksley. "It was exactly what I had been worried about," she later told *Frontline*. "They had enormous leverage. . . . [$4 billion in capital to back up derivatives supposedly worth $1.3 trillion.] All these big banks had extended unlimited loans to LTCM, and they hadn't done their homework. They didn't even know the extent of LTCM's exposure."

Tim Geithner, then at the Federal Reserve Bank of New York, organized a bailout among the fourteen banks that had loaned money to LTCM, buying out the company in 1998. It was like a dress rehearsal for what would happen a decade later, except ten years later, we the people bought the debt.

EconoMan's consensus did not just ignore Brooksley's warning. Congress next passed a six-month moratorium bill that specifically barred any CFTC action on derivatives for the time remaining to Born's appointment. This could not have appeared more personally vengeful. (They continued to keep derivatives unregulated.)

With her dignity intact, Born told reporters this signaled the end of her public responsibility for what was happening. She stepped down in June 1999, though she has since been recognized for seeing Wall Street's nonsensical numbers, impossible to pay.

A World of Difference

And this is where my comparison of mom's smoothly running my childhood home to Wall Street's running Washington really breaks down. It wasn't the same at all.

My mom never advised us to stop cleaning and look the other way past dirt. She never stopped cooking for all of us. She did her managing behind the scenes for our family's benefit, not her own. If anyone were shortchanged on sleep, or rewards, or credit due, my mom was. Like Brooksley, my mom never got rich from any of her good work.

By contrast, Wall Street's management looks smooth enough to be slimy. While fellow regulators and Congress kept Brooksley from doing her job, Phil Gramm introduced what became the Financial Services Modernization Act of 1999. It removed the last of Glass-Steagall limitations on the financial sector installed by FDR. By May, this bill had passed the Senate.

Six days later, Treasury Secretary Robert Rubin announced he would leave his post, and Clinton named Larry Summers his successor. Rubin left the Treasury in July, and three days after both houses of Congress approved the Modernization bill, he took a newly created chairman position at Citigroup with an annual compensation package worth $40 million.

In November of 1999, Bill Clinton signed the bill with a champagne celebration at the White House. All the cads, all the players attended. Much was made of it in the media for being a really forward-thinking move. Our economy was now more free and liberal than ever.

In those days, I didn't hear about Brooksley who had worried that we were unlearning lessons from the Great Depression—and that we were being sold some very bad cabbage. If I had heard of derivatives, I probably wouldn't have understood them. Back then, *liberal* for me still seemed a word for freeing people, not a word for freeing the money of our sophisticated economic owners. I didn't yet know that we were owned.

Who Owns You?

Wendy Gramm's and Brooksley's stories would later help me to see this more clearly, though I had already experienced being owned as property by 1999. In 1984, my college was sold to a larger military university. I didn't want a degree from them, but I had no choice. Decades later, my college faculty teaching position was sold as part of my private university's sale to yet another private university. No one had consulted me, the thought irrelevant.

In the first case, I was revenue property in accounts receivable. In the second, I was only a cost that had been shifted to someone new and bigger, a purchaser, a group of investors, a new president/CEO who would now manage my work, my life, and my time. The same was happening to other students, going into debt, and other employees at other companies being merged with bigger companies, and many middle-management workers less fortunate than I were "downsized." (Part IV shows why, and Part V offers help.)

In 1999, Enron was considered an exceptional beacon for American ingenuity, its energy swaps growing income in ways that no one but the smartest EconoMan in the room understood. He was Enron's CEO Ken Lay, who had been a big contributor to President George W.'s campaign and to two hundred legislators in the year 2000, most notably Phil Gramm.

Generous Ken, a believer in trickle-down theory, had always urged his employees to purchase the company's stocks for their pensions and watch it magically grow in their 401(k) accounts. In 2001, Enron paid 140 executives $680 million. Ken Lay alone "earned" $67.4 million, reported CNN. That same year, Enron filed for Chapter 11 bankruptcy. All the top executives sold their Enron stock before sharing the bad company news of fraud investigations.

Four thousand workers would soon lose their jobs. CNN *Money* reported that Enron stock worth $90.75/share in 2000 fell to just sixty-seven cents by 2002. Because of fine-print restrictions on 401(k) plans, Enron's nonexecutive employees couldn't sell their shares, *Forbes Magazine* explained. They could only watch their pensions disappear.

Board member Wendy Gramm, who received as much as $2 million from Enron for her audit committee work from 1993 to 2001, had already cashed out stocks worth just $15,000 in 1995 for $276,912, well before share prices fell, reported the *Village Voice*. Privy to Enron audit accounts (later tampered with by accounting firm Arthur Anderson), she possibly knew what most other shareholders did not.

We'll never learn if she did, because she and other Enron board members settled out of court for $168,000 when the University of California sued for its pension fund losses, reported by the *Los Angeles Times*. Most other losers, like Enron employees, lacked the means to take Enron to court.

A wave of Enron-accompanying corporate frauds hit home as George W. took office, including WorldCom, Tyco International, and HealthSouth, along with corporate bankruptcies that rose to new levels in 2001 and 2002. In 2004, CNN announced an FBI report was warning of a "mortgage fraud epidemic."

By 2005, the University of California would win record-setting settlements of $2.5 billion with Lehman Brothers, Bank of America, and Citigroup, all banks eager to avoid charges for "participating in a scheme to defraud investors," as the university put it in a news release. Wall Street banks appeared to consider such settlements a cost of doing business, while government regulators looked in the direction of that golden revolving door for team players.

In other words, by the time the big 2008 meltdown happened, EconoMansplainers in Washington and Wall Street were very well practiced in acting surprised, as three more formidable women soon discovered.

Quick Rehash

- The EconoMan fraternity is close knit, small in number, and more self serving than self regulating.
- Women and other outsiders who challenge EconoMan's fraternity rules suffer mean consequences.
- Different rules apply to fraternity members, who are financially rewarded even when caught in outright lies, and possibly paid more the bigger the lie.

EconoGirlfriend Conversation Starter

Have you ever had an experience with male colleagues like Born's? Have you sometimes "gone along to get along" with your husband or boss, or important-seeming friends as Gramm did?

Chapter 8: No Place Like Home

Sheila Bair meets Brooksley's bullies in 2006, and in 2008, so does Elizabeth Warren,
Wall Street banker Alayne Fleischmann, and my hometown.

W hen I was a kid, my dad loved *Pogo*, a wry political cartoon. One of Pogo's favorite phrases seems even truer to me after the 2008 TARP bailout paid by us taxpayers: "We have met the enemy, and he is us." You'll see what I mean, as this story continues.

Rotten Cabbage

When Phil Gramm retired from the Senate, he became an officer of Union Bank of Switzerland (UBS), an institution that by 2007 was one of the biggest gamers in something called *mortgage securities*. Those, of course, were the really bad cabbage that hurt my mom and sparked the 2008 collapse—worse even than Enron's fraud that sent some of Wendy's colleagues to jail in 2001.

✓ MORTGAGE SECURITIES

Leading up to the 2008 crisis, members of the trade group called SIFMA (Securities Industry and Financial Markets Association) began bundling home loans made to you and me for resale to investors as mortgage securities. Wall Street investment banks were the biggest salesmen. Investors around the world trusted this new financial cabbage, their bond asset assured of safety by a brand-new radicchio.

What could possibly go wrong? These new mortgage securities came with red radicchio guarantees called *collateralized debt obligations* (CDO). Collateral meant safety. These were rooted in

America's homes, those subdivisions of beautiful places that Americans liked to say they owned, though they didn't.

Banks did. But which bank, and for how much, soon became impossible to discover in their newly bundled bonds, identification further blurred by a newly digitized system that sounded contagious, MERS—the Mortgage Electronic Registration System.

Wall Street's biggest banks sold their new products to pension funds, municipalities, and institutional investors like universities, assuring them of safety. As we later learned, rating agencies like Standard & Poor's earned big fees from the same big banks for rubber-stamping their new products as AAA-securities, the best to bet on.

Earnings were high, investors clamored for more—and so, to keep its cabbage soup boiling, the biggest banks pushed for more and more mortgages. That's why we saw flyers on cars, offering refis and special mortgage deals. After awhile, even rotten cabbage mortgages got bundled, and soon give the world its worst indigestion since the Great Depression.

Women No Joke

One of the biggest players leading up to the bank crash of 2008 became President Obama's Treasury secretary. Tim Geithner cracked a joke, two years after the crash, at an event to celebrate women in finance. He said he'd seen a headline that read What If Women Ran Wall Street? That set the bar way too low, he said: "How, you might ask, could women *not* have done better?"

This might have been funny had women's influence on Wall Street changed the economic agenda in the years before or since the crash. There's little evidence of that. A raft of books explains the disaster. But none I've found has focused on women's collective attempts to change norms. None describes a sustained, nonpartisan, women's agenda for systemic economic change. There isn't one. Yet.

As in the nineteenth century, an occasional economic woman appears. We saw Republican Wendy and Democrat Brooksley over the course of a decade at the CFTC. Party disparities alone do not explain their different reception by male colleagues or women's overall scarcity.

Wall Street today remains a fraternity of EconoMansplaining from the top of a pyramid, out of hearing by most of us until deals are done. A 2014 Princeton study summed up our undemocratic situation this way: "The central point that emerges from our research is that economic elites and organized groups representing business interests have substantial independent impacts on US government policy, while mass-based interest groups and average citizens have little or no independent influence."

It took another decade before another woman, Republican Sheila Bair, was appointed in 2006 to head the FDIC (Federal Deposit Insurance Corporation). It had quietly kept Main Street bank deposits safe for seventy years. Bair later told the story of the bank crisis in her memoir, *Bull by the Horns*. The book's tone is remarkably similar to that of Democrat Elizabeth Warren, who oversaw the 2008 TARP bailout, described in her book *A Fighting Chance*.

Both women, from both parties, reported being dissed and discounted by EconoMan colleagues on Wall Street and Washington. They typically limited women's agency while using them. Wendy Gramm had made for some good camouflage, while Brooksley Born had served as an excellent scapegoat. After the crash, another woman, Lorraine Brown, former president of DocX, a mortgage document processor, was the first person (and one of only two) to go to jail.

Brown was guilty of falsifying mortgage signatures but was hardly the worst perp. She was merely the least powerful.

✓ TARP (TROUBLED ASSET RELIEF PROGRAM)

Signed into law by George W. Bush on October 3, 2008, TARP's $700 billion package was quick to bail out banks, slow to help homeowners. In 2016, the Government Accountability Office (GAO) reported a measly 60 percent of TARP money for homeowners ($37.5 billion) had even been used.

Meanwhile, Treasury reported that about $233 billion of its TARP loans to banks remain outstanding, still at risk. From 2007 to 2010, the Federal Reserve secretly loaned $16.1 trillion in short-term loans to US and foreign banks, including $2.5 trillion to Citigroup, $2 trillion to Morgan Stanley, $1.9 trillion to Merrill Lynch, and $1.3 trillion to Bank of America. We learned this because of the Fed's only outside audit in a hundred years. It's difficult to decipher what risks and liabilities remain.

According to the Pew Research Center, the Fed Reserve's holdings are considered debt held by the public. Sources like the Office of Management and Budget, the Congressional Budget Office, the Treasury, and the Federal Reserve show debt held by the public has risen sharply since 2008, yet the financial meltdown's part of the national debt is rarely headlined.

Time Warp

My mother believed EconoMan's hierarchies only natural—he who makes the money makes the rules. But I think even she would have objected to TARP. I'm also pretty sure she would have looked to a billionaire like Donald Trump to stand up for her and the little guys. The election of 2016 imperfectly expressed frustrations like hers. She shared a common belief that this economic system is the best one possible, its wars inevitable, and its money (and a penis) the truest measure of who is great.

Other organizational patterns, other money measures, other ways of moving forward do exist, as females like Born, Bair, and Warren all advocated. You will see other economic shapes and methods in chapters to come. But for change to happen, EconoMan would have to respect women, their ideas, and their values. What makes this so difficult now? Financial circles seem stuck in feudal times.

Sheila Bair's financial experience was formidable and her charge critically important. In 2006, the FDIC's troubled banks list already numbered fifty, and she knew about their risks. Yet she writes that she waited for months for the courtesy of a meeting with Treasury Secretary "Hank" Paulson, former CEO of Goldman Sachs.

When finally summoned, Bair was surprised to be met by his deputy. Like a wife, he served her tea until Hank dropped in to say hello, sorry, no time to chat. In those years, Hank's influence was so great, reported *CBS News* two years after the crash, that he was called King Henry. The report seemed more breathless than bothered by the estimated $800 million Paulson retired with after administering TARP.

Later Paulson did find time to pressure Bair to widen FDIC's insurance coverage to include investment banks too big to fail.

Masculinity Rules

In money's higher echelons where King Henry reigned, only men can be knights, and only the most belligerent (translate: *masculine*) traits get respect. Tough, hard-nosed, hard-hitting tactics and talk prove this—the reason, I suspect, that Sheila Bair and Elizabeth Warren both tell their stories with so many violent metaphors.

In her memoir, Bair reports on her many "battles" with fellow regulators like Paulson and with banking lobbyists. She was often "on the ropes, but still swinging," or "fighting to change course," or caught in "one of the most brutal fights in my public career." Likewise, Warren's *A Fighting Chance* used the word *fight* ninety-six times, and *battle* appears fifty-nine times—although there is no evidence that Warren ever punched anyone. She must have been tempted.

Historian Robert McElvaine uncovers anxieties that plague masculinity. In his book, *Eve's Seed: Biology, the Sexes, and the Course of History*, he notes that most cultures have constructed a hypermasculine ideal that rejects all things feminine—but not from strength, from insecurity that demands he overpower her with violence.

All later forms of authority mirrored this first power relationship, male over female, he writes, even among men and regardless of authority's purpose. Its earliest expression is found among some herd animals and primates, where dominant males practice what McElvaine calls "symbolic mounting" of subordinate males to say without language who is on top.

In his chapter titled "Verbal Mounting: Pseudosexing, the Notawoman Definition, and Obscenity," McElvaine writes that most often male pseudosexing is verbal. Men call each other female names like *pussy*, *bitch*, *girlyman*. This pseudosexing figures in warfare and other forms of violence, and it is virulent on Wall Street and in Washington.

He writes, "*Fuck you!* actually holds a meaning in direct opposition to *I want to make love to you. Fuck you!* could more accurately be rephrased as *I'd like to make hate to you.*" Sexuality is thus used to "other-ize," he writes, to establish an *us* and *them*, a method to establish male hierarchies.

This isn't just symbolic. A dark undercurrent of rape and its threat permeates all-male prison populations and the military. Real rape continues to harm and intimidate women and men.

You and I, biological females, are the original "them," the other. Bair and Warren did not readily fit in among men used to dominating. Females like these, who had experienced discrimination and accomplished a great deal despite it, tend to find male pecking orders and their sexual allusions tiresome. As a result, they were left out of the loop, manipulated, presumed, or disregarded by male peers.

That kind of gaming is a less bloody form of making hate. Like war, it requires victors to beat the other. Warren, who headed TARP's Congressional Oversight Panel (COP), described as a boxing match her first encounter with the ways of Washington in her book, *A Fighting Chance*.

"The congressman went a few more rounds," she writes. "Then his voice got hard. 'Look,' he said, 'the game is shirts-and-skins.' A vivid image immediately shot into my brain: boys with sharp elbows playing pickup basketball, everyone hogging the ball, one team in shirts and the other bare-skinned. (No girls on either team, of course.)"

Lords of Finance

Bair also suspected political games. In *Bull by the Horns*, she writes that the guys might not have liked her "playing in their sandbox." By the end of 2007, her troubled banks list had grown from fifty to seventy-six. Three banks had already failed with eleven more expected to follow. The FDIC-insured assets at risk of her covering had climbed from $8 billion to $885 billion.

Bair could see from mid-2006 data that FDIC-insured banks held $3 trillion in real estate and mortgages, including subprime mortgages. Coming their way was what she called "a tsunami wave." Subprimes typically reset or raised interest rates and payments after a few years. This often meant foreclosures. More banks could fail.

Where had the subprime mortgages come from? Since Wall Street had discovered how to bundle mortgages as securities, profits had multiplied. Everyone wanted to be in on the new game. To meet Wall Street's demand, and with the big banks' full knowledge, unregulated mortgage brokers began to enter lower-income neighborhoods to push subprime mortgages as "affordability" loans.

These often targeted those who had built up equity in their homes. Persuading granny to replace her old fixed-rate mortgage with a new one, featuring lower payments from deferred or adjustable interest, left her with a time bomb. Ticking in the fine print were those steep payment explosions from readjusted or deferred interest. Rate resets were really intended to force another refinance deal. Loan companies made their money on closing costs and fees, so the more mortgage deals, the more profit.

Back in 2000, the US Treasury and HUD (Housing and Urban Development) knew enough about these loan abuses to call on the Fed to issue new loan standards and avoid financial fraud. Fed Chairman Greenspan declined, several sources told *Frontline*.

With fresh assurances no one was watching, the biggest banks and their mortgage brokers next targeted African American and Hispanic neighborhoods for predatory mortgages.

> ## ✓ REDLINING
>
> The government first practiced *redlining* in the 1930s for its home loans, marking a neighborhood map for special treatment in red. Private banks followed suit, routinely denying loans or raised interest rates, regardless of an applicant's credit history. The Fair Housing Act outlawed redlining in 1968, but a new kind of discrimination appeared in the 1990s. *Reverse redlining* targeted certain neighborhoods for subprime mortgages, sold even to people qualified for less expensive fixed-rate mortgages, and even to those expected to foreclose—predatory practices.

More Shirts, More Skin

When banks and mortgage brokers ran out of qualified buyers in a neighborhood, there were plenty of unqualified ones, and plenty of mortgage processing companies to make the papers look good. And if these still looked dicey by the time they reached Wall Street, no worries. Alayne Fleischmann, a young female securities lawyer at JPMorgan Chase, would learn that a bad cabbage loan could still be sold as a rebundled mortgage security with added radicchio promises.

A deal manager in 2006, Fleischmann was charged with quality control. She told Matt Taibbi at *Rolling Stone* that bank management prevented her from doing her job, and that higher-ups bullied those who tried to catch fraud. She wrote memos describing specific practices that evaded bank accountability, and listed specific groups of bad mortgages.

She was soon laid off, Taibbi reported, and only later learned that some of the bad cabbage she'd flagged had been deliberately unloaded on investors.

Meanwhile, Sheila Bair at FDIC had a sensible proposal for saving neighborhoods and investors. In March of 2007, she urged the American Securitization Forum, a group she describes in her book as "30-something white Wall Street deal-makers," to allow their loan servicers to renegotiate mortgages, as community banks typically did.

Those in the audience who weren't glaring at her were casting sideways glances or rolling their eyes. A hand shot up in the back of the room, she writes. "The gentleman started lecturing me. . . . 'You give them a break,' he said, 'and they will just go out and buy a flat-screen TV.' So why, I asked, if he felt that way about 'these people,' did he extend mortgage loans to them to begin with?"

A year later, in March of 2008, Bair attended a foreclosure-prevention forum in southern Los Angeles. Up until then, she writes, she'd thought of the crisis in abstract macroeconomic terms. Seeing its face, she struggled to keep back tears: "In stark contrast to the arrogance and disdain I confronted on Wall Street, there I saw families with young people in their denims or uniforms. No Armani suits in that room. I saw fear, confusion, and exhaustion . . . people terrified of losing their homes."

The Bailing Begins

That same month in 2008, Bair learned from *CNN*—not from fellow regulators Tim Geithner and Ben Bernanke at the Fed and Hank Paulson at the Treasury—that Bear Stearns, a Wall Street investment bank, was going bankrupt. No surprise, Bair writes, as they'd invested in "toxic" securities, but she was astonished to hear that JPMorgan Chase would purchase it—and with government help.

Only the FDIC had authority to arrange bank sales. "Yet here the New York Fed was," Bair comments, "putting government money at risk." She'd been bypassed. In her view, the bank and its owners had failed at *due diligence*. If Wall Street investment banks weren't allowed to fail, if the government could be counted on to bail them out, why be careful?

✓ DUE DILIGENCE

This is the economic term for doing your homework. If you enter a deal and invest, it's your job to learn everything you can about the dealmaker, his product, and what you're risking. Don't sign a contract you don't understand with anyone who hasn't earned your full trust—and even then think twice.

✓ MORAL HAZARD

Economists use this term to describe a situation where two parties have differences in incentives and differences in information. It describes ethical dilemmas of ill-gotten profits and their methods in a liberal economy, but buyers and taxpayers beware—the hazards are real and all yours.

Geithner's rescue of Bear Stearns was unprecedented, and eventually Bair would call him "the bail-outer in chief." He made backroom deals involving the FDIC's money without her input. When Hank Paulson drafted his TARP request, Bair says she was never consulted, until a meeting she describes as an "ambush." Paulson, Bernanke, and Geithner give her their script, proposing more FDIC funds be used for investment banks. (This had not been allowed under Glass-Steagall, undone in 1999.)

She later told Joe Nocera at the *New York Times Magazine*, "They would bring me in after they'd made their decision on what needed to be done, and without giving me any information they would say, 'You have to do this or the system will go down.' If I heard that once, I heard it a thousand times. . . . No analysis, no meaningful discussion."

In her book, she describes giving them a counterproposal: FDIC would insure all "new risk," but not the toxic risk she'd long been warning about.

Window Dressing

In November of 2008, kingly Hank went to Congress with a one-page Treasury memo proposing TARP. That same month, Elizabeth Warren was named to head the five-member Congressional Oversight Panel (COP) for TARP and its $700 billion in bank bailouts.

"Our authority was limited," Warren admits in *A Fighting Chance*, despite its COP acronym. "No ability to subpoena witnesses. No power to blow a whistle to stop the flow of money if we thought something shady was going on." Nor was Treasury required to explain its decisions to COP.

COP only gathered information and reported while Warren learned the ways of Washington. Bank lobbyists filled its hallways. "Sometimes I wanted to shout curses at the gods of finance over what I couldn't accomplish," she writes. "But the fury was tempered by the sadness I felt. . . . So many families had suffered."

Warren's "girly" insistence on feeling her feelings put her at odds with EconoMan techniques, as Dodd-Frank reforms were undertaken. Warren writes, "Lobbyists bombarded members of Congress with complex arguments filled with obscure terms . . . saying that if you get this wrong, you will bring down the global economy. It was the ultimate insiders' play: Trust us because we understand, and you don't."

Warren went on to champion legislation for a new Consumer Credit Bureau to enforce more rigorous standards, defending the little guy up against banks grown larger than ever. In 2012 she ran for office, becoming the Senate's most outspoken and best-informed critic of economic kings and "the gods of finance."

First-Class Fallacy

Bair calls the most toxic part of the mortgage securities meltdown the *tranche*, a French word for ditch, which on Wall Street was sold as a slice. Tranches divided investors into classes. A-tranche investors, who paid more for their slice of securities, were promised a full return, even if B-tranche and C-tranche investors lost their money through foreclosure. This is like promising first-class flyers a guaranteed safe landing, even if coach and cargo lose their wings and crash.

Despite such stupidity and meanness of spirit, tranches gave A-investors no incentive to renegotiate mortgages, as Bair had proposed. They threatened lawsuits whenever B and C tranchers sought to. The top tranche was bent on mounting everyone, staying on top—until foreclosures grew so numerous, defaults so enormous, that everyone lost.

No investors were as greatly hurt as the people and cities on the ground, but this insidious and un-American notion remains embedded in Wall Street's structures—whether pyramids or ditches, its A-tranche hierarchy is bought and paid for. Originally, the word *invest* from the French meant "to clothe, wrap, or cover." That more caring way to think about money's purpose gets belittled by EconoMan's hypermasculine money culture.

Warren writes of when she realized TARP wasn't what Americans had been sold. She was on a panel with Geithner at the Treasury, and asked him why so little was being done for homeowners. He explained that foreclosures had to be paced as TARP was "foaming the runway" for banks to land safely.

The A-tranche still expected to fly first-class. Bankers' bonuses and their asses had to be protected.

Meanwhile, American choices between bad and horrible, once regular options for the poor and powerless, had come to middle-class Main Street. The tracks of ownership and property, its cruelty in our heritage of slavery, followed us. In the same era when whole neighborhoods were being reverse redlined, while American homes were repackaged and resold around the world, the mortgage my husband and I had signed in the late 1990s with our small Vermont savings bank was resold to a mortgage company we knew nothing about, and then quickly resold again to Wells Fargo, a bank we hated.

We were astonished. How could they sell us? Why would they sell us?

I understand better now. Our being sold really says it: like most Americans, in so many ways, we were on the auction block, owned by our debt. I saw this sea change in an article written by Jonathan Mahler for the *New York Times Magazine* in 2011 about the town I'd grown up in, Benton Harbor, Michigan.

In the 1950s, my family lived in a newly developed area in town called Fairplain, which I now understand was code for "white neighborhood." Our town had drawn workers from the south, including many African Americans to its manufacturing jobs. Whirlpool Corporation was the biggest employer. Family summers always included picnics on Lake Michigan at Jean Klock Park. "Colored people" could swim there at the far end of the beach.

That valuable shore property had been a memorial gift to the city in 1917, named for the deceased daughter of a local newspaper publisher. Jean Klock's parents wrote in their bequest, "Perhaps some of you do not own a foot of ground. Remember then, that this is your park, it belongs to you. . . . The beach is yours, the drive is yours, the dunes are yours, all yours. . . . See to it that the park is the children's."

Visiting the Jean Klock dunes in 2010, I couldn't have imagined what I saw, the same thing Mahler later wrote about. The park's expanse had shriveled, hedged in by a high-end beachfront housing development called Harbor Shores with a private marina and a Jack Nicklaus signature golf course, membership only. I saw no children playing there, and no African Americans. The public park's playground and grills looked abandoned.

Race Divides

In the 1960s, Benton Harbor had been a bustling home to twenty thousand people. The city is now half its former size, with 90 percent of those left African American. The factory jobs left in the 1980s. Only Whirlpool headquarters remain. Harbor Shores had been pitched as a way to rescue the boarded-up downtown, I later learned. Whirlpool had a hand in its development, and some say a fist full of payoffs.

The Rev. Edward Pinkney, former head of the local NAACP said so, and not too long after winning a city election he found himself facing charges of voter fraud, involving four dates and signatures. Pinkney was convicted by an all-white jury in a town 90 percent black—and of a felony, not of the more fitting misdemeanor even if guilty, which many believe he is not. Freeing him from jail became a cause for the Green Party.

Harbor Shore's design addressed nothing of what was found in a 2000 study of Benton Harbor housing. It had warned of a high rate of predatory lending, and high rates of bank denials for remodel and repair loans to African Americans. With its housing stock losing value, Benton Harbor town tax revenues fell. Banks that on one hand refused homeowners' funding charged the city over $100,000 in overdraft fees.

By 2011, reported Mahler, 70 percent of Benton Harbor's residents were renters, not owners. The whole state, he wrote, was in terrible fiscal shape. I'd noticed that, too, on my visits. Cities I drove through along the Great Lakes looked war-torn. Detroit was a ghost. My son-in-law's father owns a newspaper in the county nearest Chicago and says the post-2008 recession has been going on in Michigan for the past thirty years.

In an episode on NPR's *On Point*, Tom Ashbrook led a discussion among real estate experts in the light of 2015 news that construction and mortgage figures were slightly up for the first time since 2008. But only higher-end homes, like Harbor Shore, were being built. More Americans were renting. Expert panelists agreed to seeing a "seismic shift" in the American dream, the one Mahler saw, too.

Michigan's Republican governor Rick Snyder, a venture capitalist, "heavily tax-incentivized" Whirlpool's new $68 million headquarters under construction in Benton Harbor, Mahler says. Its new campus faces the city of St. Joseph, across the river.

The two towns are racially separate and economically tranched, though both have fallen on hard times. Per capita income in St. Joe is $33,000 a year. Benton Harbor's is $10,000, making it Michigan's poorest city, with 60 percent of its citizens on some sort of assistance. Mahler calls Benton Harbor and Michigan a harbinger of things to come, as other states gutted of good-paying jobs struggle to redefine their economy.

Nationally, 2008 resulted in families losing 28 percent of the value of their equity and assets, the Urban Institute found in 2014. But African American and Hispanic families, like those Sheila Bair met in South Los Angeles, lost the most. Only the A-tranche, the wealthiest, have made gains since then.

Shades of Slavery

Only the A-tranche make the rules in Benton Harbor. It was the first city to get an Emergency Financial Manager (EFM), empowered to override a city's elected government. What an EFM did to Flint's water has become a terrifying story for the whole country, but for me, more frightening was learning the EFM's source was my home county of David "Starve-the-Beast" Stockman.

A thirty-year anti-government campaign has overthrown democracy in a dozen Michigan cities, including Detroit. I had met the enemy, and he is us. Like Dorothy in the *Wizard of Oz*, I'd glimpsed behind EconoMan's curtain to find men that I'd looked up to pretending to be kings. They had brought Michigan its financial emergencies—and then used them to override elected officials responsible for answering to all the people.

Except for photos of demonstrations to free Reverend Pinkney on a website his wife put up, women of all colors seemed weirdly absent from my hometown money news. There are signs ahead our omission is changing. It needs to, and quickly.

Quick Rehash

- Wall Street's mortgage securities were the last bit of cabbage that blew up a pressure cooker already filled with radicchios, greed, and testosterone.
- Sheila Bair and Elizabeth Warren, representing both major political parties, had similar takes on what they saw, which was arrogance of a privileged few and a law-bending exploitation of a public trust.
- The color of American money is white, and its masculine masters own more and more of us with debt, having made the rules to keep us confused.

EconoGirlfriend Conversation Starter

Has anyone you know experienced a foreclosure? How do they feel about it? How do you feel about it?

© Peaco Todd & Rickey Gard Diamond, 2017

Chapter 9: Proof of the Global Pudding

*EconoMan's neoliberal free markets threaten the planet with unsustainable
numbers of billionaires who could bring another Big Bust.*

Growing up, I was taught that manners are moral, and that if you couldn't say anything nice about someone, it was better not to say anything at all. Already I've badmouthed the great neoliberal economist, Milton Friedman, as well as the schools of Keynesian, classical, Marxist, and mostly male economists.

I have served up a rude cabbage-radicchio soup metaphor to explain EconoMan's overpriced and overconfident, gassy, lying bubbles of 2008. I've protested his toxic global farts, waved away and always blamed on someone else. I've insulted both major US political parties, calling them players and jackasses.

I want you to know this goes against my grain and my feminine upbringing. It probably does yours, too. We've been taught to be nicer, so I will here resort to a kinder metaphor, another of my mother's favorite homilies and foods. Whenever she said a sharp, cutting thing, which happened rarely and only with over-ample evidence, her chin would rise, her mouth would tighten, no-nonsense, because there it was, right in front of you: The proof is in the pudding, she'd say.

By now, we've had about forty years of neoliberal free markets in a global economy. I've been saying that neoliberal ideas sold by the Washington Consensus have been cruel and damaging, but an economist might answer—So? The real question is—Have neoliberal free market policies delivered the economic rich dish we were promised?

Following is some pudding proof for the answer.

Global Pudding Proof

Since 1960, we have witnessed an explosion in the growth of economic inequality worldwide. The inequality rate here in the United States, edging up in the 1960s, zoomed upward in 1980—about the time that neoliberals' free market ideology became the only game in Washington. Now it's even practiced in Beijing and Moscow.

I'm going to serve this pudding up as the filling in a cherry cream pie. Why? To make it more concrete and friendly. When economists examine how a nation's wealth is distributed and changes over time, they talk about numerical data in terms unfamiliar, like *ratio* and *quintile*. You needn't worry: a quintile is merely a uniform measuring cup, measuring 20 percent, or one-fifth, of a whole. A ratio is simply the ring that joins two measuring cups. Both tools help reveal monetary relationships within a society.

✔ RATIOS

Ratios describe a comparison between two or more numerical values, often by using a colon. If five people are in the room, three women and two men, the female/male ratio would be 3:2. You could also express this as a fraction of the whole five, and say 3/5 are girls and 2/5 are boys. Or you could say the same thing as a percentage, by dividing 100 percent (the whole) by five parts to create a quintile, or 20 percent. In that case, 60 percent are female and 40 percent male.

✔ QUINTILES

Your mom taught you to cut pieces evenly and share, and economists do this, too. A quintile divides a whole population into five equal sets for comparison. Picture a pie sliced into five pieces with the whole pie representing the total population. The first slice is for the poorest people, the second slice for the near-poorest people, and so forth. Next, economists fill the pie with their data cherries, say in this case income and asset numbers. Each equal-sized pie slice of population gets the cherries they earned and own.

Why do economists look at ratios and quintiles? To more clearly see the movement of cherries among all five pie slices over time. Economic mobility—or people's ability to move from the thinner poverty pie slice with few cherries, to the fuller middle-class pie slice—can then be seen. In recent times, more of the hard-earned cherries in four of the US slices have moved to the fifth highest-income pie slice. That pie piece has become an ultra deep-dish serving. Even that slice mostly goes to the top 1 percent. Picture the 1 percent's share as a freakishly giant atomic cherry.

Unsweetened Parfait

In 2011, Stephanie Seguino, an economist specializing in international development at the University of Vermont (UVM), told me in an interview that the most important issue for women to learn about was income inequality. Then she gave me a ratio, saying: "Looking at income ratios around the world in 2005, for every $1 of income at the bottom 20 percent, the top 20 percent makes $105. This is huge."

Frankly, it didn't sound that huge to me, but here is a picture of what she meant about the differences in proportion of income, using those quintile measures. I've put the pudding in a parfait glass instead of a pie plate, representing everyone's income, worldwide. Its graphic quintiles make the top to bottom ratio she was talking about more understandable.

Based on UN figures for 2008, the biggest, darkest portion shows us the top quintile's income, compared to everyone else in the four remaining bottom quintiles. We four quintiles, 80 percent of us, look much more alike than different.

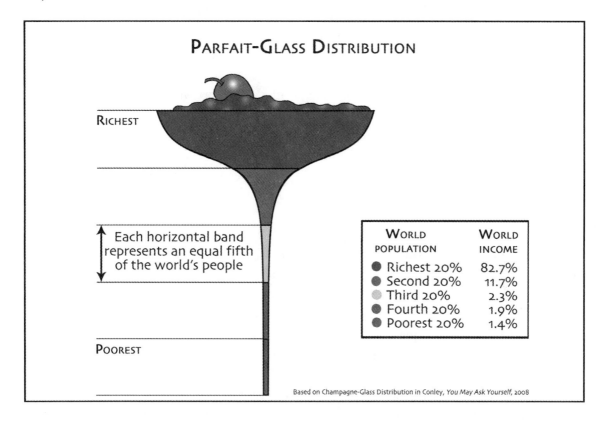

PARFAIT-GLASS DISTRIBUTION

RICHEST

Each horizontal band represents an equal fifth of the world's people

POOREST

WORLD POPULATION	WORLD INCOME
● Richest 20%	82.7%
● Second 20%	11.7%
● Third 20%	2.3%
● Fourth 20%	1.9%
● Poorest 20%	1.4%

Based on Champagne-Glass Distribution in Conley, *You May Ask Yourself*, 2008

This picture does not include owned assets, the other part of wealth that most Americans saw reduced by over 28 percent in 2008. Seguino says that when those are included, the differences are even greater. Yes, more citizens of wealthy nations, like the United States, France, and Switzerland, place higher than most citizens of Africa and South America. But even if you think yourself in that second global quintile, closer to the top of this graphic, there is a huge difference between the rim of that glass where EconoKings dip in their tongues, and you, the narrow stem that holds it all up.

Given what we've already learned about the huge worlds of difference between thousands, mi-millions, and bah-da-BOOM-ba-billions, more than likely you are further down the stem than you think. This 2008 graphic's information is already old, and it measures incomes, not assets and not net worth. Picturing net worth inequalities would require a bigger bowl, a skinnier stem, the reason you're feeling the squeeze.

A Growth Industry

Millionaires and billionaires are what financial people call High Net Worth Individuals (HNWI), defined as those with over $1 million in spare change—cash or accounts quickly convertible to cash. Their population has increased dramatically since 2008. I think using the word *individual* here is another version of sexist language, similar to the way news stories will say an "individual" with a gun was arrested, rather than saying it was, *oh jeez*, a man, again. This helps EconoMan avoid detection as a hypermasculine and cultural construction.

These men's numbers start to add up after awhile. Let's start with millionaires post-2008, the year that set so many of us back. By 2012, they bounced back big time. The world had more mi-millionaires than ever that year, reported CNBC, a soaring 16 million of them. The United States had added the most, totaling over 7 million US mi-millionaires. But that was nothing. By 2017 *Business Insider* reported 33 million "people" worldwide were now millionaires, more than double the number. Those people were EconoMen. Estimates came from the Credit Suisse Global Wealth Databook.

Now let's look at billionaires. In 2012, *Forbes* reported a record-setting number of 1,226 bah-da-BOOM-ba-billionaires, with the United States topping the list with 425 all-American mostly guys. Two years later, a 2014 report from Wealth-X and UBS Billionaire Census claimed another new record, 2,325 billionaires with the United States, China, Russia, and India generating the biggest crops of them. (I'll here rudely note that all four of these nations tolerate rising numbers in poverty, with politicians turning a blind eye.)

Three years later, in 2017 *Forbes* reported a "record 2,043 billionaires worldwide." Was that a setback? More likely they had just missed some that UBS had found earlier. In yet another CNBC report for 2017, a Chinese source, The Huran Global Rich List, claimed 2,257 billionaires. These discrepancies in billionaire numbers undoubtedly are due to what the last researcher admitted, saying billionaires "go to extraordinary lengths to conceal their wealth."

Putting dollar amounts to this slippery global population is even harder. In 2012 CNBC reported millionaire net worth at $4.62 trillion. In 2017 CNBC claimed world net worth of billionaires at $8 trillion, a doubled amount.

Converted to time? I'm not exaggerating when I say that our tolerating the neoliberal practice of a few men hoarding most of our pie cherries and parfait pudding really takes us backward. We're not even talking King George royalty, here. We're talking Nebuchadnezzar and Pharoah. No, worse than that. Take those last estimated dollars and convert them into seconds, and you will find your-self projected backward in time 1,718,670 *years* to the Jurassic period.

T. rex might make a good movie, but it doesn't make for a happy planet.

Tipsy Times

The distance between the world's top quintile and the poorest, first expressed to me as a ratio by Seguino, at $105:$1, gave us the global parfait glass picture. But if we were to look just here in the United States between the top 1 percent of Americans and our median quintile, not the bottom, as the Economic Policy Institute did in 2010, the ratio was $288:$1, nearly three times as large a bowl, teetering from the weight up top. Back in 1962, they say that the US ratio was $125:$1. Its 2010 ratio more than doubled, a proportion that keeps showing up.

The OECD (Organization for Economic Cooperation and Development) pointed to similar US changes in their 2011 report, Divided We Stand: Why Inequality Keeps Rising, naming US inequality among the highest of their thirty-six members. Only Chile, Mexico, and Turkey are now more unequal.

Meanwhile, US poverty rates have grown, narrowing the stem. We have fewer middle-class Americans. It is rude to say so, but a relationship exists between one quintile going up and the other four going down, one pie slice getting fat and juicy, while the others flatten. Neoliberalism and development policies promoting free markets work well for a few HNWIs, those *high net worth individuals*. But for most of us, free markets cost dearly.

New York University sociology professor Laura Norén believes this stemmed glass graphic works because it enables people to see the fragility of the system as it operates now—as we learned in 2008. It doesn't take much to snap that narrow stem where four-fifths of the people on earth live.

Without a more solid footing on that stemmed glass, the global champagne-shaped economy tips and crashes easily. Its shape is really an inverted version of EconoMan's pyramid, its wide base (namely us) upturned and hollowed out.

Increasingly, those in the stem (you and me, and most of the people you know) are con-scripted into the role of what my mom called "cleaner-uppers." TARP is an example of that. Yet even after TARP's save, the parfait glass top quintile got bigger, and those two bottom quintiles got squeezed narrower. This is why many predict another even bigger financial crisis. We've done little to change the overall tipsy picture of income distribution.

I believe little can happen, so long as most women don't understand what is so wrong, espe-cially for them.

No Peace Without Prosperity

The parfait graphic works because of the symbolism, its elegant long-stemmed crystal a marker of ease and luxury. People know who uses stemmed glasses and who reuses jelly jars. We've already seen how, in the wake of humiliating war debts, Hitler's grandiose vision of a Third Reich arose. After the economic obliteration of Iraq came the rise of ISIS with its dream of a Caliphate. Post–economic meltdown in the United States, Trump promises to make America great again. These are masculine corrections to an imposed impoverishment, reclaiming glory from a ferocious past.

✓ THE WORLD BANK, THE IMF, and WTO

In 1944, with France liberated in Europe but WWII still raging, Franklin Delano Roosevelt convened a highly secret meeting at Bretton Woods, New Hampshire. Delegates from forty-four countries, all men of course, created global institutions. The *International Monetary Fund (IMF)* sought to disarm national currency exchanges waged as war while the *World Bank* rebuilt war-torn regions to alleviate poverty. They also eventually reached a General Agreement on Tariffs and Trade (GATT). Tariffs are national taxes on international trade, which had also been used as weapons. In 1995, GATT became the *World Trade Organization (WTO)*.

Despite a gentlemanly intent to regulate international economic relations in such a way that another world war would never again be repeated, these institutions were rooted in undemocratic notions of pay-to-play, a little like tranches. Economist Richard Peet explains in his book *Unholy Trinity* that the number of votes a nation can cast is based on how much capital it puts in. The United States has always had the most votes, and policies have advantaged US currency and US corporations.

Globalization has exported capitalism to all the earth's nations, but unfortunately it is a particular kind of capitalism that creates billionaires and poverty, linked together in a frightening ratio. Peet writes that all three global institutions—the IMF, the World Bank, and WTO—have amplified international resentments, and failed in their stated mission of shared prosperity and peaceful trade.

Subverted by neoliberal ideas within its ranks of EconoMan expertise, this trio has sought to deregulate the world economy, override state interventions, and encourage private "individuals'" moving capital and assets outside national boundaries in an ongoing and chaotic economic war. Peet describes their familiar EconoMansplaining: "All three have learned that a little spin and some confessions of partial failure ('we have a lot to learn') excuse many abuses in the exercise of power."

This power had escalated when London bankers first invented offshore banking in 1962, creating a bond to circumvent national capital controls and enable the wealthiest to evade taxes. Fifty years later, their bonds, free of taxes, now chain the rest of us to private and public debt.

Two-Faced Measure

Economists have long been measuring inequality of income with a widely recognized and uniform measure called the *Gini coefficient,* named for Corrado Gini (1884–1965), the Italian statistician who came up with this numerical expression of monetary relationships within a nation's pie or parfait.

A zero would mean all is equal, and everyone has the same numbers of cherries in their slice. A score of one would mean 100 percent of all the cherries went to one guy. That hasn't quite happened yet, but the closer we get to one, the more unequal the distribution.

The US Gini got more unequal over time: from .32 in the 1970s to .36 in the 1990s to nearly four, at .394 in 2016, an increase of 30 percent, and compared to Finland and Norway's .257 that year. Like Seguino's ratio, this may not sound huge, but "appearances deceive," says a late 2012 article in the *Economist*, noting a dramatic new concentration of US money has exceeded the first Gilded Age. Income for the top 1 percent has doubled since 1980, up 10 to 20 percent from a century ago. "Even more striking, the share going to the top 0.01 percent—some 16,000 families with an average income of $24 million—has quadrupled from 1 percent to almost 5 percent."

These numbers are not isolated. Money going to the very top is a worldwide trend, but here is why American women need to care. Too little for the majority has made for an era of global disruption, huge migrations of populations, and wars over energy sources, food, and water. This disruption is why the US Central Intelligence Agency (CIA) and its spy-wonks track Gini-coefficient ratios country-by-country, as does the UN, the World Bank, and the OECD. All are aware that people deprived of what they need to live will tend to object—sometimes violently.

Yet current US policy—or rather our lack of it—allows the freewheeling operations of economic vultures on Wall Street. Vulture traders and hedge funds also watch these Gini-coefficient numbers, country-by-country. They are looking for the weakest to prey on. Hedge funds and private equity firms, which trade in currencies, interest rates, and bonds, carry on enormous amounts of international trading that nations count on to survive. But nations do not regulate them. No one does. They are strictly private, and increasingly are laundering money and escaping taxation.

For these companies run by EconoMan HNWIs, personal profit making transcends national goals. In the United States, his top marginal income tax rate dropped from 70 percent in 1981 to 35 percent in 2010. In reality, he serves no one cabbage soup, pie, or parfait—only one dry food for all: paper, only paper debt to eat, and even that is disappearing. Today his wars are waged with electronic blips, a fast-moving churn of digital currency, and bonds forced down national throats, deprived of rightful tax revenue.

Top Heavy

Inequality among nations spells trouble. Little-guy nations have less power in the international markets and in the political realm, where national trade agreements get made. Such inequalities among nations affect development internationally. For instance, those heading the Central Bank of the European Union and the International Monetary Fund refused to restructure or renegotiate loans to the Greek government, rather like A-tranche mortgage security investors refusing a haircut in 2008.

A *haircut* means a reduction in profit, a smaller return to those wealthy enough to extend a loan, in some cases to nations. Ostensibly, any contract involves both the responsibility of the lenders' due diligence and the borrowers' good faith. But as news reports showed us, Wall Street loans extended to the Greeks, which included those nasty radicchios, essentially doubled Greek debts when the 2008 crash happened.

A haircut in 2008 or today would hurt the wealthy much less than would impoverishing the future of a whole nation. Refusal among the wealthiest to renegotiate with the less powerful reveals that little has changed since the crash. This is why women need to educate themselves about Econo-Man's power, and prevent the violence that history tells us ultimately could happen—but needn't.

Wealth inequality among nations destabilizes nations and international agreements. It prompted the Second World War, and those wars that have followed, though headlines and political rhetoric seldom illuminate real economic issues underlying social differences. EconoMansplaining masks money so well, making it so complex, that other explanations seem easier: it's the Jews, it's the Muslims, it's race, it's religion.

Of course our differences matter. Diverse points of view could potentially become our strength if we listened to those now unheard to discover what unites us. Then national governments that better represent all of us could "promote the general welfare."

Wealth inequality within a nation damages Main Street's commerce, just as inequality within a city or a family provokes worsening conflicts around regional, racial, ethnic, and gender issues. Whenever a few have the most power, too many have too little.

Violence is not people's first response to deprivation and injustice. First they suffer. They suffer physically, mentally, and spiritually. Often they will tolerate suffering a long time, especially when lacking an understanding of forces at work in the larger macro-economy.

Arguments, protests, and violence will break out to answer faceless economic forces that squeeze them. Already they explode. We are seeing a growing anger now in the United States. Young people who perceive a diminishing economic future will revolt. Without adequate investments in their education and social safety nets for families, unrest will grow as technology redefines work.

As a result, American women must take income inequality very personally. It matters to all of us that the ratio between the top 10 percent of Americans to the bottom 10 percent of Americans was 10:1 in the mid-1980s, rose to 12:1 in the mid-1990s, and was nearly 15:1 by 2011. No one disputes these figures from OECD. But they are faceless. Look around you for concrete situations in your family, your region, our nation, to illustrate these abstract numbers.

For me, it began with us women in that Michigan welfare office in 1979 where my story began. We there never dreamed that the fine print in our nation's trade agreements, and in those made by the World Bank and by the International Monetary Fund, had anything to do with our daily lives and how we lived it. Like growing numbers of women, we just wanted to stay out of poverty. Even while working, many of us remained poor.

My Michigan hometown has drawn in stark clarity for me the dramatic differences between poverty and wealth, riches grown so arrogant they threaten America's noblest ideas of government by consent of the people. No doubt, you and your family have memories and stories, too, that illustrate differences you've witnessed, changes that you'd like to help make.

Weather Fore-costs

Desperate for some gleam of hope, you might be thinking of the improvement women have seen in the ratio between women's wages and men's wages by now. In my lifetime, it's gone from fifty-nine cents earned on a man's dollar, to eighty-seven cents. That's an improvement.

But remember, ratios only describe the relationship between two pieces of data. If the one dollar that our men have been earning is a smaller one, we're hardly better off. As a recent Pew graph reveals, the hourly earnings for those aged twenty-five to thirty-four nearly meet, but largely because men's wages have fallen so dramatically since 1980, not because women's wages have greatly gone up.

One provider for a family is no longer routinely enough. Two economists from Brookings Institute, Michael Greenstone and Adam Looney, challenge the conventional analysis of men's wages from 1970 to 2010; everyone agrees the median fell by 4 percent. That's bad enough, given that overall costs did not fall. But Looney and Greenstone found that in 1970, 94 percent of prime-age men had worked. By 2010, only 81 percent did.

When all working-age men are included in the analysis, Looney and Greenstone found the real earnings of the median American male have fallen by 19 percent since 1970. Those with only a high school education fell by a shocking 41 percent.

That helps account for those missing cherries in lower quintiles. The total pie of American income for those below the median now comes in a shallow tinfoil pan, not the sturdy glass pie plate of my mother's time.

Some fear a change in the American character is the cause, with more women and men going to jail, dealing drugs. Others blame women without husbands, living in poverty. Until the post-2008 protests in Zuccotti Park, American women had seldom railed against macroeconomics. Economics just *was*, like the weather or God. But in fact, specific EconoMan Americans have transformed our nation's landscape both politically and economically. The rule changes that grabbed more pie and parfait for the High Net Worth Individual destabilized American family connections and millions of homes.

Staying Well-Connected

Why should women care about economic issues and news that so seldom includes them? Surprisingly, given the gender of most billionaires, women around the world are largely responsible for producing the cherries and pudding.

The *Economist* in 2006 credited women with the lion's share of global economic growth in an article, "The Importance of Sex," rather like Herodotus praised women as "queen bees" when he first coined the term *oikonomia*: "Add the value of housework and child-rearing, and women probably account for just over half of world output. It is true that women still get paid less and few make it to the top of companies, but, as prejudice fades over coming years, women will have great scope to boost their productivity—and incomes."

It's a promise long awaited—and a wrong one at that. If women merely impersonate the money power now in control, jockeying for individual clout in that rigged Monopoly game, we will shortchange ourselves, our families, and leave our Mother Earth bereft.

A lot of our American lifetime's economic growth has come at the expense of our more desperate sisters in Mexico, Indonesia, and Bangladesh. We who have benefitted at least a little from the neoliberal bullying of our leaders are entitled to demand more democratic leadership here that negotiates more fairly internationally and at home.

At stake is a very personal bottom line. Wherever we women find ourselves defending the right to plan our own pregnancies, to own our own bodies, we can know that a government grows more dangerous for all its citizens. Controlling women is the first order of business for any orderly and submissive slave state. Where freedom extends only so far, woman's debasement enshrines the power of her owners.

Only when more of us can look straight in the ugly eye of EconoMan will women more clearly perceive our collective mistreatment—and our collective power. Women's power must persist in being different—not dividing, but joining; not abstract and theoretical, but concrete and embodied.

Our power bleeds with regularity without violence. Our strength stretches us with roars that birth unfathomable new loves, astonishing new lives. Our connections pump in brainy bodies full of heart, in tears of sorrow and joy, in breasts and hands that share food, in listening ears and laughter and song.

Reports about economic inequality, however they may be shaped or sliced or colored, are not disputed. These are facts, regardless of how much EconoMan deadens us to them with his abstract numbers and opaque language. There are solutions too, less often talked about here in the United States.

The OECD emphasizes the importance of public policies for addressing the dangers of extreme inequality. Job losses are real, and wage increases are needed by most, so government incentives for creating good livelihoods might help, as could increased unemployment insurance for bridging to them. They recommend "human capital investments," too, meaning affordable or free education for young people and older workers who need new skill sets to ready them for technological changes. Affordable or free health care is another sensible investment. Social safety nets for the poor help relieve desperation and its violence, enabling people in crisis to keep a clear head precisely when they most need it.

Yet none of that can happen without first dismantling what the *Economist* calls "crony capitalism," the term used in the Gilded Age for EconoMan, and really a misnomer. A crone is an old woman, and most old women I've met are more generous and wise than mean and self-centered. This crone has to ask, how does EconoMan screw *you* exactly? Oh, let us count the ways, and create an economic to-do list for American women to take on while we still can.

Whenever I talk with my girlfriends about the taboo topic of money troubles, I learn I am far from alone. Ending economic abuse will require our believing our own stories. If you recognized yourself in the title *Screwnomics*, already you've begun. We all have stories to tell—though as I discovered, we're discouraged from ever thinking our female life decisions are economic ones. That is what makes women's longer economic history in Part III so important and surprising.

Quick Rehash

- Since 2008, the number of millionaires and billionaires has exploded worldwide, more than doubling, and the United States has the fourth highest inequality after Chile, Mexico, and Turkey.
- Booming US incomes at the top have increased because of increasingly nontransparent and unregulated deals, capital gains, and big tax cuts, along with creation of tax shelters, frequently offshore.
- The majority of Americans have lost ground due to job losses from technology; shrinking wages for all but high-tech and financial workers; and high costs for education, health care, and housing. Women's salaries and wages have helped camouflage the damages.

EconoGirlfriend Conversation Starter

What money stories are you comfortable sharing with girlfriends? What uncomfortable ones would be harder?

Wow! Here's progress! The US Census Report says women earn 80 cents to a man's dollar now.* That ratio's the best ever!

*From 1973 to 2014 her median income went from 30,182 to $39,621

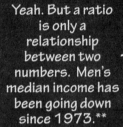

Yeah. But a ratio is only a relationship between two numbers. Men's median income has been going down since 1973.**

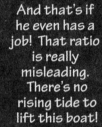

And that's if he even has a job! That ratio is really misleading. There's no rising tide to lift this boat!

It's always sink or swim, kids!

Guys, it's a _wading_ pool!

**From $53,294 to $50,383

© Peaco Todd & Rickey Gard Diamond, 2017

PART III

HIS STORY OF WOMAN

Females Are for Sex and Food—Or Else.

Chapter 10: Mom's Sugar Bowl

1776–1965

Woman's industrial story transforms her production from a credit to a debit.

When I was a girl in the 1960s, my mom and her mom, my Grandma Elsie, both seemed like weirdos. They had good-paying office careers and dressed up every day for work, wearing girdles, hose and high heels, and red lipstick. What made them weird? They were married and had kids. In those days, women didn't have office careers unless they were husband-hunting, or old maids and spinsters. That's what we called an unmarried woman.

In those days, we girls at our pajama parties would ask each other a rhetorical question. Will you give up your career when you get married? The expected answer: Yes, of course, if you love him.

Besides, having a career back then usually meant being a receptionist or a store clerk, so it wasn't all that hard to give up. Plus, being a good wife (everyone knew) was a full-time job. Becoming a mother was not an option, but an expectation before birth control, part of the package of being a good wife. You "gave" your husband children, and ideally these were sons. I am not making any of this stuff up. It was in the air I breathed, growing up.

I was embarrassed by my mother's working because she was. She never volunteered the information and, if pressed, grew red admitting it. Worst of all, my mother eventually made more money than my stepfather, which was *really* embarrassing. She had to make it up to him in many ways, pretending to leave all the money decisions up to him, although even a kid like me could see she was really running things.

He regularly asked her when she was going to quit her job and stay home because (everyone knew) this reflected badly on his breadwinning. He got laid off regularly and more easily became unhappy changing jobs, so my mother always vaguely answered him with a truism: *Beggars can't be choosers.* In other words, she never chose to work.

When my mom died, an old schoolmate of mine expressed admiration for her independence and confided how she'd viewed my mom as someone special when we were girls. My friend's mom had been a full-time mother, and I had admired *her* for home-baked cookies after school. So I was surprised my mother's shame and mine were not the common feeling in town—although I also think my friend's view a retrospective one, informed by the women's movement and what came afterward.

Rainy Day Backup

Before she got her fancy job, Mom had paid her dues. She first worked as a waitress during one of my stepdad's layoffs in the 1950s. She decided she liked having her own "pin money," the cash she kept in the sugar bowl, a measure of safety. She turned to a young black woman to help her with my brother and me. She must have found Maybelle by word of mouth, since my mother's race prejudices remained fully intact.

The only black person I had ever seen up until then was the neighboring farm's hired hand, who drove a tractor in the vineyard behind our house. I was seven or eight and have vivid memories of Maybelle's beautiful red nails, her elegant hands and soft-spoken voice, and her willingness to paint my fingernails when she gave herself a manicure.

When Mom got home, she glanced disapprovingly at my nails and, moments later when my stepdad came in, asked if I'd like to come with her to take Maybelle home. I jumped at the chance. Standing on the car's back seat floor, leaning forward between them, I was surprised when Mom suddenly braked and pulled over at the top of a hill. She let Maybelle off on a busy street with a rush of cars.

Neither woman seemed to think it as strange as I did. My mother always worried about my crossing streets. But we were taking Maybelle *home*, I protested after she got out, curious about where she might live, watching her dodge traffic. "It's only a short walk for her," Mom answered, pointing to a low spot down the hill where shadows were already forming.

"Do you see down there? That's the Flats. White people don't go into that neighborhood after dark. See how awful those houses are? I don't know how people can live that way, especially Maybelle, when she keeps herself so nice."

I didn't know what to make of it, either. I had never seen a slum before and wasn't sure what I was looking at, a neighborhood more tightly packed and run-down than the houses at the top of the hill.

How little money must Maybelle have made for her caregiving time with me? She had worked for a white waitress, who herself had worked mostly for tips, which she kept in her sugar bowl for emergencies. Mom had given Maybelle a fistful of coins.

Maybelle didn't last long. When my stepdad got second shift, he became our next babysitter on evenings Mom worked. Our best hope, my stepfather used to say in those days, was that the union would come through and get him needed raises. Then Mom could quit her job.

Who's Dependable?

The work of the home in those days was considered so essential for the public sphere of commerce and America's democracy, that male labor unions—also sorted by race and often blocking any but white membership—regularly demanded a "family wage," one large enough to support what the unions rather ungraciously called "dependents." It's a term still in common use today.

Only Marxist economists had discussed housework in economic terms, naming it "labor reproduction work." But of course (everyone knew), Marxists were the worst weirdos of all. And even Marx thought women's work at home was an economic exception to labor's wage struggle.

A household with a woman doing labor reproduction work at home meant matched white socks without holes in the toes, a nicely decorated living room for the breadwinner's relaxation, a yard with flowers, and well-organized cupboards in a shiny, stocked kitchen.

In contrast, a household with a woman who worked for pay served as a convenient symbol of what families should avoid: children who roamed the neighborhood after school like me, ate questionable food, left dirty dishes in the sink, and kept lights on past a decent bedtime. That these were also often poor households, sociologist Ruth Schwartz Cowan points out in her history of household technology, *More Work for Mother*, only underlined the general warning.

> ### ✓ OPPORTUNITY COST
>
> Whenever you must choose between mutually exclusive alternatives in the microeconomic world, the value of the road not taken is called the *opportunity cost*. First described in 1914 by Austrian economist Friedrich von Wieser, this cost theory is thought to aid efficient decision making, as we cannot be in two places at once or spend one dollar twice.

Opportunity costs include time, pleasure, and nonmonetary benefits, so if Mom chose to care for her children full-time, she suffered an opportunity cost to her earnings. Her choice of market labor carried an opportunity cost of time at home. When only a mom is considered hearth keeper and homemaker, either way she loses something. But these costs can apply to men as well, especially the caring ones.

Three Shifts of Work

Unions won an eight-hour work shift at factories that might include all three shifts, but this didn't apply at home. The work of home's sphere was and remains essentially different from wage work in many ways. It demands the housekeeper-parent be on call twenty-four hours a day, and it's never truly finished. And, no, you can never quit it.

Home requires work, but the pay is lousy. The work is varied and demands a range of skills from nursing to gardening, to finding bargains or cobbling a meal together—all managed and coordinated to deliver an increasingly high standard created by the twentieth century's mushrooming field of marketing and advertising.

Unlike the paid worker in the labor market who grew more and more specialized over time, the home worker (and all of us are home workers to some degree) must remain what Ruth Schwartz Cowan calls a Jane of All Trades. Housework is the first work that children will do, and many of its tasks, such as setting the table or picking dirty socks up off the floor, require no specialized training.

The work of home and of childcare, however it is done, creates what sociologist Arlie Hochschild calls the *second shift*, using that term as her book's title, for today's unprecedented numbers of women working for pay, and also working at home. But three shifts is truer, since you're on call around the clock.

It is worth noting here that the word *housework* never appeared until production was separated from home by industrialization. It would not have made sense before that, since work was always done at home on the farmstead. That separation of home from wealth production led to new ideas about women. The Industrial Revolution was background to our US war of independence and our later westward expansion, but we need missing pieces in this history—the part about us women—to see what this revolution meant to us.

Adam Smith's description of an early pin factory appeared in 1776 in *The Wealth of Nations* and is very relevant, because in those times husbands were expected to give their wives a household allowance eventually called *pin money*. Even factory-made pins remained expensive, and pins were essential when clothing was still made at home. Without access to resources or legal protection, this pin money cash kept in a woman's sugar bowl was often her only safety net. The term even entered into law by that name.

Her Products Pocketed

The Industrial Revolution (everyone knows) was the greatest thing since sliced bread—an industrial product itself, sliced bread. It spanned the eighteenth to nineteenth century's inventions of the steam engine, its noisy factories, its metal tooling, and newfangled transportation. Railroads connected isolated farms and ranches, and factories changed food production, its processes, and distribution.

The accompanying discovery of cheap energy from coal and oil for all these machines led to Edison's twentieth-century electrical discoveries, and, soon after, to Henry Ford's assembly line and affordable automobiles. The heroic mass production of all sorts of consumer goods raised the standard for modern homemaking.

We hear much less about what happened to women's wealth production in those centuries and before. Historian Elizabeth Wayland Barber in her book *Women's Work: The First 20,000 Years* shows how significant woven textiles and clothing were from prehistoric times, really women's domain since she first invented spinning and weaving.

Thread and woven cloth were the first of her wares to be appropriated by the Industrial Revolution and transformed into a market commodity, delivering profits and ownership away from her and her family to capitalists and to a lion's share of wages of men. Her production of a garden's home produce and her flock of chickens would eventually be replaced by green grocers, her herbal home remedies transformed into purchased potions that made men great fortunes, her home-prepared foodstuffs replaced by corporations run by men, producing Heinz 57 Varieties and Campbell Soup.

Women's central role in transforming agrarian raw materials into manufactured wealth was thus diminished over time. Wealth production and home were separated. Woman was demoted from a producer of material goods to what later male economists named a *consumer*. The word feels neutral today, meaning "shopper," but its root means to eat, drink, use up, waste, and destroy. A consumer was a taker, not a maker—and she newly paid for the privilege. Profits, the production of assets and surplus, thus left her homestead, which by then had also moved into town.

Lest We Forget

Women's real economic history gets blurred in a national amnesia actively created and packaged by the most widely circulated magazines. Martha Stewart's domestic embroidery of today has nothing on *Godey's Lady's Book*, which promoted feminine ideals and middle-class standards for homemaking and child-rearing from 1830 to 1896, during the same period that the word *house-work* first appeared.

In it, a dogma took shape about the parallel universes of men and women, their "dual spheres" of home and work kept separate yet supposedly working in concert as God intended. One sphere was masculine and rational, both wondrous and brutish, that tough, dirty world of money and commerce. The other was a strictly feminine realm overseen by the figure that became known as the Angel of the House.

The Angel cared for all she encountered, charitable and generous, while she nourished and tended the less fortunate, the ill and aging, and the children, ensuring their moral upbringing. Her house was spotless. Unbothered by budgets, she cut the crusts off white bread to make little tea sandwiches. She knew that "the hand that rocks the cradle rules the world," a truth quoted from a popular poem's refrain without so much as a blush in the post–Civil War years that enthroned the Gilded Age and its first billionaires.

✓ **THE FOR-PROFIT**

By buying stock, capitalists own the means of production, for example, a textile factory. Production costs include wage labor, raw materials for production, overhead in property, and taxes for public services like roads and water. New technology boosts wage labor's production, and capitalists can then sell resulting goods at a price higher than their costs, becoming *for-profits*. Production costs are tax deductible, but surplus earnings or profit go to business owners who may or may not put their profit back into wages or the business.

✓ **THE NONPROFIT**

Government can and does exempt some producers of goods and services from any tax payments if they can document a shared public good, allowing them to become *non-profits*. Such enterprises most often have a mission of caring and helping, and seven out of ten nonprofit employees are women. Salaries and wages tend to be lower than in the private, for-profit world, but individual employees pay payroll taxes at the same rates as employees at for-profits.

✓ **THE UN-PROFIT**

The *un-profit* is my name for workplaces that continue to be excluded from dual-sphere economic thinking and policy making. Households with dependents do get a small reduction in their taxes called a *tax credit* for their provision of social good. But most families who left the farm stopped thinking of their homes as a private enterprise, encouraged to function as consumers and debtors, not as production centers for maintenance of healthy human beings.

Today, workers earning low wages, most often women, must document their income annually to gain special *earned income tax credits,* widely considered a good policy. Yet her household carries a social stigma. She remains poor. Were homemaking included in US economic policy, the same woman could as easily be viewed as a valuable nonprofit, contributing to our social good and its orderly function, freed of tax.

Earned income tax credits might then be seen more clearly as taxpayer subsidies for businesses, encouraging low wages. Excessive business profits squeezed from workers' wages might then become a social stigma. Imagine.

Angelic Shadow

The nineteenth century's Industrial Revolution multiplied the families who were too poor and powerless to aspire to the Angel ideal of home as oasis. Sociologist Stephanie Coontz pointed out in *The Way We Never Were* that the spread of textile mills required industrial amounts of raw materials produced by slave labor in the South. Early factory laborers worked fifteen- to eighteen-hour days with no weekend. Nearly half their numbers were children. Immigrants "went into service" at the age of eleven or twelve.

Writes Coontz, "For every 19th century middle-class family that protected its wife and child within the family circle, then, there was an Irish or a German girl scrubbing floors in that middle-class home, a Welsh boy mining coal to keep the home-baked goodies warm, a black girl doing the family laundry, a black mother and child picking cotton to be made into clothes for the family, and a Jewish or an Italian daughter in a sweatshop making 'ladies' dresses or artificial flowers for the family to purchase."

Godey's Lady's Book sentiments tried to distract from those restless women who kept popping up, protesting the larger world outside woman's private sphere. Isabella Baumfree escaped from slavery in 1826 with her infant daughter and went to court to rescue her son from the white man who "owned" him, the first black mother to ever win such a case. She later named herself Sojourner Truth, an abolitionist, and among the earliest to speak out publicly for women's rights.

The abolitionist Grimké sisters, who grew up in a slaveholding family, drew crowds with the novelty of a woman giving a speech in the public sphere. Another more privileged abolitionist, Elizabeth Cady Stanton, happily married with seven children, went to an anti-slavery convention, only to be barred from seating along with all other females. She began to see what Sojourner saw.

At Seneca Falls in 1848, Stanton and the Quaker preacher Lucretia Mott organized the first women's rights convention. It was there Stanton suggested, to the shock of every radical present, that women ought to have the right to vote. Meanwhile Harriet Beecher Stowe, who never espoused anything so unfeminine as Stanton's "extreme" views, wrote a blockbuster novel, *Uncle Tom's Cabin*, which Abraham Lincoln would credit for starting the Civil War. A woman writing was still shocking, but at least it took place in the private sphere of home—where women belonged.

Going Public

Those who dared organize in the nineteenth century, first locally and then nationally, came to see that changes they sought could only be accomplished in the public sphere. Without legal changes there, women would remain the private property of fathers and husbands, just as slaves were still property.

Laws that prevented women owning or inheriting property, winning custody of her children, or serving on a jury were part of her first evidence, brought forward for public debate. Yet in the public imagination, women lost their femininity by entering that civic realm. *Godey's* carried the message: If a woman abandoned her true mission in the private domain, then all "mankind" would be lost. Only she, the mother and godly wife, could exert great enough powers at home to make it the one place left on earth untouched by industrial economic disruptions.

Shortly after slavery was abolished in the agrarian world, the Angel's torch-bearing icon, the Statue of Liberty, was installed on an island next to Ellis Island in 1886. Declaring American shores a haven in a world turned upside down by factories and capitalist-driven production, Lady Liberty hovered over the heads of those huddled masses. She became the Angel of the American national duplex house.

And if meanwhile, the biggest businessmen of her time, busy building the first skyscrapers, took their liberty by exploiting newly freed African men and the immigrants who came for freedom's promise—well, that was simply the way economics worked. Rights were only rights and only went so far. A living had to be made.

So men sorted out paying jobs according to an unspoken racial and class hierarchy to determine what kind of labor was most fitting, and guarded their rightful breadwinning role wherever they worked. There was still plenty of wealth to be had if only you worked hard enough. And were male.

Mid-Westward, Ho!

Immigration is part of my story, and possibly yours. My grandma Elsie's folks, the DeWispelaeres, emigrated from Belgium around the turn of the twentieth century, escaping Europe's economic turmoil that would lead to WWI. They discovered the streets of America weren't paved with gold, as had been rumored in "the old country," as they called it. Helped by relatives who worked in new factories, they bought property in South Bend, Indiana.

They ran a small dairy, and built a house with a hand pump in the kitchen. There was an outhouse, and hot water got heated on the iron stove for baths in a tin tub. My grandma, the oldest child, thin as a rail, delivered milk and butter with a horse-drawn wagon before she went to school. My great-grandma and her four daughters raised a flock of chickens, which meant twice-daily egg collection, butchering, and plucking, added to milking, churning, and delivery, plus endless cooking and cleaning.

My grandma Elsie later said that all that work was why the three oldest sisters got married as soon as they could. It was understood their younger brother would inherit the farm. Women were barred from all but the humblest jobs for pay, and most often they worked in private homes, providing domestic services or doing piecework. Textile and clothing industries welcomed them but only when girls. Once married, they kept house.

The common household size when my grandma was born in 1900 was seven people. With that many to cook and launder for, sociologist Mignon Duffy writes in her article, "Doing the Dirty Work," private sphere jobs were needed. After the Civil War, most middle-class homes employed at least one domestic servant, while wealthy families had a staff. By the 1880s, even lower classes had servants, one for every eight American families, and in some cities one in four.

By 1900, private households still employed almost 1.3 million domestic workers; yet as a percentage of the population, the numbers of private-sphere female workers remained small, were paid little, and were expected to stay invisible. A domestic workforce of female relatives, like sisters, eliminated the need for hiring help.

The marketed illusion of female exception to man's harsh world of labor was harder to maintain whenever a woman was a farmer, or had darker skin, or was an immigrant, or became widowed, abandoned, or divorced. Without access to decent wages, any woman and her children could quickly become destitute.

Mixed Progress

The Ford Museum in Dearborn, Michigan, will show you a different view. Sparkling like a ray of chrome sunshine, a wondrous glut of so-called labor-saving devices for the home and "the little woman" (as wives were referred to in those times) accompanied the Industrial Revolution. Supposedly protected from that dog-eat-dog world of money, she was isolated further with a new generation of toasters, washing machines, and stoves that reduced any need for domestic help.

Elsie and my mother, Peggy Mae, once married and on their own, prided themselves on doing their own housework. When I became a teenager, my mother enlisted me, thinking it necessary training for my future life of cleaning, knowing that this, and hot meals served on time, were the real measures of any middle-class woman's competence, not a job.

Elsie first worked at a WWII war munitions plant, but she didn't bow out the way she was supposed to when the soldiers came home. She eventually became a company accountant at Whirlpool Corporation when such jobs were possible with on-the-job training. My mother, who never went to college, followed in her footsteps, eventually becoming an accountant and then controller of a small corporation.

Neither woman ever expressed joy in their positions or their money. I suspected, first with kid intuition and later as a worker myself, that Mom did enjoy both. I remember a rare smile, tinged with guilt, when she brought home an expensive new lamp for the entry that she said she shouldn't have bought. She had to qualify her choices, her competency.

Like others of her generation, she worried a woman's money was dangerous; it gave her and Elsie some freedom—too much, perhaps. They had both divorced their husbands, another source of shame. Like wax buildup in the corners of your kitchen floor, a selfish indulgence in making filthy lucre might prove you were shirking more important family duties—while taking a job away from a rightful male breadwinner.

Females needed male permission to work. One woman of my grandmother's generation told me that when she first landed a job in town in the 1920s, the department store gave her paycheck directly to her dad. Money matters (everyone knew) might sully or confuse a young woman. Equal pay was never expected, pay never a subject of polite conversation, which is still largely true today.

My stepmother told me of a job interview she had in the early 1970s. The employer, without consulting her, first checked in with her husband, my father, to make sure it was all right with him that she be offered the job. I mean, what if Dad came home and his dinner wasn't ready on time?

Double Duty

That last story is not so old. I suspect many American women today continue to be haunted by their Angel of the House. How else to explain the success of Martha Stewart and her impossible Victorian standards? Or the popularity of television shows about rich housewives, and cupcake wars, and the domestic drama of a Mormon with multiple wives?

The year I graduated from high school, 1965, the idea of a woman working for contributions she could make to society, and even for her own happiness, broke out like a virus, first in Betty Friedan's book, *The Feminine Mystique*. And everyone, especially Mom and Grandma Elsie, knew Betty Friedan was a weirdo.

In those days, both women still gave regular lip service to the ideal of becoming full-time homemakers some day. Intelligent women, neither thought their jobs outside the home liberating. It only doubled their work. They did it for the same reason men did: money. And money was, and still is, a banned subject.

I doubt even Betty envisioned that women would soon be entering the job market in droves, few of them "women-libbers." More families needed the money. The 1980s brought women a backlash and nostalgic stories about professional women who had decided on stay-at-home mommyhood, while fewer than ever had that option.

We've yet to discover what is "natural" for either changed sphere, the private one supposedly feminine and the public one supposedly masculine—the more money at stake, the more masculine, I've noticed. While each generation has changed norms, sexual dualities still plague us with designations of value and work, and whose time is paid, underpaid, and unpaid, and what it means to be a liberated human being. Whenever a motive remains largely cultural and unconscious, it is all the more powerful—as I think is the case with judging women's life decisions.

Not so long ago, women and money didn't mix. Her coins were only pin money, even when supporting her family without a man. Now more often, a growing number of men would live in poverty without her paycheck. The unconscious wish to diminish the threat of her earnings to men's status could help account for her nearly universal smaller paychecks. But today, her pay equity would be one very simple way to improve the lives of most Americans.

There are other solutions in chapters ahead, on our way back to the future, through women's economic past. By now younger readers are probably asking, why on earth did women put up with their lack of liberty for so long?

The next chapter attempts to answer that question.

Quick Rehash

- An imaginary division between gendered realms—a feminine home ruled by an Angel and a masculine marketplace ruled by men's money—still masks economic hierarchies sorted by race, ethnicity, and gender.
- Opportunity costs are particularly weighty for American women who span both realms of work without economic support for her caring labor reproduction work in the great un-profit, a bankrupt leftover of that nineteenth-century Angel ideal.

EconoGirlfriend Conversation Starter

Are you haunted by an Angel of the House? What does she want you to do? Who does she sound like? Is she a relative? Or a media ideal?

Chapter 11: Egg Money

40,000 BCE–1965
Woman's ancient story reveals her eggs as the first property, Gaia as the
Greeks' first creator, and Juno's gold coins as Rome's first currency.

My mother seemed relieved when in 1965 I announced I was becoming a wife, intending to be supported like the ones on *The Donna Reed Show* and *Leave It to Beaver*. My new role reflected well on our family's full arrival into the middle class.

Her relief probably also had to do with her being liberated from her gatekeeper duties. I had made it to the altar without first getting pregnant. Before the women's movement, bulging surprises would shame the whole household, common as it was. My mom and dad had a "shotgun wedding" to save honor. It hadn't lasted.

Roman Catholic, Mom still insisted that even before we bought a wedding dress, we go to a doctor for the newly invented birth control pill. That I was too young to be a mother at nineteen did not come up, since she had become one at eighteen and my grandmother at fifteen. The women of my family never discussed motherhood. It was simply expected.

Yet Peggy Mae and Elsie both were protective of me, ahead of the general curve in understanding motherhood's economic penalty. How else to explain my mother's quick embrace of the pill, and my grandma's similar and immediate reaction six years later?

I told Elsie of my too-soon third pregnancy while using birth control. My doctor had taken me off the pill for its side effects, but a diaphragm and spermicide hadn't worked, and I wanted a tubal ligation that I couldn't afford.

I didn't talk about being only twenty-five and soon having two infants in diapers and bibs, the diaper pails, the stinky pukes, the achy back, and the dread of endless babies after this third one. I didn't have to. Elsie surprised me.

She said a litter of three was quite enough. She proposed a no-interest loan to get my tubes tied once newly delivered—and in more than one way. I was astonished and grateful. It never would have occurred to me to ask her for such a thing.

She died a decade later, and I regretted knowing so little about her life decisions. When I asked my mom and aunt about her, my questions touched a nerve, both of them angry, silent—though more years later, Mom said she shouldn't have judged her. I never learned the details, including an affair when Elsie was way too old, but I still remember her ready compassion for my life decisions—that, and her confident access to money.

Unspoken Stories Remembered

More than likely Elsie had become a farmer's wife at age fifteen because she had to. Families didn't talk about this, since women were either Angels, or else they were Sluts—one of many names used for a female who knew about sex. One way or the other, a farm wife would soon be pregnant anyway, performing the most crucial of her duties.

Elsie had three children, the oldest my mom. For thirteen years Elsie kept the stove going, baking, chicken plucking, canning, washing the kitchen walls down every spring, same as her mother had done before her. Then she walked out.

Grandpa was probably unfaithful, given his fast remarriage, but in those days male philandering was expected. I don't know exactly how it all happened, but somehow Elsie and two younger sisters would kick up their heels as adults and throw over the pedestal of expected farm-wife-and-womanly-sainthood. Elsie would divorce four times, her fifth marriage finally lasting when she and her husband both stopped drinking. And both of Elsie's childless sisters worked and divorced three times too.

Possibly Elsie and her sisters were sluts. They certainly knew how to have a good time and attracted the attention of a good many men. Was it the Industrial Revolution and its new wage-work money that undid Angel traditions? Was it Prohibition's overthrow? The Great Depression? Or was there something deeper and older that Elsie and her sisters resisted and ultimately rejected?

I was a young mother by the time Great-Grandma DeWispelaere died, and I remember going through the family house with Grandma Elsie when the estate was being settled. That's when I learned Great-Grandma had birthed five children in her upstairs bedroom, the last one all by herself, except for thirteen-year-old Elsie, the daughter attending her delivery, the one who told me this story.

We stood, looking at the wrought iron headboard, not talking. I remembered my own bloody labors, imagining Great-Grandma's: the smells and groans, her struggle to stay quiet, calming her young daughter. I never talked about it afterward, except to Peggy Mae, who all but shrugged. And this is the first time I have written it down to be remembered.

Gnarly, Ancient Roots

I would have to go back much further than my great-grandma to discover the economic taproot of women's fertile predicament, our "concrete situation" and its economic consequences—back before writing and history.

In 1996, I spent three weeks pursuing glimpses in museums and archeological digs of prehistoric European culture shaped by human hands. In Nice, France, I visited a site called Terra Amata that had uncovered the then-oldest known built structures within a cave, along with stone tools, a fire site of sustained use, and even petrified poop, the remains of *homo neanderthalensis,* dating back 400,000 years.

When Ice Age glaciers began to recede about 40,000 years ago, a burst of new creativity appeared, a good share of it coming from the female *homo sapiens.* Small bone tools and sinew cordage made sewing with hides possible, and over time, fiber cordage to form bags, and looms of weft and warp weighted with stones so thread could be woven into cloth.

Such prehistoric ingenuity is easy to overlook, until you imagine being naked in a world without clothing. Cunning woven baskets made the gathering of plant stuff and grains easier while holding or nursing a child. Pottery of dried and fired clay made food storage handier. I looked for female creativity on that trip.

The museum at Terra Amata had hosted a gathering of world scholars in 1991 to catalogue small figurines that have now been discovered on every continent, our earliest art. Victorian male archeologists who first found them thought the Venus figures obscene and talked little about them. Scholars are reexamining them. Early prehistoric people went to a great deal of trouble to create these small but richly detailed carvings of females.

The Venus of Willendorf, which I saw in the Museum of Natural History in Copenhagen, has exaggerated egg-shaped hips, buttocks, and breasts, and a braided crown of hair. The Venus Lespugue, found in the south of France, has similar features and shows braided cords hung on her hips, the loose tassels at the ends visible, difficult to render with stone tools. Both are more than thirty thousand years old, made from the ivory tusks of woolly mammoths.

We don't know who carved these figures, but they make clear that women played an active role in human advances. Food in baskets and pots probably sprouted. This no doubt gave some more-than-likely female humans the idea of growing plants in ground they prepared, begun about ten thousand years ago.

Agriculture is the human industry that made large civilizations possible. More reliable crops of grain led to surpluses,

The Willendorf venus, carved from a mammoth tusk, is 30,000 years old.

ground into flour. Clay ovens of the earliest known permanent settlement, Catal Huyuk in Turkey, were clearly thought sacred. The site was settled 8,700 years ago and inhabited continuously for eight hundred years. Its oven smell of warm bread must have seemed a wonder to humans more accustomed to dried jerky and roots.

Visiting Copenhagen, where acidic bogs preserved rare textiles, I saw remarkable cord skirts that were 3,400 years old. Similar cordage can be seen on those older figurines I've mentioned, often referred to as *girdles* in ancient literature, says scholar Elizabeth Wayland Barber in *Women's Work*. I remember my shock at these peek-a-boo miniskirts. They must have advertised and flaunted the sexuality of whomever wore it, like hula skirts or a 1920s flapper fringe. Our foremothers were clearly not only ingenious, but quite possibly sluts, who knew about sex.

They were obese by our standards. Barber invites us to think about the primitive times of the Venus figurines: "A woman too thin will become temporarily infertile. . . . So a fat woman is in a far better state to survive and to support her child with her own milk during seasonal famine. In short, obesity helps ensure successful reproduction." Historians theorize the cord skirts signaled a readiness for childbearing.

It Takes Two to Tango

About the same time that women began weaving and planting and baking, animal husbandry began. This activity is widely thought more likely to have been developed by men. For pregnant and lactating women, this division of labor must have been welcomed by her. She couldn't have foreseen his new agricultural role was also her doom.

You'll remember Malthus in Chapter 4 and his ideas about the mathematical difference between the amount of a land's crops which can only be added or subtracted—either a little less or a little more than the year before—while people on that land multiply with each generation. If two parents have four children, and those children have four children, the parents become grandparents to sixteen children and great-grandparents to sixty-four. If they all stay on the same plot of land, they will eventually starve.

Historian Gerda Lerner in her book *The Creation of Patriarchy* points out a similar ability of herding animals to multiply. Valuable surpluses in livestock, meat, and pelts could be accumulated as wealth by the men who kept animals. Herding more than likely also gave people insight into the bull's role in sex, his ability to pass on traits like red spots or black ones. Later plow agriculture would also require the strength of men and his oxen or horses. Lerner writes: "Thus, agricultural economic practice reinforced men's control over surpluses, which may also have been acquired by conquest in intertribal warfare."

Land was not a scarce resource then, she points out. People were. And so Lerner and many others also theorize that when the survival of the tribe depended on more workers, tribal warfare had a purpose to capture those whose reproduction could multiply the numbers of the tribe. Women could be captured more easily than armed men and were then useful for trading as wives and concubines. Women's reproductive powers thus became the first property, writes Lerner.

A man could only know if her children were his and not some other man's if he guarded her, reinforcing ownership. Over time, forceful conquest paid off with more stolen people. Slavery of both sexes added to the needed labor force for more agricultural production. So the agricultural revolution was tightly woven together with ownership of humans, and especially of women's eggs, her generative powers.

The Golden Goose

Interestingly, these reproductive powers have everything to do with coins, another huge economic advance in the ancient world. The Mediterranean kingdom of Lydia, near Greece, had a ready supply of gold, most often used for sacred purposes and for jewelry of royals then believed divine. Egypt had buried tons of it with their pharaohs.

The king of Lydia, Croesus—as in *rich as Croesus*—was the first to make coins about 2,500 years ago. He flattened little lumps of hot, soft metal with an imprint of his face. Coins first functioned as gifts, rewards for service to the king, or in recognition of some event or legal contract. Bride price and dowry were two such contracts.

These marked family alliances, not romance. Over time, the bride price of migrating peoples to purchase a wife was largely replaced by the dowry, the bride's family investment in the union, payable to the groom.

Technically the woman's property, a dowry was seldom managed by her and sometimes resulted in feuds among male relatives. Marriage was always first an economic enterprise, but it was the Greeks who first expanded a token use of coins in marriage to one that replaced barter. Uniform coins used in port towns for merchant deal making added a new liquidity as coins trickled down in the ancient economy.

By Roman times, coins were minted at the temple of Juno, the wife of top-god Jupiter and protector of Roman brides. Her mint sat atop the central hill of Rome, protected by a flock of geese that sounded an alarm when barbarians tried to rob her. She became known as Juno *Moneta*, Latin for "warning," which became our name for money.

Agricultural Backlash

Over thousands of years, male gods edged out the older female ones, eventually all but obliterating the divine female. Reproductive powers were eventually claimed as exclusively male. Aristotle, writing about 2,600 years ago, considered females defectives, only useful for providing the material for men's fully human form, the essence of which was present only in semen.

Unlike Rome's Jupiter and Juno who were married, the later Jehovah and Allah had no wives and despised local goddesses. Gaia, who the earliest Greeks had said created the world, was demoted and by our time completely forgotten. I'll come back to her later.

Today, reproductive science highlights our continued view of woman's eggs as property, though never her own. A surrogate mother earning money from her reproductive powers raises big ethical questions, unlike fees paid to reproductive scientists for artificial insemination. How dare a woman profit from her womb's *production*?

Towns, Trade, and War

The post-Roman phase of economic history leaves women all but invisible. You have to imagine her in the background, busy overseeing human life and death with food, soap, and health care, birthing babies and burying corpses. She made economic man possible, storing, cooking, and serving food, spinning, weaving, and sewing clothes.

That same old three-dimensional multiplication of people kept outgrowing the two-dimensional arithmetic of land. In Europe and around the Mediterranean, the ruins of Rome's empire fell to an emerging feudal system of royal bloodlines. From the ninth to the fifteenth century, men jockeyed for dominance and ownership of the land, often negotiated by marriage.

The unions of noble daughters, overseen by male hierarchies within the new monotheisms, added to the era's battles. Lords swore loyalties and military might to kings and sultans and khans, and in exchange won grants of land from whatever man wore the crown on his *caput*.

Lands always came with those unfortunate people lower down in the social hierarchy who only happened to live there. Peasants and serfs still eked out landed livelihoods through farming, herding, hunting, and foraging on tiny lots as tenants of nobles, and on shared land called "the commons." Serfs were heavily taxed and the men in their families were conscripted into their lordship's military exploits.

One of the ongoing arguments within economics is whether savings and wise investment is the original source of capital accumulation, as Adam Smith suggested for his pin factory. Marx later argued that what he called *primitive capital accumulation* had a longer history of violence and exploitation that advantaged ruthless men. As examples, he pointed to gold and silver extraction from the New World, the enslavement of indigenous peoples, and the conquests of Africa and India that created great piles of capital.

Even earlier though, beginning in the twelfth century, people on common lands in Europe and England had their means of production from fields and forests seized and captured through something called *enclosure laws*. These laws legally transferred public common lands to the aristocracy. Displaced to cities then, serfs were desperate to work for wages, as capital next slowly enclosed the industrial means of production.

Explorers and colonialists who came to the New World's shores during the three-hundred-year period from the sixteenth to the eighteenth century were sent there by the richest royalty in Europe for one primary reason: to extract raw materials and make money from new lands. Violence was their ultimate persuasion.

Historians estimate that by the time of American independence, Europeans had shipped home between 145,000 to 165,000 tons of silver and about 3,000 tons of gold. With gold at $400 an ounce, it is hard to imagine the wealth such tonnage delivered until you look at the era's European royalty. Their gilded castles and casks of royal coins, their pirates and privateers and newly chartered companies, all help us to picture how the old feudal exchanges of agriculture—local trade and barter—were being transformed, disrupted, and exploited.

That wasn't how New World expansionism was sold, of course. And it wasn't the only reason Europeans came to the Americas. But it was the foundational one. With gold and silver swamping Europe, prices there were rising. Kings and their friends with gold and silver from the New World bought goods from a newly important merchant class in London, Paris, and Madrid. Industrialization wasn't in place yet, so production couldn't keep up with their demand. All that flour sold for royal cake-eating raised bread prices for everyone else.

The new land of the New World offered new sources for agricultural self-sufficiency.

New Ideas

The three centuries of New World economic disruption in Europe that I've just sketched eventually led to the American and French Revolutions. These couldn't have occurred, however, without a great many radical new ideas that to us, three hundred years later, seem common knowledge.

For instance, you and I know that the church is not the same as government, the two having separate functions. The Bible can be read in the same language you speak, and can be interpreted by you, as you see fit. You can even decide to join a mosque or a temple or not attend church at all.

Likewise, we know kings do not have a direct line to God, nor are kings descended from God, or appointed by God. Kings and presidents must submit to the same laws as everyone else, because laws are applied by the consent of the governed and written by their elected body of representatives, also subject to law.

Not only that, but if you don't like your government, you can speak freely about it. And have you heard? Science, by means of evidence, not faith, has actually proved the earth is not flat and revolves around the sun, not the sun around it, as kings and churches once insisted. Violently.

Any of the ideas in the paragraphs above could have cost you your head had you expressed them in Leonardo da Vinci's time (1452–1519). But in the intellectual furor of something called the Protestant Reformation (1517–1648), followed by something called the Enlightenment (1685–1815), all closely connected with the publishing of something called books, the social contract in Europe was dramatically changed. The discovery of the New World, its gold and land, not only helped make these new ideas relevant, but added fuel to the era's conflicts and aspirations.

Enlighten-MAN

By the mid-1600s, a man with the urge and the time to learn to read could, though as books and newspapers were expensive, literate men were few. Wealthy guys could pose questions about the issues above, and discuss these with peers in coffeehouses. It was dangerous at first. Many heads rolled. But one idea led to another, and humanist thought and science began to emerge in the upper classes. The questions and claims of the newly enlightened man began to fill up more books.

I refer to the Enlightenment's man and his books advisedly, because during all this intellectual uproar, most women did not read. The few who did mainly concerned themselves with moral instruction. With a few exceptions, it took until the early seventeenth century for religious and creative upper-class women to protest their being barred from education of a wider world.

While most men didn't read or participate in the Enlightenment directly either, even the most ignorant did benefit from new liberal ideas about the rights of the common man. Women had few defenders. For the most part, for most women, the Enlightenment altered little in the old world or the new. Spinning and weaving, soapmaking, candle making, cooking in a fireplace, and salting down meat for the winter were all more crucial work than radical thought.

In fact, it was widely believed a woman's overuse of her brain would tax and steal blood from her womb, best kept occupied by the *homunculus,* a tiny and complete person thought to be present in sperm. Woman's menstrual blood was earth to man's seed, and she was thought best natured when kept pregnant. Her eggs, the ovum, wouldn't be discovered until 1837. Even then, its essential role in reproduction remained unclear to male scientists until 1876.

Mundane Terror

Our history often tells us of soldiers' valor, but much less is made of women's routine courage, practiced for thousands of years. The enterprise of baby production, so essential to the economy's well being—to the whole social contract whatever shape it took—was extremely hazardous to women. Its danger helps explain why our foremothers took so very long to demand the liberation that men were claiming.

A woman's fate as child bearer was conveniently considered her inevitable lot in all churches and faiths, which viewed a mother's screams and bloodletting as her punishment for Eve's original sin. Her only escape was a nunnery.

A typical mother in colonial times gave birth to five to eight children. Of every eight female friends and relatives a woman had, one would die in childbirth. Nearly all women gave birth at home, attended by female friends and relatives, and, if she were lucky, a practiced midwife with a flask of alcohol as painkiller.

All the while that liberty bells were ringing in the New World, and the Industrial Revolution was revving up and starting to churn cash, women's eggs continued to be fertilized, the expectation of her child production unabated. Women of the early colonial era approached childbirth with alarm, their letters calling it "the Dreaded apperation," "the greatest of earthly miserys," or "that evel hour I loock forward to with dread."

Grief was a companion to every mother's Dread. One infant in ten would die before the age of five under the best of circumstances. This all kept her very busy.

Her Credit Becomes Cost

My Grandma Elsie's revelation of her having attended her mother's delivery shouldn't have shocked me. As late as 1900, over 90 percent of all births still occurred in the mother's home, a male doctor more likely to attend her than a midwife by then. Science had introduced two drugs in 1847 that relieved pain in childbirth. Doctors delivered babies from unconscious mothers, using forceps, not hands.

Induced sleep can serve as symbolic marker of woman's near complete financial erasure by 1900. Birth had become a cash cow for a growing new medical industry. The cost of a doctor and hospital birth was probably the reason my immigrant great-grandma decided to have her five babies at home.

Two decades before my great-grandma DeWispelaere crossed the Atlantic to find her midwestern farm, a woman named Anne Higgins gave birth to a daughter named Margaret, the sixth of eleven children. It was 1879 in upstate New York, and Anne's immigrant husband was a stonemason making tombstones. There was nothing ironic in his need of these. He and Anne suffered the death of seven children before Anne died at age fifty. She had survived eighteen pregnancies in twenty-two years.

As daughter Margaret grew up, she helped raise the surviving younger siblings. When she married and became Mrs. Margaret Sanger, she worked as a visiting nurse. Seeing her mother's grief-filled life repeated in the women on New York City's East Side, she began publishing a newspaper, the *Woman Rebel,* in 1914.

I'm quite certain that my great-grandma, by then in South Bend, never saw it. Postal authorities confiscated the paper, calling Sanger's information about contraception "obscene." Sanger responded by writing the pamphlet, "Family Limitation," an even more blatant argument for women's control of their own bodies and health.

Indicted, Sanger used an alias to escape prosecution on a ship bound for England. There, Sanger expanded her ideas about a woman's liberty to include her sexual pleasure. How could any marital relationship thrive, she demanded, when death and dread accompanied every woman's sexual encounter with her partner?

Returning to Brooklyn in 1916, Sanger opened the first birth control clinic and was promptly arrested. Her trial made headlines, airing her issues. In 1918, after Sanger had served her sentence, the New York Court of Appeals ruled to allow doctors to prescribe contraception. Once contraception was monetized and controlled by male doctors, it apparently stopped being obscene.

Sanger's later Planned Parenthood was born about the time that fifteen-year-old Elsie gave birth to my mother, Peggy Mae. I'm sure Elsie never went to Planned Parenthood. It was mainly supported—and this seems amazing in light of today's news—by wealthy Republicans.

The word *control* in that phrase *birth control* provides a hint of what was at stake. It might keep riffraff like Elsie, who was Catholic and a Democrat, from overproducing. What good Catholic would put up with that? So the Dems, with a large Catholic population, said a big *no* to birth control in those days. It's almost as if birthing is political!

Consumption Junction

After the First World War, the automobile, movies, radio dance music, and bold new writers loosened old Puritan attitudes about sex. Women won the right to vote in 1920, but her voting transformed her world less than her family planning did. Homemaking remained an ideal, but now she was a *consumer*, the opposite of *producer*, purchasing most goods. Her shopping became managerial, her domestic and childcare work less labor-intensive for a shorter span, and housework grown more isolated.

✓ CONSUMPTION

The term *consumer* was used to mean a wastrel in fifteenth-century England, but by Adam Smith's time it became an economic word. By 1919, the US Bureau of Labor was tracking changes in the *Consumer* Price Index (CPI), measuring costs for urban families, and their rates of *consumption*.

John Maynard Keynes included a mathematical formula, called the *consumption function*, in *The General Theory of Employment, Interest and Money*. It showed that generally, as income increased, so did consumption, though he also found consumption rates were always less than income rates.

Milton Friedman later added to Keynes's ideas with the *absolute income hypothesis*. He found people tended to base consumption on their sense of expected permanent income over their lifetime. Windfalls had little effect.

Recent *behavioral economics* is consumer theory gone further. It suggests that all kinds of behaviors play out in a global economy. Consuming patterns are not strictly logical or consistent, as economists' mathematical formulas asserted.

Our consumer decisions today testify to power imbalances of race, class, and gender. Andrea Dworkin believed gender the first key to understanding patterns of spending, commenting in her book, *Pornography: Men Possessing Women*, "In the hands of women, money stays literal; counted out, it buys what it is worth, often less. In the hands of men, money buys women, sex, status, dignity, esteem, recognition, loyalty, all manner of possibility."

Elsie's Sharecropping

Even farmer-producers were becoming consumers, who bought milking machines and tractors that made expansion of farms both possible and necessary. My grandparents would leave their Indiana farm for cheaper open land out West that eventually became the Dust Bowl of the 1930s.

They returned home busted and unable to buy a farm, so they rented one, an arrangement close to sharecropping. Somewhere amongst crop failures and Grandpa's becoming a truck driver, and Japan's bombing of Pearl Harbor, Elsie and my grandpa got divorced.

Times were hard, and landless families like Elsie's were at loose economic ends, like earlier European serfs, more numerous than ever. Moved into town, no longer a producer, now wage-paid consumer, a divorced Elsie faced feeding her fully hatched eggs, her children, on a paycheck even smaller than my fifty-nine-cent one had been.

In a modern industrialized world, she and her kids were no longer the productive labor assets they had been on the farm. Welfare payments presented far more hurdles then, the largest one being family pride.

So Elsie's kids were divided up.

I learned this too late to ask her about it; my only sources were her three children who had suffered from the split-up. Peggy the eldest, my mother, went with Elsie. My mother's sister, Pat, went with grandpa when he remarried. And their youngest, a new baby boy, Robert, was taken in by one of Elsie's childless sisters.

For decades, Elsie and her sisters kept secret from Robert his true identity. I can't say the revelation for him was a joyful one, nor for Elsie and her sister, though they finally made their peace, all of them. I've since learned that this secret child-sharing was not an uncommon practice during hard times before there was public welfare.

Elsie's was a life decision that everyone in the family had an opinion about. Her daughters forgave her only late in their lives. I, who had faced a similar desperation, with more help than Elsie had ever found, could only imagine the furies her divorce and this loss of her kids might have let loose. Enough to fuel alcoholic abandon, perhaps, and a rage at any man who ever dared think he could own her.

Times got better after WWII. My grandparents recovered a middle-class life and their children, too. But something in the hearts of my family's women had shifted, I think. Nothing in women's sphere seemed certain anymore, and money was at the heart of it. Elsie and her sisters never depended on the property of their reproductive powers to negotiate a livelihood dependent on any man. My mother, too. You couldn't count on that—you couldn't put *that* in a bank.

Not that they ever talked out loud about such an offensive idea.

Getting Real

The actual cost of women's bearing and raising children in our private un-profits is unseemly to discuss in public. For a woman to talk about children and money in the same sentence remains distasteful. Angels aren't allowed to think in those terms.

But America's stinginess toward its mothers shows, for those willing to look. While other developing countries are lowering maternal death rates, the US rate is rising, the highest among thirteen peer nations, according to the *Lancet*. We're talking rates six times as high.

We all have mothers, yet where can we locate her part in our Constitutional contract for the nation's promotion of our general welfare? Certainly not in her wage penalty, well documented by now. *US News* reported in early 2017 that mothers earn seventy-one cents to a father's dollar—the same wage gap as 1990. Today 70 percent of mothers work, says the US Department of Labor, and of them 75 percent work full-time. Her welfare is not in the increased hours that mothers in poverty work today in minimum wage jobs. Certainly not in our remaining the only industrialized nation still a world away from subsidizing parental leaves for new parents, or legislating sick days and family leave, or mandatory vacations, or flextime, or universal childcare support.

There are financial solutions for providing everything we need, economist Stephanie Sequino once told me over lunch. Healthy children, wherever they live, are like money in our planetary bank, assuring a future. Having a child is a very private decision, but raising her well takes a shared public trust.

People no longer are rare—land is, water is, resources are. Worldwide, birth rates go down as women gain in education. This is good for nations' families, good for the earth and shared prosperity. In a world more interconnected than ever, the essential tasks traditionally done by women, the private day-by-day maintenance of healthy life and death, cannot be separated from her work in the public realm where money is made. How, then, can we better manage it all?

Quick Rehash

- Women's reproductive powers made her the first sought-after property, and kept her so busy that over time, despite her ingenious innovations that made civilization possible, men's accumulation of surpluses and weapons won him dominance.
- Originally tokens to honor marriage and other contracts, coins and money began to be used in trade, more flexible than barter.
- Women's production of goods at home was gradually monetized and overtaken by capitalist industrialization, demoting her from producer of wealth to consumer.
- Women's education and birth control have begun a new Woman's Enlightenment.

EconoGirlfriend Conversation Starter

When did you first think about having or not having children? Were you encouraged to think about their cost? How does it feel to consider their cost?

Chapter 12: A Penny Saved Is a Penny Earned

1965–Now
Female double duty today creates inefficiency and makes caring a cost she must pay.

I used to complain when my mom had no time to help me with homework or play a board game. I knew how to milk her guilt. Mom worried. She didn't know that economic term you've learned, *opportunity cost*, but she lived its reality. And so do you. It goes like this:

You cannot have your cake and eat it, too. You cannot be in two places at once. You cannot be an Angel of the House in the same hours you are a competitor at work. So you weigh what matters, you adapt and readapt to find equilibrium and ideally some happiness.

To counter her work self-reproach, Mom indulged her kids' consumer wishes, making sure we had candy, trendy fashions, music, and bikes, the better to belong and fit in at school and appear normal. Our whole family depended on her efficient managing at home. She'd work late or delegate what to do, while tending everyone's emotions, counseling our upsets and soothing any hurts. Whenever she barked orders or failed to look pleased, she was found wanting in her Angel duties.

My stepdad had a workshop in the basement. In the same way Mom found time for gardening to recharge her happiness, he loved to putter in his basement workshop, creating wooden knick-knacks. Once he made Mom a mood meter that was round like a clock but with only one indicator hand. She (or her critics) could set its dial to warn us: Was she happy, angry, nervous, moody, sleepy, sad, or cranky?

Her favorite setting was *cranky* to keep us on our toes. But our family's balance depended on her. Her real mood set the tone for the whole family, and no one but Mom was required to meter and regulate emotions.

Home-Grown Capitalist

However much her salary cost Mom in guilt and crankiness, her personal ledger's bottom line showed her income numbers were greater than her capital costs. Working was more profitable for her. My mother, the little capitalist with coins in a sugar bowl, had first hired babysitting labor and then invested in new technology, like instant potatoes and a car, for greater efficiency, so she could sublet a full eight hours of her time for money.

Her entrepreneurial investments thus increased her production, if production is measured by output of dollars—which is how most things are measured now. The pennies Mom earned with her efficiency, her careful planning and management that saved our family money, were harder to see, near invisible, as were those good feelings she generated with generosity, giving herself away.

If my mother's maneuvers sound businesslike, as if she were running a private enterprise, to see it that way you'd be technically right. And yet all the work that maintains any private home like hers and yours and mine is never considered a private enterprise, never commercial. Why not? Because a home is far more private than private enterprise, supposedly the inner sanctum of our economy.

Its consumer dollars only drive the whole economy's demand, but home consumers must never expect any credit for this, only debits. As consumers, whether mothers or not, women pay for the privilege of taking care of life.

Costly Caring

Mother or not, a woman pays a higher price for care. She is expected to be beautiful as well as clean, using moisturizer, hair products, salon cuts and colors, makeup, and a variety of shoes, skirt lengths, equipment, and tampons, all on a smaller paycheck. Keeping fit is important, so there are gym fees or Pilates or yoga classes to purchase.

Care requires keeping a roof over her head. American households annually spend the most money on housing; the median house price in mid-2017 was $345,800. On average *Realtor Magazine* says she'll need a down payment of $38,000 to finance the rest. At the current 3.92 percent interest, she'll pay $17,460 a year, or $523,800 over thirty years, not counting insurance and property tax.

Say she only rents. Annually she needs at least $9,588, or $799 a month, though this varies dramatically depending on region and bedroom numbers. After that, transportation is her biggest cost. The National Household Travel Survey calculated a national average of $7,302 a year.

Moms today have fewer kids, no doubt connected to their cost. Household size has shrunk from 3.3 people in 1960 to 2.5 people in 2016. Every year the US Department of Agriculture (USDA) reports what families can expect to spend raising a child to the age of eighteen. The average cost of a child born in 2013 stood at $245,000, not including college or pregnancy. By 2016, it was $273,405.

Despite her baby production being the baseline for all future economic production, an American mom personally pays for giving birth. In 2013, Truven Health Analytics reported US births the costliest in the world, about $30,000 for a vaginal birth, $50,000 for a C-section. Her out-of-pocket costs average $3,400 per birth, depending on her insurance, another cost. Moves to reform US health care in 2017 actually sought to make maternity insurance separate, expected to raise its price.

The National Conference of State Legislators reported the average family's annual health insurance premium was $18,142 in 2016. Employees paid an average $1,250 toward their employer-group policy, which included more deductibles. *Business Insider* cited a Kaiser Family Foundation report that year on skyrocketing out-of-pocket costs averaging $1,478 a year.

Care requires that everyone eats. Average households spent about $7,000 on food in 2016. (Add on about $2,900 a year for an extra kid.) *Business Insider* noticed that $3,200 of that amount was spent on restaurants and fast food like Hot Pockets. To save money, they suggest cooking more at home, without a blush or a nod to the increased hours all Americans now spend on the job.

Whether she is a well-paid high-tech manager on her computer or a retail worker trying to sync up two jobs—maybe three or four if she has a partner—she's plenty busy while shopping for, caring for, and washing down kids, cars, rugs, dishes, clothes, and herself, day after day, throwing something in the Crock-Pot when she can.

The Bureau of Labor Statistics (BLS) set the median household income in 2016 at $56,500, but she will likely earn less, as wherever she works, whatever her field, she earns less than men doing the same work, says the Institute for Women's Policy Research. A full-time, minimum wage job today earns a whopping $15,080 a year before taxes, the federal rate unchanged since 1990—the reason some states and cities have increased it, with many saying $15.00 an hour should be the bare minimum. She'd then gross $31,200 a year. Sound too generous?

Women are the sole or primary support for 40 percent of children, says the Pew Research Center. So consider her need for childcare, difficult to find and easily taking another 20 percent of her income. Then there's the possibility she has education debts to pay for herself, and quite possibly she has an aging parent who needs care. God help her if she or someone in the family gets sick.

Like my mom, today's women are looking at their personal ledgers. How profitable are her dollars, the way production is now measured, if her dollars and time keep coming up short? What creates this shortfall?

The general welfare requires shared capital investment in our roads and bridges, but also in our caring and our homes. Other nations universally recognize and support families' importance. Alia Dastagir at *USA Today* reports that US women legislators on both sides of the aisle have put forward legislation in 2017 to start a needed US revisioning of public policy for including family needs.

US Senator Deb Fischer (R-NE) proposed the Strong Families Act to give a tax credit to companies offering at least two weeks of paid family leave per year. The FAMILY Act (for Family and Medical Leave Insurance), sponsored by US Senator Kirsten Gillibrand (D-NY) and US Representative Rosa DeLauro (D-CT), proposes a national fund providing workers with two-thirds of their pay for up to twelve weeks. Funded by employee and employer payroll insurance, its cost is less than $1.50 a week. But it's only a beginning.

Women's Limited Partnership

Women need to revise the old story of the Angel of the House, kept separate from the economy, to a more fully economic tale of our home's essential production of life, liberty, and the energy for the pursuit of our happiness. The separate spheres of that first hundred years of male industrialized economy—the "private" domestic circle of the nineteenth century and the "public" sphere of money and power—persist in US ideology, keeping the ultra-private un-profits of our homes invisible and uncounted. This private and public division of work was always a masculine sleight of hand, but as with all good lies, there was also some truth to it.

The division of labor between the sexes was familiar and longstanding. There remained plenty of work to go around, and male protectors were needed to withstand male violence, always a risk then and now, I'm afraid. Meanwhile women remain the only ones who can swell up to twice their size and then burst blood and a brand-new baby through an opening the size of a doorknob.

We need to rethink our old ideas about *private* and *public*, and make sure we understand what we mean when we use those terms. Whose interests are served? For instance, in the twentieth century, male capitalists and male laborers both made money in the public realm by means of private enterprise, which sounds contradictory—until you consider the EconoMansplaining source. This old story has a particular point of view.

Using the term *private* as in private enterprise, an entity making money, rationalized why all the cash—whether capitalist profits or laborer wages—rightfully belonged exclusively to its male owners. Using *private* as a private sphere kept a woman at home and rationalized that the invisible pennies she saved him with her efficient management rightfully belonged to him, too.

Public-private partnerships are all the rage in political circles today. What exactly does that mean? It's a recognition of what already goes on regularly, generally leaving the ultra-private un-profit—namely you—out.

For example, when Main Street needs to be repaired, taxpayers chip in their tax dollars to help pay the workers who do the roadwork. If it's a large road, these public tax funds might come from Washington, your state, and maybe your town or city. Without tax funds, store owners and suppliers, employees and customers, would be stuck in mud ruts, instead of easily parking on Main Street to enter privately owned private enterprises to exchange currency for goods and services. It's a public-private partnership.

Public funds, our shared taxes, may also pay private firms to do the needed roadwork. That's a matter of efficiency. Depending on the size of the job and its complexity, publicly funded work crews might fill a few potholes cheaply enough. On the other hand, a specialized private firm with a new asphalt-paving machine might be more efficient for bigger jobs.

These are the kinds of decisions that town councils or administrators make all the time. Most often, in most towns, roadwork and other jobs are a mix of private and public entities. Many arguments over taxes and government are about where exactly these two streams of money, shared public tax money and private capitalist money, should meet in search of the greatest efficiency.

A private enterprise also pays taxes, so you could say a share of taxpayers' income earned in both realms, the public and private, is reinvested in the publicly shared town, which then may contract with private enterprise operations for services. Money thus ideally goes round in a circular flow between public and private, benefitting all.

Then There's Her

But now let's look at what remains missing and invisible—namely, you and me and our invisible pennies of efficiency, the product of our time and attention. In my example of a functioning Main Street, the road's surface got repaired so that stores were accessible and the economy kept functioning. Private enterprise owners, whether they were road-paving companies or downtown merchants, earned a profit from increased traffic downtown. Store clerks' time, their wages, were paid by private storeowners, and town administrators' time or the town road crew's time was paid by public funds. The time that workers took to repair the roads was paid either by a private company or the public town. In either case, taxpayers footed the bill.

The only person expected to function without any compensation for her time on Main Street is the shopper, the consumer, most often you and me. She alone pays for all of it, whether through her fair share of public funding or spending her privately funded wages for goods and needed services. Her sales tax funds the government's public pot of money while her purchases fill the private till of Main Street storeowners.

Making efficient purchases for her household, she connects everything economic and ultimately pays for the economy's healthy functioning, all while remaining invisible, her time available for free.

Now women's role has been expanded in that old economic story, a tragedy in the making unless she calls out its pretensions as laughable. EconoMan's definition of efficiency is not at all what you'd think.

As we saw in Chapter 10, production was made more technically efficient by industrialization, gradually moving production out of the home and into the market. Production was then measured as outputs, and increases were and are always sought (*why* is found in Part V) in a competitive market.

EconoMansplains that freely competing markets, guided by that invisible hand, just naturally bring supply and demand into balance with a fair market price. Italian neoclassical economist and engineer Vilfredo Pareto (1848–1923) developed principles that defined human welfare in terms of this market competition, describing an equilibrium that only occurs in a theoretical economic world of mathematical perfection. His ideas about "efficiency" are still widely accepted today.

> ## ✔ PARETO EFFICIENCY
> Pareto basically said that an allocation of resources is efficient if as a result, one individual is better off, and no individual is worse off. In any situation, therefore, a number of *Pareto efficient* outcomes are possible.

For example, if a seller values a car at $1,000 and a buyer has $2,000 to spend, any price the buyer pays up to $2,000 is *Pareto efficient*, since the seller is better off and the buyer has a car he values at $2,000, rightly or wrongly. If the buyer is stingy and pays a price of only $1,100, it is still Pareto efficient; in fact, it is *Pareto optimum*, because both the seller and the buyer are better off.

And if both happen upon a $100 bill in the parking lot, they can either decide to split it, or the stronger one can keep it all. Either situation is a *Pareto improvement*, since at least one person is better off, and no one is worse off.

Notice that the unfortunate person who had lost the $100 bill never appears in this economic calculation, probably because Pareto efficiency is only concerned with outputs and technical method. The losing owner is irrelevant and invisible, much like the invisible pennies saved by thrifty management at home, and the invisible return of good feelings when you and I share what we've shopped for.

As far as Pareto is concerned, if you didn't share, your purchases are still Pareto efficient because you and the store are better off. Your family was without dinner to begin with, so they shouldn't complain since they are no worse off. In other words, unlike the actual life you live, Pareto's efficiency claims to be entirely separate from ethics, equity, wisdom, or the joy of sharing. Remember, economics is abstract, a purely rational science, superior to any generosity of spirit or intuitive feelings, which are, as you know, *girly*.

But a good question that feminist economists seem to repeatedly ask is this: Who exactly is served by ideas and principles like these? Competitive production alone never makes a woman more efficient. If she attempts too many things all at once, like bake six pies, catch up with a project on the phone, watch her kids, and change the oil in her car the same afternoon, things will go awry. Then time and resources are wasted, and waste is inefficient.

A living productivity, as opposed to a competitive productivity, tracks a different equilibrium.

Economic Mismatch

The real-world economy is very different than that described in standard economic theory, writes economist Sabine O'Hara in her article "Everything Needs Care: Toward a Context-Based Economy," from a book I'll revisit in the next chapter. She explains that there is only so much arable land to grow human food and so much water to be polluted or used up. By concentrating only on output and ignoring the biological sources for that output—human and ecological inputs—we are using up nonrenewable resources and harming nature's ability to renew life. That is the ultimate inefficiency.

O'Hara writes, "As restorative and reproductive capacities are impaired, efficiency levels cannot be sustained without ever increasing investments. The results are self-evident. Half of the world's wetlands, temperate and tropical forests are gone; more than half of all arable land is suffering some degree of deterioration and desertification; oceans are dying and 75 percent of marine fisheries are either over-fished or fished to capacity."

Without care and attention, earthly communities that support our human ones will come unraveled, and so will we. A rise in human poverty in exhausted environments where people formerly sustained their lives is another marker of our threatened future.

EconoMan finds competition unerringly good. By contrast, biologists find competition a state that brings harm to species. If two species compete for water or a particular food, natural selection requires that one species ultimately dies out—or else adapts. Equilibrium within an ecology results when species efficiently interrelate and reproduce only enough offspring to sustain numbers.

I learned more about adaption when I went to Cape Cod for a field trip seminar on the horseshoe crab. Our biologist guide talked about the intricacies of our natural world's equilibrium. We were there for a particular full moon when the female horseshoe crabs come onto the beach to lay eggs as they've been doing for 450 million years. An orgy of the species' smaller males were in hot pursuit to fertilize her thousands of eggs.

Birds actually time their migrations to make the same date on this beach—and as we watched them, churning the sand with their beaks, the biologist pointed out the long-billed godwits, the short, stubby-billed plovers, and the medium-sized bills of the dunlins. These birds had all adapted to better share in the feast, and even the surviving eggs benefitted from all those different-sized bills, driving them deeper into sand safety.

The division between human economics and a living environment is as false and convenient as the old two-gendered-spheres doctrine of work, divisions benefitting only EconoMan and his Pareto improvement for one. Like your life-maintenance work and time at home, the earth's life-maintenance work in the oceans, the soil, and the climate is omitted from EconoMansplaining. That both these invisible realms are gendered female is no coincidence.

Mutual Problem Solving

Another feminist economist, Irene van Staveren, writes that a peer of Pareto, Charlotte Perkins Gilman, showed in her fiction how competition is not the only economic method or even the most efficient one. Her sci-fi tale of an economy without men, the novel *Herland* written in 1915, makes the case that both paid market work and unpaid life-maintenance work at home can be motivated by cooperation and mutuality, all made easier when connected to heart-incentives that help define who we are.

No man is an island, no woman a totally free agent. The people and places we love—or hate if that's all we can manage—shape our edges and fire our imagination and decisions. In my own early economic story, striving to be that dreamed-of full-time mom, I saved invisible pennies by practicing thriftiness, finding bargains, cooking from scratch, planting a garden, sewing our clothes, and bartering yard sale exchanges.

By the time my children were in school, I entered the workforce to earn copper pennies of the public world, as my mother had before me. One income was not enough by then, even with thrift. My edges and dreams changed.

When I remarried, it was to a man who wanted to help me succeed at my career as much as I helped him to succeed in his. We two shared our household tasks. One morning, in the frantic rush to work at the college where I taught, I lamented the good old days when professors had secretaries.

"And I need a wife!" I said. "Someone who makes sure I have clean underwear and matched socks in my drawer, and has my breakfast all ready so I can concentrate on getting to work, all ready to go."

My husband was utterly sympathetic. "I know," he said. "I need one, too!"

Workers today operate at a disadvantage. Few have the benefit of even a part-time Angel, an affectionate person with time to care, someone who dotes on our successes and soothes our failures. Despite our best intentions, our better selves are kept busy working for someone else's profit, not our own. The on button of competition is always on.

In failing to credit the indispensible importance of our mutual collaborative services to any economy, that old male economic story with its simplistic dualisms—supply vs. demand, capitalists vs. labor, capitalists vs. government, capitalists vs. capitalists—has overlooked what is most essential. Being essential is different from being important.

We need a new script for a comedy, not a tragedy. Comedies always have young lovers who, despite crazy odds and weird characters, finally find each other beautiful.

Juggling Concrete Blocks

When more young parents are expected to do too much for too little return to those ultra-private enterprises, the un-profit we call home, their ability to be efficient becomes harder. Finding invisible pennies requires close attention and time, as well as energy recharging that only comes from whatever brings you happiness—gardening, friends, hobbies, playing with your kids.

A think tank interested in more life-friendly models, the New Economy Working Group says that two US streets have become metaphors for describing two very different economic models with different values and methods: Wall Street and Main Street.

> ## ✓ WALL STREET
>
> Wall Street values huge bankers and traders who finance the global economy, international trade, and the equally huge multinational corporations they own. Its sole purpose is to maximize profits, using financial methods, centrally planned and organized. Wall Street is far distant from the resources they allocate and activities they own. Being distant, often across the world, its managers don't live with the social consequences of their actions.

EconoMan's capitalists need not look closely at the people whose lives they rent out on the other side of the world. Feelings, skin colors, and justice have nothing to do with his ultra-rational efficiency decisions, based only on Pareto improvements that are usually his own. By contrast, capitalists on Main Street must define their economic decisions in a more limited, time-and-place-bound way.

That smaller capitalist will get only those employees and customers who live nearby. She makes do with these limits or else collaborates with others—or she develops new inventive services or relationships that expand possibilities for surviving and thriving. With her life at stake, too, connections cannot be ignored.

In these days of global economics, Main Street businesses have much more in common with laborers than they do with international corporations or their capitalist investors. It isn't surprising that more women's businesses are found on Main Streets around the world than on Wall Street.

Most often, women's businesses aren't even categorized as small businesses. They are deemed part of the informal economy, or if regulated, they are called *micro-businesses* for very small operations, often a source of self-employment. In the national and international economic story, their numbers are a fairly new phenomenon.

Both women and men work more hours than conventional measures of the labor market suggest. But hundreds of international time studies show that women everywhere spend much more of their time than do men in informal, unpaid household production work. They rest fewer hours.

Women's life-maintenance duties at home mean that she earns less in the job market. For the most part, women don't do the same work as men. Most of our wage work is care work and relationship-maintenance work. Two-thirds of working women are clustered into just 54 of the 534 occupations tracked by the US Department of Labor.

Human service sector wages, writes Sabine O'Hara, are among the lowest paid. Low pay reinforces those stereotypes of gender and ethnic roles we've seen already sorting us out into hierarchies. Ninety-seven percent of childcare workers and 94 percent of domestic workers in the United States are women, and 37 percent of them are African American, 15 percent Hispanic.

If these jobs paid as well as truck drivers, we would see a lot more men taking an interest. But as it is, O'Hara reports, the elderly, the poor, the young, and the powerless do most of the paid and unpaid essential care and maintenance. Care remains discounted and unnoticed in the private domestic realm, and overshadowed by work in the marketplace.

Half the Story

A clear point of view is crucial to telling any story. That is a story's grace. Many points of view are really possible. The writers of my generation have shown how the meaning of a story's events changes dramatically depending upon the character through whose eyes you are viewing events.

The standard economic story so far has generally, and quite simplistically, drawn on a plot of competitive tension between two male sets of characters. The male owners of surplus private funds, the kingly capitalists currently called "makers," do battle with male laborer unionists, who—depending on the story's plot—are either the underdog or shiftless "takers" that undermine money genius. Villains and heroes have changed over time—sometimes quite suddenly and dramatically.

A relatively new character, still male, appeared in the modern twentieth-century economic story, introduced by gentleman Keynes. Government created a new triangle plot with labor and capital, all still competing for dominance—bad guys vs. good guys, winners and losers. Who gets to control private *and* public money now?

In other words, up to this point, the overly simple economic story of only half the population is about one tiny part of human and earthly reality. Little by little, the gender of labor and capital and government characters has changed, becoming more female—yet whenever our money is laid on the table, it's the same old masculine action tale up on stage, muscling in on Pareto improvements for one, with shouts, dares, and threats of violence.

Their story gets nastier, their bravado riskier. We could all use a good laugh by now, and some passion that isn't hate. So thankfully, there are new economic stories forming, with fresh players and a more complex plot and point of view. Their tales awaken a shimmering awareness of life's interconnections, still ahead in Parts IV and V.

Quick Rehash

- EconoMan's competitive market equilibrium may prove a mathematical efficiency when scoring an improvement for one, but has little to do with life as you live it, trying to find balance.
- The marketplace cannot safely be separated from the biological work of nature, including the biological work of our homes; it does so only at all our peril.
- Economic cooperation and mutuality are more efficient and sustainable than endless warring competition and growth.

EconoGirlfriend Conversation Starter

Assuming waste is inefficient, what waste do you see in your own life, or your community, that you wish could be lessened? What concrete change do you think might help?

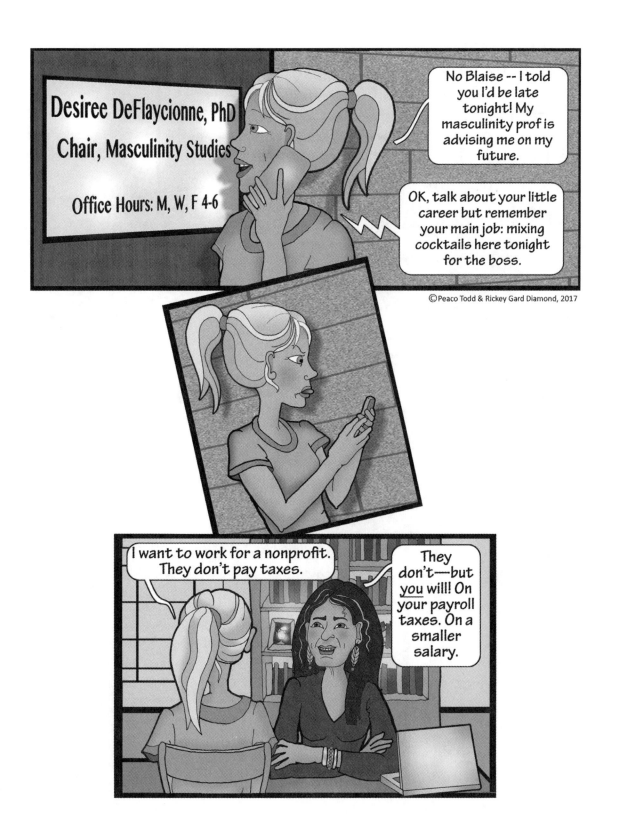

PART IV

HIS EMBODIED FICTIONS

Collective Bodies of Nations, Corporations, and
Labor Must Always Perform as Men at War.

Chapter 13: Out of the Mouths of Babes

A sexier accounting of commerce and nations would include the essential female.

In the 1950s, no advice books existed for parents who got divorced. There was only embarrassment and suspicion. My mother and dad both suffered from unspoken judgments and feelings, and Dad complicated matters by remaining devoted to me, regularly traveling long distances. At times there were tensions I didn't understand but could feel in the air.

Once when I was about ten, Dad took me to an ice cream emporium. Somehow our conversation revealed that my mother had a new job. Dad asked what she did now. Mom had told me when asked that I should use a certain word, but in the spotlight of my father's attention, the word changed shape, and I told him that Mommy was a countess now.

"A countess?" he said, smiling. "I see. Does she wear a tiara to work?"

My face turned scarlet. I didn't know what a tiara was, but I knew I'd made my mother a joke somehow. I felt a shared shame for her and me. No, no, I'd goofed up, I confessed. She worked with numbers and counting all the time. What was the word?

An *accountant*?

That was it. But my dad was right, too, I realized much later, when I could laugh about the memory and his joke. My mother's aloof dignity and her no-nonsense beauty made it easy to imagine her royalty. No one dreamed she was scared of being thought a hillbilly. I never understood her compensations for that fear until I was much older.

This confession is an account of what happened to me, a story told from my point of view. My selected details fit my purpose of showing how easily language can be misunderstood, and how appearances are not necessarily reality. It left out a world of context: ice cream flavors, flashy décor, my dad's tie, and how tight my barrettes felt from Mom signaling our neat non-hillbilly-ness.

A numbered account is another form of story, its language numerical. That numbers can distill so much is both a strength and a weakness. A young father taking his daughter out for ice cream can be explained numerically: minus twenty dollars for gas, minus two dollars for ice cream, plus four hours driving. But as with any account, a great deal has to be left out. Setting down black-and-white certainty feels magically solid and reassuring when swirling tensions, nervous laughter, and blushes demand something be known for sure. Yet deciding what's most essential always depends on your intent.

Double Meanings

As economist Jane Gleeson-White explains in her fascinating history of accounting, *Double Entry*, numbers in ledger books, bookkeeping, and pie charts are no less skewed to a purpose and a point of view than any other story. It's important to consider whose account it is, told from whose point of view. Determining a numerical account's point of view and purpose can also help you to see their limits.

Numbers have a long history of occult and mystical associations. Strange clay tokens found in ancient storerooms mystified, until recently deciphered as a nine-thousand-year-old accounting system by French archaeologist Denise Schmandt-Besserat. Firing clay for pots was a female endeavor, and she and others now hypothesize that women began symbolic counting to mark menses, pregnancies, seasons, and gifts.

As communities grew larger, social hierarchies and ranking appeared, redistributing goods with trading. Clay tokens led to symbol systems inscribed with a stylus on flat clay tablet accounts in Mesopotamia, the Indus Valley in India, in China, and in Meso-America. Their symbolic numbers and writing were associated with the highest ranks, and over time males increasingly headed these.

When the Greeks began to use coins for trade, numerical record keeping was essential. Roman accounting records, called *tabulae rationum*, even served as legal documents. Their two pages listed debits or disbursements on one side, receipts and credits on the other. Roman numeral accounts survived Rome's fall, still kept by society's elite, lords, kings, and monks of feudal Europe.

They were first exposed to Arabic numbers, the kind we use, when southern Spain became a Muslim caliphate, about 1,300 years ago, writes Gleeson-White. The Church in Rome considered its symbols dangerous. Hidden knowledge of the sacred had long been part of math's mystique, and early universities of Europe were nearly as leery of math as they were of women. They sided with the Roman-numeral church and banned both. So did banks and guilds until about five hundred years ago.

Merchants Lead the Way

Today, we take Arabic numerals, its zeros and the decimal point, for granted. Its system makes quick calculations possible and proportions visible. The most important result of Rome's four Crusades was unintended, says Gleeson-White, giving rise to eastern trading routes. Turks, Arabs, Hindus, and the Chinese already used the abacus and the new number system, exposing merchants of northern Italy to their simplicity.

Milan, Pisa, Genoa, and Florence all grew powerful en route to the Holy Land, but farthest east, reigned Italy's richest merchant city, Venice. In 1492, a monk named Luca Pacioli published a math "how-to" book. In it, he explained practical techniques for creating perspective in paintings, using Arabic decimals with ten fingers, and the Venetian method for keeping business accounts.

The four financial statements Pacioli described over five hundred years ago were adopted around the world and are still familiar to accountants today.

✓ DOUBLE-ENTRY ACCOUNTING

Pacioli's Venetian method recognized the dynamic contained in any commercial exchange. The purpose of its accounts was greater transparency of the whole enterprise for efficiency and balance. The method's *duality principle* held that a loss in one place is always balanced by a gain in another.

This principle led to double-entry bookkeeping. For every debit there is also a credit, and for every addition, a subtraction. This double effect can feel like a hall of mirrors but is actually representing a yin-yang whole. Selling a product thus increases income but also must decrease inventory assets. Paying the electric bill increases expense and also decreases cash assets in the bank.

Double-entry bookkeeping's time structure is important too, grounding its numbers. Its four summaries (the balance sheet, the income statement, the cash-flow statement, and the statement of retained earnings) show all credits and debits for each three-month quarter and finally each year. It is a numerical account, a story of sorts, but like any story it necessarily leaves out a great deal.

Not So Simple

As universal and standardized as Pacioli's accounting has become, Gleeson-White points out that accountants themselves do not agree on how to define global-sized multinational corporate structures today. Even basic terms like *costs* and *valuation* are, she says, "highly contestable figures. . . . Numbers can be negotiated to make management look good."

The importance of the balance sheet with its measure of future viability, highly regarded in the past, for instance, has shifted in today's pressured global markets. The focus is now on the income statement, which measures the immediate earning capacity.

In that context, the auditors of large accounting firms like Arthur Andersen and Ernst & Young missed huge corporate deceptions in recent years, including Enron, WorldCom, and Lehman Brothers.

In the 1970s, the biggest firms began offering business consulting services, more profitable than audits, and at least in theory kept separate. But as global corporate structures grew complicated, and five huge international firms came to dominate the profession, academics in the field began to describe a neoliberal shift in concepts, transforming the auditor from "judicial man" to "economic man."

One of Gleeson-White's sources, Prem Sikka, a professor of accounting at the University of Essex in England, calls auditing "a weak link in this chain" of accounts and measures, in a paper on the history and rhetoric of auditor independence, published to inform the US Independence Standards Board.

He explains the profession's exposures to conflicts of interest this way: "You have one floor of big accountancy firms doing an audit and another floor giving advice on how to bypass rules and regulations and how to flatter their financial statements. And accounting firms make money whichever way things go. . . . Like Russian roulette, 99 percent of the time, you get away with it."

Making management look good was not Pacioli's goal. Seeing more clearly was. After Enron, Congress passed The Sarbanes-Oxley Act of 2002 to strengthen auditor independence and transparency. Yet as Wells-Fargo's 2016 fake bank accounts made evident, despite auditors, a ruthless corporate culture using overly complex financial tools will still try to sell lies.

Too narrow a definition of profit engenders duplicity, not the duality of Pacioli's business realism. Newer thinkers advocate numerical accounts that deliver the balance and wholeness that Pacioli originally sought. Without this, trust becomes impossible.

Who knew accounting could be so exciting? Changes in it could literally save the planet and your future.

On Account of GDP

You may not have heard of something called *national accounting*, but no doubt you would recognize its result, Washington's most often cited number, the Gross Domestic Product, or GDP. Politicians love to talk GDP in the same way Wall Street likes to talk about income statements and immediate earning potential.

This numbered account emphasizes an imperative to grow, while confusing paper dollars with a healthy economy. GDP only adds up money made from market transactions. Its numbers equate your value to your salary or wages. By GDP's account, men are far more important than are women because they make more dollars. GDP accounting helps keep things that way.

✓ GROSS DOMESTIC PRODUCT (GDP)

The GDP began as the Gross National Product (GNP) when American economist Simon Kuznets at the US Department of Commerce created a new report called "National Income: 1929–1932." It gave government a new economic profile of sales income industry-by-industry. When WWII broke out, it revealed industrial production abilities that enabled more efficient coordination of war production.

GNP, which measured dollars of Americans no matter where they live, was replaced by the GDP in 1991 in the United States, as more multinational corporations appeared. GDP measures all dollars produced within a nation's boundaries, including by foreign companies.

Both Kuznets in the United States and Keynes in England said income data alone was an inadequate national measure. But after the war was won, and Keynes had died and Kuznets resigned, a new generation of male elites from both countries, including accounting statisticians, adopted a detailed set of standards for national accounts, producing a uniform measure of money.

The United Nations formed in 1945, and through international negotiations, began to gather numbers on economic activities globally with a uniform pattern for accounts. Required for any nation joining the UN, national accounts make financial analysis and comparisons easier. But as usual, the agreements important men made among themselves largely omitted women.

✓ UN SYSTEM OF NATIONAL ACCOUNTS (SNA)

Revised several times, the SNA "how-to" handbook provides a macro-overview of nations' economic processes that underlie both GNP and GDP numbers. They record dollars that originate in production, and then track their flow to consumption, saving, and investment by consumers, businesses, government, and foreign nations, adding up all dollars to measure growth. Only dollars are measured, as if a nation's sole purpose were financial.

GDP's Privilege

Ranking nations by money may be less bloody than ranking them by battle. But for most people, economic wars over international resources remain a gory mess. Today GDP remains largely unquestioned by the US general public. It's a boring subject, complex enough to make the eyes cross.

To wake you up, I'll call its system of accounts the numerical tales of privileged global elites. They weave a royal robe of GDP threads to cover the naked power that money alone wields. Robert Kennedy gave a remarkable speech about the GDP's misdirection in 1968, just weeks before he was assassinated. He said that GDP's materialism failed to account for the things Americans most valued, such as "the beauty of our poetry or the strength of our marriages, the intelligence of our public debate or the integrity of our public officials."

It wouldn't be until the 1990s that women's challenges to GDP details gathered steam. Among the earliest to draw attention to its masculine bias was one of the first female New Zealand parliament ministers, Marilyn Waring. (Earlier I discussed the work of Sabine O'Hara, one of a generation of feminist economists influenced by her.) Waring had worked on New Zealand's national budget, and she dared call the GDP dangerous nonsense.

Her 1995 book, *Counting for Nothing: What Men Value and What Women Are Worth*, argued that national accounting concepts originally designed to win WWII were not what was needed today. The GDP counts the sale of weapons as a plus, while ignoring the care that makes life possible. She described the cost of failing to account for the reproductive labor of Mother Nature, and the life-maintenance work of women and men around the world.

Those who subsist on the land or work at home do not work, according to SNA methods. Their work is invisible to the GDP. Likewise, national accounting methods give no value to a forest of trees replenishing the soil and air. A tree only counts when it is cut into lumber and sold on the market for dollars. Only market dollars count.

From the beginning, Simon Kuznets had questioned these data gaps, too. He thought the national accounts should include the value of unpaid housework and community work, despite the difficulty of estimating its monetary value. When the US Bureau of Economic Analysis (BEA), part of the US Commerce Department, refused to calculate those estimates, writes Gleeson-White in *Double Entry*, Kuznets resigned in the late 1940s.

Many others saw gaps, too, though not necessarily framed as a woman's issue as Waring saw it. An Indian economist she admired, Amartya Sen, had developed a Human Development Index to measure the value of life expectancy levels, numbers of adults able to read, and education enrollments. These measurements too were omitted by the GDP.

✓ BOTTOM LINE

The number at the bottom of a company's income statement, after all expenses have been subtracted to find a net sum, is commonly called *the bottom line*. Companies try to increase that bottom line number by either growing their income, or becoming more efficient through cutting costs or production time, aimed at increasing the surplus, called a *profit margin*.

In 1994, British businessman John Elkington first coined the term *triple bottom line*. He argued that a sustainable future required businesses to account not only for *profit*, the traditional bottom line, but also to measure its social relations in a *people* account and its environmental impact in a *planet* account. Businesses without a triple bottom line, accounting for three Ps—profit, people, and planet—he said, are not accounting for their true cost of doing business. Ben & Jerry's Ice Cream in Vermont was among the first US businesses to use and promote this kind of 3-P accounting.

Yet only nations or states can more fully account for nonmarket reproductive work that still remains largely invisible. Thirty years after Waring's book, economist Sabine O'Hara, in her essay

"Everything Needs Care," says it is no accident that both realms of reproduction, in our homes and in our ecosystems—which make the economy possible in the first place—remain neglected. Like Waring, O'Hara argues that a built-in economic bias exists that values extracting resources, not conserving them. That bias values work, but not resting or staying alive.

I've named that persistent bias EconoMansplaining. Its point of view has a purpose. It deliberately omits the importance of human emotions and a world of wisdom traditions that have long guided human decisions. It devalues the efficiency of loving, caring, and sharing. When only dollar amounts are allowed in EconoMan's accounts, any personal interactions with his numbers are kept off stage. In this way, a public claim can be made for purely rational, impersonal, scientific analysis.

This conviction that overvalues rationality persists, despite recent brain science that has shown us how critically important emotions are to what is called "executive function," the ability to make good decisions, to evaluate and sequence priorities, and to learn while maneuvering in concrete situations.

Feeling is, in fact, an essential part of human reasoning and learning—even when we try to ban feeling and call ourselves experts. Especially then, when feelings are kept hidden, we might ask why. Like my mother the countess, who feared being thought a hillbilly, perhaps EconoMan overcompensates.

Change in the United States cannot happen until more women understand how the economic game gets played with a deck stacked against her. We need new data cards, new ways of accounting to create a fuller economic story. They already exist, but the United States seems stuck.

Concrete Situations

By 1993, the UN was encouraging nations to create *satellite accounts*. Such accounts would relate to the national account but not replace it. In 1994, the US Commerce Department's Bureau of Economic Analysis (BEA) that generates the GDP proposed some environmental measures to track nonrenewable resources like oil and other energy. Congress promptly defunded it. Of the three satellites first suggested thirty years ago, environmental, household, and tourism accounts, only US tourism has sustained data numbers.

We lag behind other countries in our environmental accounting, and are even further behind on accounts of household production. Without acknowledging and accounting for invisible pennies of efficiency earned by our families' attention and caring, we're overshadowed by EconoMan demands for more growth, whatever the cost.

Let's say a woman makes more money than her husband, and together they both decide that when they have children, he will stay home and take care of the children and their home.

Or let's say a woman and her husband decide that one will work the night shift while the other works days, so that both can share the load and the joy of that second shift of work at home.

Or let's say a woman and her partner decide not to have children but to invest themselves in caring for the children already born in their world, choosing careers of helping and teaching.

In any of those situations, such thoughtful, caring, and deeply moral decisions will be invisible to our GDP. Such positive solutions, such rational, creative, and caring decisions with healthy outcomes for the nation will not be visible anywhere, since no dollars were exchanged—oh, with the exception of choosing a caring profession with a lower salary. That actually hurts the GDP.

Yet these families' efficiency, won by keeping their balance while leaning toward happiness, counting debits and credits, plusses and minuses, enables an invisible economy's sustenance. I know this because the domestic choices I've asked you to consider are real ones, all three present in my own children's families.

GDP only adds, it never subtracts. Using Pacioli's duality principle would better help us to see the whole. Let me show you the potential minus side of one concrete situation above, so you can better understand GDP's false guidance.

Let's say that family-friendly husband of my first example above were to say to the heroine of our story, Hell no, I won't stay home. He punches her in the nose, and she has to go the hospital, and then has to pay for childcare out of pocket. The GDP would count that childcare cost as growth, with the special economic bonus being the punch in her nose that required a visit to the emergency room.

The exorbitant fees for that visit's cost and the paltry paychecks earned by the childcare provider both count because the GDP counts as a plus every dollar amount attached to any market transaction. Stupid and mean ones can be even better for the GDP. If that woman went straight to a divorce lawyer—great! Then the lawyer's fees would count, and so would both spouses' psychiatric evaluations, plus the salaries needed to maintain a court of law. The most ideal situation, by GDP's reckoning, would be for all their children to develop costly addictions and eventually be jailed in a privately owned and profitable penitentiary.

I am not making this up. In the GDP, every dollar spent, every piece of goods and services exchanged for dollars—all of it is a plus, and never, ever a minus. When did big losses, meanness, violence, and stupidity add to anything good in your world?

✓ GROSS NATIONAL HAPPINESS

Three amateur economists from Vermont—Linda Wheatley, Ginny Sassaman and Paula Francis—have been working to help transform the heart of our current economy. They were inspired by Bhutan, a tiny country in the Himalayas that has declared that *Gross National Happiness* (GNH) is more important than Gross National Product. Linda, Ginny, and Paula formed a kitchen table study group and recruited other interested members to look at this different economic model. Within a year, they had named their group Gross National Happiness USA and organized a conference, hosting GNH officials from Bhutan. GNH-USA has since organized four international conferences, most recently in Burlington, Vermont, in 2014.

Not everyone loves the idea of finding additional measures to the GDP. "The happiness movement is at best utopian; at worst, it's silly and oppressive," economist Robert Samuelson wrote in an op-ed piece in the *Washington Post* in 2012. But more nations and US states are recognizing the limits of that single measure of market dollars, reaching out for additional numbers to enumerate additional values.

Vermont economist Eric Zencey of the Gund Institute at the University of Vermont, another of the early organizers of Gross National Happiness USA, helped to persuade Vermont legislators to adopt an additional set of measures called the Genuine Progress Indicators. In an interview he said, "It's only common sense. . . . Sound business practices include subtracting costs from benefits. . . . This is just double-entry bookkeeping to the economy as a whole."

✔ GENUINE PROGRESS INDICATORS (GPI)

GPI is a new kind of public accounting with twenty-six indicators for measuring how the economy is doing in terms of natural resources and social costs, as well as per capita income. Maryland, Vermont, and Oregon were the first states to adopt these as additional measures to their Gross State Product (GSP), although only Maryland reviews its data annually. Additional states are gathering GPI data. By 2014, nineteen states were looking into GPI to help guide state policy decisions. Unlike GDP, which counts every dollar as a plus, the Genuine Progress Indicators (GPI) also calculates social and environmental costs. It counts the value of household production and costs to leisure time.

GDP Mirrors Twice as Large

In 1929, Virginia Woolf wrote in *A Room of One's Own* that we "women have served all these centuries as looking glasses possessing the magic and delicious power of reflecting the figure of man at twice its natural size." Women like Marilyn Waring gave that up, and possibly prompted more EconoMan resistance and compensation.

Waring worked closely with Australia's leading economist and statistician Duncan Ironmonger, a leader in time-use accounts. He more accurately renamed the GDP the Gross Market Product, or GMP, and home production the Gross Household Product, or GHP.

Waring writes of Ironmonger's first analysis in 1992, in the foreword of *Counting for Nothing*: "Gross Household Product was $341 billion, while the Gross Market Product was $362 billion. In accounting for more than 48 percent of total production, the household was the single largest sector, exceeding the production of manufacturing by a multiple of ten, and the value of all mining and mineral extraction by a multiple of three."

She believes the magnitude of these household numbers probably helps explain why they were at first confined to UN satellite accounts, so as not to be taken too seriously. When the United Kingdom did its first household satellite account in 1997, it uncovered routine production, not just consumption. Households routinely turned raw materials into finished meal products. Even assigning an average wage for food worker employees to home food production time made visible the largest industry in the country, writes Waring.

EconoMan and his market-only dollars wouldn't reflect back twice his size if American women counted our vital human work at home. If the sheer weight of our collaborative devotion became known in Washington and throughout the country, we might more clearly see who and what really holds a nation together.

Old Royal Fancies

"But he has no clothes," the child said in that fable about the vain Emperor who was fooled into thinking himself grand while parading naked in his imagined gold-threaded robes. These were robes, I add, that were sold to him by men who might very well have been EconoMansplainers. Why does GDP persist, despite widespread knowledge that its skewed information is wrongheaded?

In the foreword of her book's second edition, Marilyn Waring gives us another clue to the willful blindness about our accounts, quoting Leo Tolstoy: "I know that most men, including those at ease with the problems of greatest complexity, can seldom accept even the simplest and most obvious truth if it be such as would oblige them to admit the falsity of conclusions which they have delighted in explaining to colleagues, which they have proudly taught to others, and which they have woven, thread by thread, into their lives."

There are no physical limits to the current GDP. There are only dollar numbers in the abstract, expected to continually grow from millions to billions to trillions. But there are real limits to the earth's resources, just as there are to the resources of your checkbook, your day's time, and your lifetime. You have at your disposal 16 waking hours a day, 365 days a year, multiplied by an 82-year life span—or 478,880 waking hours in your life. That is not such a huge number.

Our nation has been using badly designed accounting tools. They make management look good, but hide debits to our planetary resources over eons, including our human ones. More accurate accounts would show us the reasons why our mood meter is stuck on cranky, our time and our caring stretched thin, unnoticed.

✓ TIME ACCOUNTS

Time accounts are now being done around the world. In some countries, such as Britain and Canada, women's organizations have promoted time studies to more fully describe women's complex lives and varied needs. Time data has helped influence and maintain policy decisions that support women's work and value family and community connections. For instance, subsidized childcare, family leave, and bereavement leave all help de-stress Canadian family and community life.

In Canada, data on time use and other important human measures help guide its citizens. Here in the United States, the ATUS (American Time Use Survey) gets little policy attention. In

2010, France appointed gentlemen economists Amartya Sen and Joseph Stiglitz to devise new life-quality measurements for France, and now the OECD tracks a wider range of data on developed countries, including the United States. You can compare our scoring there (which shows our children suffer). Our northern neighbor's Canadian Index of Wellbeing (CIW) makes its data available online, too, measuring health, living standards, community vitality, environment, leisure and culture, education, time use, and democratic engagement.

There is even a Social Wealth Economic Indicators (SWEI) measure, developed by the Center for Partnership Studies, and described in Riane Eisler's 2017 article, "Roadmap to a Caring Economy: Beyond Capitalism and Socialism." SWEI is the only metric that focuses on women and on care work, which are left out or marginalized in other measures, even the happiness one. It includes nature's economy, the household economy, and the volunteer community economy, that biological foundation that makes all economic development possible.

So why is US data stuck? On page 562 of the US Affordable Care Act was a provision for the development of three hundred "key national indicators" through the American Academy of Science. Why three hundred indicators when others get by with less than a dozen? More masculine warring over money, I think. Who will win and be biggest—scientists, economists at the BEA, or Congress? Like that Emperor parading his nakedness, believing he is covered, EconoMan will seek always to be the greatest—greater than a child who easily sees through lies and spots fools.

So how exactly can women make change? You are making it now. You are learning about revisions underway, and why these matter. You have seen the big holes in how America's EconoMan accounts for things. Like me, you're probably asking, whatever can he be thinking? Maybe, as my mother would *never* say, he is using his dick for brains. It's worth considering next.

Quick Rehash

- Numbers tell worthwhile stories, but always for a purpose with a point of view.
- GDP overvalues dollars at the cost of its life sources, all minuses now as invisible as women's essential unpaid services of care.
- Nations need a balance sheet, not just an income statement.
- The United States could easily adopt additional measures, given women's will and desire to do so.

EconoGirlfriend Conversation Starter

Which kind of account do you find the scariest: a numerical account or a verbal account? Which do you prefer and trust more? Why, do you think?

Chapter 14: His Manly Largeness

A sexier account of corporations would include the essential female and essential male for much more than its current norm of verbal mounting, quickies, and concubine slavery.

When I first moved to Vermont in the 1980s, I worked in what was called the War on Poverty while I finished a graduate degree in fiction writing. A war hardly described what the poor needed, though our defense in Washington kept Reagan and Stockman from slaughtering program budgets for food stamps and Head Start.

I can't say my getting a writing degree was a financially savvy decision, but I loved writing, and I paid the rent by its practice, working on newspapers and grants, eventually becoming a professor and teaching. In the evenings or early mornings, I wrote what I most loved, fiction. Unlike journalism that could skew a story by what it left out, fiction took an exacting point of view, revealing feelings and inner conflicts and choices—or else their denial and a tragic refusal to feel or face them.

I'd started on my writing path back in Michigan, publishing a bit. A high school friend heard about it and asked my advice about a novel she was writing. I'd taken a fiction course by then and thinking myself literary, I advised her: Don't overdo the dialogue. Make your heroine a little less idealized. Give her some warts.

Oh boy, was I wrong. Soon after I moved to Vermont, I discovered just how wrong. My friend sent me the embossed cover of her first book, *River of Love*, with news of a contract for more. While I was in grad school and working full time, she quit her job at the electric company. She eventually wrote a whole shelf of romance books.

It was a lesson in humility for me, the would-be artist. My friend delivered what her readers wanted—hot desire, courage, the fulfillment of dreams. In the trade, her books belonged to a genre called "bodice rippers" for their lustiness, yet her writing about sex was coy and modest. Whenever her heroine was swept up in the arms of her lover, she felt against her thigh, not his erection but "his manly largeness."

That phrase stuck with me. Eventually I came to see how "manly largeness" pointed to what is so wrong with our economy today. Oh, those lonely longings for largeness—the hard embodiment of our joining physicality, blood surging hormones, moaning for the climax. Of the story, I mean. A passionate joining is exactly what a love-starved economy most needs.

Love Joins

The dangers of economically discounting our deepest desires is revealed in stark contrast by the writings of psychologist Rollo May whose *Love and Will* became a best seller in the 1960s. The book's subject is *Eros*, the name of a Greek god but also a word used by psychologists to describe the sum total of our instincts for survival. May writes that without Eros, that mythological character who symbolizes a passionate will that motivates people, civilizations fall apart.

As a powerful driver, the determination of Eros provokes us to become better, more beautiful and devoted than we ever dreamed we could be for the sake of winning our beloved—whatever our lovesick dream of a beautiful future. But when we put aside the pursuit of our deepest desires, May cautioned, when we settle for relieving tension by just "getting off" or going through the motions, then we miss the emphatic erotic that longs for our connection to our greatest largeness. Spiritual faith and ideals can provide this and so can human relationships that inspire our best.

May also warned that Eros denied in us leads to a deadly but dependable progression. First comes apathy and boredom. Next comes an attempt to fill an empty inner space with addiction to more, more, and more. Ultimately violence breaks through numbness, the last ditch effort of a people to feel, *please*, feel something. Suddenly American addictions to food, sex, shopping, and drugs, with the virtual world's daily violence, its screaming news and zombie tales, begin to make sense.

Eros, the god of Greek mythology, appeared in Hesiod's *Theogony*, a classic poem written nearly three thousand years ago as a kind of *Who's Who* for the Greeks' Mount Olympus. In it, the three Fates tell how the earliest Greek stories held that the goddess Gaia, not Zeus, created the world.

Soon after Gaia, another powerful deity appeared—Eros, the sexy young man. These two were not siblings or married, but called *protogenoi*, a kind of initial yin-yang power that created and sustained. At the heart and tender crotch of Gaia's life was sexy Eros, a mythology with uncanny psychological accuracy.

And God Said, Sex!

Microbiologist Ursula Goodenough explains in *The Sacred Depths of Nature* that sex began more than 570 million years ago. Before sex, single-celled bacteria and amoeba could only divide to reproduce. As a result every cell was just like every other one. Sex newly required the joining of two different genomes. It demanded biological relationship, and that made all the difference.

Each genome, a sexual cell with a single set of chromosomes, is like half a deck of cards with DNA instructions, Goodenough explains. Sexual mating reshuffles the genetic cards, dealing a whole new hand for the next generation to better fit a changing environment. Sex gave life its flexibility and a fine-tuned diversity for adapting as needed.

The living relationships of human sex grew more complicated as societies did, too, and so tragedy inevitably entered our stories. Ironically, sexy Eros regressed under the Roman's military might, becoming the baby we now know as Cupid. He's cute but not sexy and hot like Eros. As for Gaia, we'd all but forgotten her until 1979.

That year a British chemist named James Lovelock (a name so fitting, I couldn't have made it up) published a book, *Gaia: A New Look at Life on Earth*. In it, he proposed a new ecological theory that "living and nonliving parts of the earth are a complex interacting system that can be thought of as a self-regulating, living organism." Lovelock had once worked for NASA's space project and, like the rest of us, could finally see how rare and dazzling our planet was.

Lovelock had also worked with Lynn Margulis, a female biologist (a relatively new species in science history). They observed microbes interacting with minerals in ways that enhanced and sustained life, creating atmospheric gasses and modulating water's acidity. To specialist scientists focused on minerals alone, or microbes alone, the notion of the earth as a unified, interactive organism seemed preposterous, until later upheld by research.

Not a Female

Now everyone knows Gaia, our beautiful planet, but unfortunately the Eros of the Greeks remains infantilized. Martin Scorsese's 2013 film, *The Wolf of Wall Street,* based on the life of Jordan Belfort and his high-flying stockbroker career, showed us men acting like high school boys, looking to get laid, and jerking off. As we see in the film, sexual innuendo permeates behavior and figures of speech on the trading floor.

The selfless devotion that Eros inspires, the heartsick longing of deep desire that requires giving oneself away to the beloved, is scorned there. EconoMan's love for money is about appearing larger than he is, not about his tender vulnerability, which women actually do find sexy. EconoMan's sexual mania isn't interested in what women find sexy. Rather, it proves to other men that he is not a woman.

We met not-a-woman masculinity (and verbal mounting) in Robert McElvaine's book *Eve's Seed*. To this mindset, to be a woman is to be mounted and controlled. In male hierarchies, you get larger or get screwed. If masculine sexual insecurity is, as McElvaine says, often behind the drive for power and war, if it has given us penis-shaped skyscrapers and missiles, then we need to inquire. Who exactly are those guys now atop an all-male pyramid, screwing all those below them and constantly measuring their largeness?

The Wolf of Wall Street's picture of this male world reveals an endemic misogyny that historian Robert McElvaine would recognize as sexual insecurity: men so busy proving they are not female, they miss their fuller humanity. Criminal psychologists would see symptoms of a psychopath in the hypnotic verbal fire hose of deceptions. Saddest and most tragic of all would be Rollo May's diagnosis of Eros denied in them.

Purchasing sex is nearly as common on Wall Street as buying stocks. The movie's men sell short their deeper, more vulnerable feelings and dreams, transformed into drug addiction to numb the cruel job of "taking" people. The word *taking*, like screwing, comes with undertones of forcible sex.

More damning revelations come from Kevin Roose, writing for *New York Magazine*. He crashed a meeting of the Beta Kappa Phi, a secret brotherhood of the 1 percent, taking photos with his phone before he was caught and thrown out. New members suffered the hazing humiliation that often comes with entry into all-male hierarchies.

As part of their initiation, very wealthy men had to put on comedy sketches, and play to their audience, the country's very most wealthy men in black-tie formality. And here's the important part. The newbies were required to attend dressed in drag, wearing gold sequined skirts, high heels, wigs, and makeup. As pseudo women, they more clearly exalted their mount-ability to the top tuxedoed dogs already part of the club and—above all—not female like them.

None of this theater and ritual had anything to do with biology or with male desire, committed or fleeting. Beta male status was symbolically reinforced, and their dirty jokes made women and homosexuals the biggest butt of their laughter. And then, see, it's quickly over—all just kidding. If you didn't have fun, girl, then maybe you can't take a joke.

Or maybe, like me and other mount-ables of the world, you are ready to make some large, embodied changes. Women who mean business, who are honoring their deepest desires, cannot be expected to fall for a shared corpus with half-conscious assumptions so silly.

EconoMan's Babies

It gets clearer that EconoMan's imagined battles for piling up dollar numbers serve to publicly measure his manly largeness. He justifies his own dominance by misusing the phrase, "survival of the fittest," based on false notions about Darwin's evolutionary theory. It's all natural, he says. He is simply the best.

But for Darwin, the *fittest* didn't mean the biggest, the cruelest, or the most ruthless and powerful. Darwin's fittest included both sexes, responding to an eco-reality around them with love and will, to make the biggest cooperation possible, not just for themselves and their pleasure—but for a future.

Pleasure is a compelling incentive of sex, of course. But without the ingenuity of two healthy genders connecting, a species could kiss tomorrow goodbye. Darwin's fittest meant species' devotion to their babies' survival, even sometimes switching roles to come up with surprising combinations and solutions. The result is an astonishing diversity of life forms and sexual practices to enhance the chances for the next generation.

You never hear EconoMan concerning himself with how his babies are doing, much less anyone else's babies. You never hear of his yearnings for much beyond the increase of his naked numbers and the growing of his manly largeness. His billions have become the biggest codpiece he can find. His multinational, corporate *priapism*, what doctors call an erection that just won't quit, grows painful for all of us.

Wall Street does have a strangely pregnant connection, however, with a substitute progeny that economist Michael Hudson writes about in his book, *Killing the Host*. Hudson studied the financial world of ancient civilizations and tells how it was widely understood that interest charges would double an investor's money at regular intervals. The ancients, he tells us, equated that doubling with biological growth.

The Babylonians referred to *giving birth* to new money grown from interest-bearing loans, while the Sumerians referred to interest charges as a *mash*, meaning a goat kid. In Greece, the new money was *tokos*, a birth, and for the Romans, it was a *foenus*, derived from the Latin word *fetus*. Yes, you read that right.

In Greece, debts were even calculated by the moon, much like pregnancy, gestation, and menses. The nice thing about it, though, was this new money "baby" grew without any need of a woman's body.

Today's EconoMan still holds interest-bearing powers to double his money-kids, outstripping us flesh-and-blood moms. But unlike the ancients, he denies money's ties to nature and represses the integrity of deepest desires. Instead, he's addicted to gambling.

Capital's Body

Whenever I went back to Michigan to visit Mom, the Fox News channel came with dinner. We avoided talking politics, but I'd sometimes get an earful about America's need for the rich. They were our "job creators." What would we do without them?

Becoming rich was part of our American Dream. When I was a girl, my family would gather to watch a popular TV show called *The Millionaire*. Its fictional storyline was much the same each week: a fabulously wealthy benefactor named John Beresford Tipton, Jr. would hand a cashier's check for one million dollars, tax free, to his executive secretary for delivery to a person neither had ever met.

We never saw Mr. Tipton, only his arm as he handed over the check, but Mr. Anthony described his boss with awe and affection as we gazed upon beautiful Silverstone, his sixty-thousand-acre estate. From here, Tipton "spent the later years of his life pursuing many hobbies, often tied to his fascination with human nature and behavior," Anthony explained. Tipton himself likened his hobby to a game of chess.

We never questioned why his wealth entitled him to play games with human lives and expect Anthony's report on what happened. Instead, we admired Tipton. The phrase *job creator* was unborn, still in the future, but money's trickle-down was already visible, instructing us in the order of our universe and our American dreams. We judged the tales of Tipton's guinea pigs either comedy or tragedy. We never judged Tipton.

He remained untouchable, despite his wealth's likely source, his corporation, a word whose Latin root, *corpus*, literally means "body." Tipton's viewers never laid eyes on him at work or saw anything his companies produced.

By the 1950s, when *The Millionaire* was filmed, wealthy men like Tipton had largely removed themselves from shop floors. Rich men were now shareholders in a stock market become a speculator's game, with Tipton's chess board a fitting metaphor. But like capital, incorporation and stocks had a much older story.

To incorporate means to embody a collective purpose. Guilds of skilled artisans did it in the Middle Ages and so did later groups intending to build fleets of ships for mercantile reasons. Capital raised through such collective organizing was affixed as head of the new incorporated body whose moving arms and legs were operated by hired hands.

With this new legal physique, financial risk was limited, usually for the amount of the investment. Today any group of people who have joined to work as one body, for any purpose, can incorporate. Towns, churches, nonprofits, and businesses all do.

✓ CORPORATION

Incorporation is not mentioned in the US Constitution, but states have something called *Articles of Incorporation* giving rules for becoming a legal entity upheld by the courts. At first, states limited their charters and debated them in legislative sessions, even revoking them. But by 1819, corporations had grown big enough they could take a state to the Supreme Court to skirmish for power. Both states and corporations were artificial embodiments, at first organized for collective cooperation, but being exclusively male, the operational norm soon became one of warfare.

A steady progression of legal precedent has granted corporations increasing power of personhood, culminating in the 2010 Citizens United ruling that equates money with free speech. Its decision permits the wealthiest to speak loudest of all about our supposedly democratic elections. It begs resolution of whether corporations are a legal fiction, a kind of metaphor for lawful collective organizing, or are literal bodies with voice. If the latter, then unlike their human creators, they are gigantic and will never sleep or shut up.

Muscular Bodies

It is fair to say that in the beginning, corporations that issued stock enabled shareholders to take more risks than they otherwise might, a cooperative good. The creation of stock also organized capital for bigger ventures than one person alone might accomplish. Previously only divinely endowed kings or popes had the power to raise such large funds.

So stock was in some ways democratic—but only for a small group of propertied men, like the Constitution's original voting franchise. A group of wealthy men could contract together to embody a corporate mission or intent, but in reality these men usually had ties to existing powers already, whether kings or high churchmen.

✔ STOCKS & SHARES

Stock began in a time when few could read numbers, and so simple notched sticks kept track of accounts. In England, these were called *tally sticks*. Splitting a notched stick in two provided a record of exchanges between two parties, carrying proof of a payment or debt. It was used in courts of law when disputes arose.

Later refinements made tally sticks into two halves of different lengths. The longer one, given to the creditor that supplied goods or capital, was called the *stock*. The shorter one went to the one who owed payment, giving debtors "the short end of the stick," otherwise known as the *foil*. Shareholding grew out of this business relationship.

Stock can mean the inventory of a business or the stock on its shelves, but the stock of a corporation is a share of its ownership. A corporation gains collective capital from its stockholders and in return is owned by debt. Unlike bonds, which are time limited, the dividend or return on stocks ends only when the investor sells. The law limits investment losses but not its gains, in another example of "he who makes the money, makes the rules."

If our physical bodies organized and operated the way these artificial corporate bodies do, our capitalized head would scream from the pain of cutting off its smallest digits, namely those workers easily fired or laid off. But incorporated bodies do not actually grow their own hands and fingers, or even their tiny brains. Instead, they rent—or hire—them. Their legal attachment to the hands that produce corporate goods and services is more loosely stitched, a little like Frankenstein's monster body.

While capital can and does organize as a collective body to accumulate wealth, EconoMan tends to consider any similar organizing of his hired hands a threat and overreach. American corporations first grew large when a group of Boston capitalists built textile mills in Lowell, Massachusetts. They employed many single young women in the 1830s. When capitalists cut wages, the mill women organized a "turn out" in 1834, the first labor "strike," as later male unionists renamed the action.

By 1885, satirical American writer Ambrose Bierce was describing incorporation as "the act of uniting several persons into one fiction called a corporation, in order that they may be no longer responsible for their actions." Stockholders grew richer and protected their small group's power as the twentieth century marked industrial progress. The corporate self-servicing seen in Bierce's cynical joke regularly blew up the economy, outdoing itself with the Great Depression. Corporate power got dialed back during FDR's period and the post-WWII era.

Those huddled masses of the poor who had come to American shores, our immigrant grandparents, enjoyed a liberty to pursue happiness, which for most included more money. We prided ourselves on working hard, running businesses and farms, buying and selling, taking our chance as Americans.

In truth, my mom's sunburned Belgian family and my browner Sicilian stepdad had become part of "the white race," a mythology that privileged our chances over Americans of African, Hispanic, Asian, and Native descent. The only television fare in my childhood that approached the popularity of *The Millionaire* were Injun-shooting cowboy shows like *Death Valley Days*, hosted by actor Ronald Reagan, eventually elected president.

Reagan began loosening economic regulations, and American corporations grew bigger and bigger, rustling up operations overseas. By 1992, CEO and presidential candidate Ross Perot was alerting us to that "giant sucking sound" of jobs leaving the United States. CEOs like Perot had always been paid handsome salaries, around twenty to forty times the average workers. Traditionally CEOs maintained corporate health by investing profits in buildings, equipment, workers' training, development, and wages. CEOs were nearly exclusively men, but were held to a sense of responsibility.

As we approached a new century, a new kind of investor and CEO began to flourish, financed by Wall Street banks that had become more ruthless as Nomi Prins showed us in Part II—giving rise to that cultural reality I call EconoMan. By 2010, New York University economist Edward Wolff, using Federal Reserve surveys, found that 80 percent of corporate stocks and bonds were owned by the top 10 percent of Americans, and of this, about half was owned by the top 1 percent. By 2015, CEOs were making eight hundred times as much as their average workers.

Highway Robbery

Les Leopold, in his book *Runaway Inequality*, describes these new ruthless players—Wall Street bankers, neoliberal investors, and their CEOs—and their financial effect on corporations. The media at first called out "corporate raiders," writes Leopold, but as all these men grew richer, they were newly heralded as hedge fund and private equity firm managers with new norms hailed as efficient—that economic word used to rationalize one person's improvement, without any need of sharing.

They invented leveraged buyouts. This meant purchasing companies with borrowed money and then using corporate resources to pay off the new debt, while also buying back the company's own stock. Why would they do this?

Most importantly, because they could. In 1982, Reagan's SEC had reversed regulations to allow it. Stock "buybacks" can manipulate stock prices and misrepresent a corporation's real value.

If there are fewer shares available, Leopold explains, the remaining stock's value goes up, even while a company's real production value goes down.

Something else had changed in corporations during the thirty-year period from Reagan to the 2008 meltdown, writes Leopold. CEOs began to be paid in *stock options*, unheard of in the 1970s. The pay of CEOs, newly promoted to the investor class through their stock options, transformed the older, more gentlemanly capitalist practice of "retain and reinvest" to the neoliberal player's "redistribute." This repeated phenomenon Leopold calls "financial strip mining." By 2008, when the stock market crashed, 75 percent of corporate resources were directed to stock buyback.

Such short-term greed could flourish only in a time of financial deregulation and in an Econo-Man culture that encouraged banks, stockholders, and CEOs to wage economic war for their individual, self-interested advantage. Previously healthy American corporations that had paid workers decent wages abandoned hometown communities for cheaper production with overseas workers and markets.

Another disruptive change brought technology to manufacturing. Chad Bown, a senior fellow at the Peterson Institute for International Economics, told NPR in 2016 that US manufacturers simply don't need as many workers for increased productivity. "It's a lot more robots and computer equipment, and many, many fewer people." The windfall that labor-cost savings brings to capitalists is hoarded, I'm afraid, not shared.

What Leopold calls the "financialization" of corporate America has seen Wall Street's job sector of only 6 percent of American workers capture 25 percent of the nation's profits. In 2015, *Bloomberg News* and *Rolling Stone* reported that 320 American corporations, including its biggest high-tech firms (Microsoft, Apple, Google) are stashing $2.1 trillion in profits overseas in low-tax countries to avoid bringing that money home to help pay for the government they claim as theirs.

Is Big Money Sexy?

Since EconoMan's fortunes at the top are largely masculine ones, let's pause to consider what drives this apparently gendered impulse. Does this masculine behavior, this ambition to appear big, have anything to do with a wish to be noticed by females? Do women find money largeness sexy?

Consider what biologists and evolutionary psychologists have theorized about differences in mating strategies among males and females across species. A female mammal must invest more effort in gestation, birthing, and nursing of the young, so she tends to be more selective. Males' essential part takes little time, and so mathematically speaking, by mating with as many females as possible he will likely have more surviving offspring.

Across cultures, human studies have confirmed these general mating differences. Males tend toward short-term strategies, are more likely to bed whomever will have them, and are attracted by curves, not cleverness. Females tend to prefer longer-term relationships and are more drawn to a male's social status than his looks, for its potential access to reproductive resources.

A 2011 study of American college students reported in the *Journal of Personality and Social Psychology* found that a man driving a souped-up sports car sent a clear mating message that females accurately interpreted. He had money and sperm to spare, and was looking for many short flings, not a long-term relationship. Young women could read these signals, and some wanted an adventure. However, other experiments revealed these same signals did not make a man attractive for long-term relationships. Young women knew that, too.

Human social life being complex as it is, there are diverse responses to the conspicuous alpha male, including those of beta males not as monetarily muscular. Sneaking strategies are also pursued across species, with non-alpha males and plenty of females willingly assisting in diversifying the gene pool.

In a time when women need men less for economic support, this all gets complicated. If she doesn't need him for resource support, if she has status in her own right—what exactly are female mating desires today? The social environment is changing. Overpopulation is a fact. The human female is in the process of sorting all that out. This matters because female desires have generally led the way to survival.

Two to Tango

That old romance of my mother's era said you married a man who supported you, and the Mr. Tiptons of the world owned corporate stock as a long-term commitment. It never was a realistic or complete picture of the conspicuously rich shareholder, or of men who held jobs in his service. There was always much more to men, known only to the women in their lives.

Let's admit it: centuries of mothers and wives helped develop EconoMan's ego in the capitalist head of those manly largeness corporations and the men who serve him. As Marjorie Kelly puts it in her groundbreaking book, *The Divine Right of Capital*, we may be hard pressed to find an enemy in this embodied system.

Most of us participate in it, whether as owners and stockholders or as purchased wage earners, with a pension or 401(k) if we're lucky. The problem is not in our participation but in our assumptions. We are blind, Kelly says, to the traditions of corporate law and language that present today's corporations as "persons"—and, I would add, as persons of a particular entitled class, race, and sex.

A Canadian film *The Corporation* makes the case that, if really a person, he behaves like a psychopath, devoid of empathy and guilt-free. Psychopaths pretend these feelings, deceitful, but will explain actions like your murder as necessity, seeing others as mere instruments. Professor Jeffrey Hancock of Cornell University says the giveaway is how psychopaths talk. His researchers describe it as "being hypnotized," or "drinking from a fire hose," exactly the way EconoMansplaining can feel.

But women have now named this experience, and as they enter the economic world stage, they tell new tales we have never heard before. Some are of the dangers women have faced at the hands of controlling, cruel men, tales of underdog courage. But often come additional, more intimate stories of caring and sensitive men gone unnoticed before, the beta sons, fathers, and lovers who populate valiant women's lives.

Concerned with the long term, women appear to be wondering: What is it that females of the world, including our mother Gaia, most need now, if it is not money largeness? More mutual respect? A new reshuffling of our genetic deck? A whole new end game?

Women need to answer our own discriminating nature if men and the economy largely owned by them are to change. I can see that they are already beginning.

I interject that question of sex to remind you of whose body is embodied in those traditions. Whose legal physique is taken on? The female body often displays and sells corporate products, but the super-large, corporate individual with his money codpiece, who claims to be eternal, has a masculine bod. His giveaway sausage trait is his constant dollar measures of how big he is and his anxiety when he isn't as large as the next corporate bodybuilder.

Let us be sexually clear. These competitive male corporate bodies, enslaved by their stock-debt, belong almost exclusively to the richest, most powerful men: masculine legal bodies do not operate to impress females. The manly corporation serves his shadowy owner, our EconoMan Mr. Tipton, in an unhealthy bromance.

Reshuffling the Paradigm

Corporations, unions, and government have all worked in recent years to become more inclusive of women. By themselves, small demographic shifts are unlikely to transform our current economic war story. The hierarchies on stage, whether corporate or union or government, tend to be more male the higher up the pyramid you go, and the more golden the pyramid, the more exclusively male.

We are told those large corporate "persons" must not be seen as a privileged class of white men with an unhealthy amount of self-interest. That would be class and race warfare. But finally noticing the gender and race of these uneven power dynamics, talking more openly about what is now largely unconscious and accepted as a norm, could result in something far sexier than warfare-driven, life-denying legal fictions.

Reshuffling the chromosomal decks, adding more diversity of sex and race, increases a species' odds for adaptability. We could partner to organize an economic environment better adjusted to the earth's real one. We might include female mating strategies and concern for earth's living offspring, not just male ones with an interest in money-babies only. More quickie, one-night stands won't serve our future's interests so much as committed, long-term ones.

Male war-making hierarchies work well enough in an emergency. But developmental hierarchies, like the more gender-diverse ones within our families, have a more democratic purpose, despite uneven distributions of power and knowledge. Traditionally, parents care for children and make the rules. Yet healthy families develop and pass on their power; eventually, children care for parents.

Marilyn French in *Beyond Power* first identified this difference in hierarchical purpose. In warfare, what's important is *power over* someone else, but in *power with*, you help develop caring independence and mutual respect. It's a longer-term commitment. Riane Eisler further identified these paradigm differences in her book *The Real Wealth of Nations*, showing us economic-dominator models of the kind I've been describing and sexier partnership models that we'll look at more closely in coming chapters.

Change, But Not Really

In feudal times, kings and lords of the castle could expect to own peon slaves and sexually use any servants they desired. Our language continues to acknowledge its metaphorical reality. When we have gotten the short end of the stick, whether we are male or female, we say, Hey, we just got royally screwed.

To be fucked or screwed is essentially to be female, to be owned and possessed like a concubine, a daughter of the vanquished, whatever your actual sex. Beta men who resent being screwed over have traditionally gotten even without challenging that definition of female. But now real women are entering public realms formerly off-limits, becoming new players in our economic theater. The challenge of our future will be to develop broader definitions of what it means to be fully human.

Women and the gay among us have already begun to get out of old gender boxes and end their restrictions, reclaiming strengths once available only to men, or only to women. Yet our ideas about masculinity, especially in the loaded realm of money, continue to be oversimplified wherever men—and now women—seek higher status.

Right now, to be a member of a hierarchy—and our society is full of them—by normative rule means that all lower people, men and women, may be verbally mounted, humiliated, and used by others on their way higher up. All are accountable to the top guy, and all but he can be penetrated, at least metaphorically. If his corporation gets caught at a crime, someone lower down the pecking order will go to jail, not him. Whatever that person's actual gender, he or she will be a girly man, willing or not.

That is why I think of those within the masculine corporate body as concubines. In some important way, I don't think it only a figure of speech. A concubine is an owned sexual property. When those higher up in the hierarchy choose to use her, she has no say-so in their joining's intent. Will their relationship be short-term and fleeting? Longer-term and cooperative? Whoever is on top determines that, leaving those lower down with few options but sneaking satisfactions.

Forward, Not Back

Corporations seek the liberty of the free market, but for whom is it liberty? Only for owners, an old medieval norm, Marjorie Kelly argues in *The Divine Right of Capital*. "It is the liberty of property: freedom as the right to the undisturbed possession of property."

✓ PROPERTY & REAL ESTATE

In the thirteenth century, the word *property*, meaning "ownership," came into common use and began to include *real estate*. Importantly, *real* in this usage doesn't mean the opposite of fiction. It literally means *royal*. Any *estate* or property ownership depended upon your relationship to royalty. States and nations both began as royal lands of the king. Here in the United States, state laws vary, but generally real estate rules are more closely enforced than other property because land is limited and taxed.

Interestingly, Kelly trusts the same inner drive that Rollo named Eros to self-regulate our work, saying, "Our economic drives are part of the natural order and are trustworthy." But she argues that corporate governance structures gloss over the "institutionalized power of wealth."

Darwin's natural selection is the ultimate natural order. Its self-regulating requires cooperative exchanges of gendered differences. That's the dimension missing when corporate bodies are half-realized only as legal largeness, masculinized, and constantly warring. But there is evidence of big changes underway that more closely mimic nature's greater diversity and more fertile relationships.

Kelly, in a later book, *Owning Our Future,* writes of an emerging change in the shapes of business ownership. Instead of the "extractive economy" of the past, she predicts a coming "generative economy." Generative is a more polite word for fecund, or fertile. Generation requires the teeming contributions of male and female genders, cooperating together. As I'm suggesting, a more sexy economy could even be a good bit of fun.

In 2015, the Council of Economic Advisors for the Obama White House issued a surprising report that highlighted opportunities for expanding business as usual. In 2012, 36 percent of US business owners were women, they said, up from 29 percent just three years earlier. Most of these were small sole proprietorships. Few have more than one hundred employees. Micro-businesses tend to be in the fields of health care and services, the sort of businesses that must remain local and rooted, not shipped out of the country. Nor can they be easily replaced by technology.

Less than 2 percent of women-owned US businesses generated more than $1 million annually, but women's incorporations were a fairly new species. One notable investor represented in the report, First Round Capital, found that businesses with at least one female founder performed 63 percent better than all-male teams.

What will women's appearance as owners, stockholders, and managers bring to the corporate world now defined as manly largeness? In an all-male world, to be female is a state to be avoided, to be automatically mountable. But that is a male-imagined fiction. It won't hold up in a new business world with real-life human genders.

Women are far more creative than that, as you'll see next.

Quick Rehash

- The collective creation of corporations is a cooperative good, but exclusive ownership by would-be capitalist kings has promoted a fraternity of ruthless self-interest, verbal fire-hosing, and perpetual money wars.
- Darwin's "fittest" were not the predators at the top of the food chain but all species that adapted to their environment by creatively joining the sexes, drawing on the passionate will of Eros to secure future offspring's survival.
- Humans all have a responsibility to discern their deepest desires, but women's erotic and economic discernment now has a special role to play in shaping humanity's future.

EconoGirlfriend Conversation Starter

Have you ever been verbally mounted or witnessed this behavior? Have you verbally mounted anyone else? Or wanted to? What were the circumstances?

*2010 Citizens United v. Federal Election Commission

Chapter 15: She's in Labor!

A sexier account of labor's story embraces the value of
We, the erotic pronoun larger than all of us.

In the summer of 1965, thirty-five thousand young men each month were being drafted for the Vietnam War. Marriage could still exempt him. My best high school friend Susan and I both wanted to save our boyfriends. We married straight out of high school, but by late August, President Johnson changed policy. That fall, our new husbands got sent off to boot camp.

I was living in a trailer on Paw Paw Lake but facing expenses on my own now. I invited Sue to come live with me. I would charge her less rent than her landlord and with her added bit, I could pay the electric bill. We both had office jobs and at night came home to cobble together cheap dinners, taking turns, experimenting. Our collaboration was the best idea my nineteen-year-old brain had ever had.

In the evenings, we read books and talked about everything in the world. Earnest churchgoers, we discussed sermons and civil rights marches. We shared novels like *Love Story*, never questioning why the girl had to die. Romeo and Juliet had died. Tony in *West Side Story* had died. Our husbands might die. Dying was young love. *We* were young love.

Another of our friends, married to a soldier, was already a widow. Sue and I withstood our impending tragedy, primed once a week for optimism by our favorite television show, *That Girl*. Marlo Thomas tossed her hat up in the air on her way into work out of joy and pure sass—a model of the modern young women we both were now. We giggled over books about sex, advising us to be submissive, agreeable, and sexually adventuresome. We talked about school, the future, and our faraway husbands on tenterhooks, waiting to be called up and shot at.

Meanwhile a bigger pot of societal changes bubbled and boiled around us—Panther power, the feminine mystique, *That Girl*. Yet little of it talked about why Sue and I had to work and scrimp together—we needed money. I don't think Sue and I ever talked about money once we settled on the rent.

Neither of us saved our boyfriends from Vietnam or our too-early marriages from breaking up. Eventually, we would both divorce, part of generational trends. At that time in 1965, only 42 percent of women aged sixteen to sixty-four had jobs, half the rate of 85 percent among men, according to the US Bureau of Labor Statistics. By the year 2000, 68 percent of women would be employed, with the numbers of working mothers unprecedented.

Labor's Gender

By the time Sue and I went to work, the demise of labor unions in this country was underway, but we were little concerned. Labor's face was a male one, and news stories centered on his battles, his bullies—the reason my mother disdained unions. She took pride in being management now, not labor, earning a salary instead of clocking her hours—though she did resent working weekends every quarter, closing out the books, while factory men got time and a half for extra work time.

> ### ✓ SALARY
>
> The word *salary* comes from salt, which was once allotted to Roman soldiers, possibly for food preservation. It's behind the expression, *She's worth her salt*. Today, a salaried worker is paid an annual sum distributed monthly or weekly. She must make more than $433 a week under the Fair Labor Standards Act (FLSA) to be exempted from overtime pay for longer work hours.
>
> ### ✓ WAGES
>
> The word *wage*, related to the word gauge, dates from the Crusades when it meant "a reward for service." Wageworkers are paid by the hour and are entitled to overtime pay for work over forty hours, but not much else. They are easily laid off and their numbers of hours easily reduced. Eligibility for benefits may change and so can her shift schedules, complicating life at home.

Sue and I would have been surprised to learn that labor solidarity had first begun with American women and had long been supported by outspoken women labor leaders. Women's labor history wasn't taught in our schools or part of news in newspapers and on TV stations owned by families richer than ours.

Most male union leaders weren't that interested in talking about those women, either. For most of the nineteenth and twentieth centuries, union leaders had spent more time shutting the doors on women workers than engaging them in leadership. Women had organized separate unions, or auxiliaries, but were often segregated from power. That's beginning to change.

While I was growing up, there was much warring between union workers and corporations. The Taft-Hartley Act had limited union contract negotiations, and in the context of the 1950s anti-communism scare, unions focused on money, oversimplifying labor issues. Big labor in Detroit battled for higher wages, overtime pay, and membership dues. Jimmy Hoffa and his truckers drew battle lines for more money, with literal violence and help from Mafia ties.

What would Sue and I have thought of a more inclusive story of labor leaders, including women who said, *We want bread, but we want roses, too*. Immigrant textile worker Rose Schneiderman first used that rose metaphor for a life worth living in a 1911 speech. She and her cohorts sought good wages and working conditions but also spoke about the larger meaning and purpose of work. They wanted time for renewal and leisure, time to pursue the roses of education, music, art, family pleasures, spiritual self-development, community, and civic connections.

Women like Sue and me knew nothing of Rose Schneiderman and her movement. By mid-century, television, consumerism, and keeping up with the Joneses for status display had displaced those old, forgotten ideas.

The Time of Your Life

Today, the amount of time that middle-class and working-class American families rent out for wages or salary is possibly more alarming than their wage decline since 1970. Two-earner households increased by a fifth in the years between 1986 and 1998 and now outnumber single-breadwinner homes, three to one, reports the Bureau of Labor Statistics. Because the work of the household itself remains, couples and children report feeling more stressed. Single parents can feel close to desperate. Combine unpaid work at home with our giving away time on the Internet, and we are busier than ever.

✓ WORKDAY

The eight-hour workday was first proposed in the early 1830s in Britain where industrialization began and when sixteen-hour days, seven days a week, were expected. Over seventy years, workday time limits were won piecemeal by occupational trade unions, like United Autoworkers. Eight hours became a government standard in the United States in 1940, but is an actual rarity today. A 2014 National Gallup poll reported US salaried workers averaged forty-nine hours per week while wageworkers averaged forty-four hours. In Silicon Valley, sixty hours is a norm.

✓ WORKWEEK

The word *weekend* did not mean two consecutive days off work until 1926 when United Autoworkers won a five-day, forty-hour week from Ford Motor Company, the same year that the American Federation of Labor set it as their national goal. In a survey of full-time workers reported by *US News*, a quarter reported checking their emails during family and leisure time.

Most people are shocked when I tell them that a thirty-hour workweek standard was actually passed by the US Senate in 1933. As John Maynard Keynes had already predicted during the Great Depression, the production of all we need was taking less and less time. Our productivity trend has not reversed since then. Thanks to computerization and robotics, we are more productive than ever.

However, the financial returns on improved production has not gone to the trained and educated workers who use the new technologies. Neither has greater efficiency awarded workers reduced working hours. Sensible business arguments for improved worker performance and saner workplaces have not granted Americans relief from the pressures of twenty-first-century work schedules.

Whenever I mention this eighty-year-old legislation, the thirty-hour week, to people I think would benefit, I get an alarmed response. Wouldn't you prefer a four-day workweek to better manage your too busy life? I ask. No thanks, they say, looking scared and wide-eyed. I need to work more hours, not less—I'm short on money as it is. I can't get done what's expected in the time I have now! Even salaried people today think like low-wage earners, worried about their jobs.

A memory lapse, a loss of our collaborative labor history, has cost us. The traditionally feminine work of tending those off-market roses at home, away from the job, remains invisible, as we've seen. Right now, only money counts. As a result, the invisible roses of life are less sought after and less respected.

My mom managed her life by constantly working, delegating some tasks and giving up others, like volunteering. Now my grown daughters manage a virtual world, as well as their concrete one. Is it any wonder that cooking from scratch is now more often a subject for television competitions, than an at-home indulgence? Eating out is a market transaction, visible in the GDP as a national plus. Buy expensive pots—that counts. Cook in them? Forget it.

In family pocketbooks, any rose-like activity remains a debit in time and money. Even the families that can afford good food, music concerts, trips to the art museum, or classes in anything purely pleasurable have trouble finding the leisure to enjoy them.

I've noticed a new tactic for handling the oversized load. How busy you are becomes a talking point, and it seems the busier you are, the higher your status. Hyperactivity turns into another competitive race, but it's unclear how you win this one.

Labor Embodied

In these pressured digital times, it's more important than ever to remember the boundaries of our bodies. Like the word *corporation*, the word *labor* is linked to the human body. The question again is, whose body is it?

Some linguists note the word *labor* is related to the female *labia* and childbirth's physicality. Another link is to the image of the *labrys*, a double-edged axe.

The labrys and its handle look a bit like a woman's vulva when you squint at it right. This tool was used for harvesting grain, which in the beginning of agriculture was women's work. The labrys was also the battle-axe of the legendary female warriors known as Amazons.

Childbirth's labor surely *feels* like a double-edged axe. I sincerely believed, during a moment in each of my three labors, that I would be split wide open to my nostrils and then die from all the blood gushing out of me. Women seldom talk in public about this, but I suppose that's the reason why in fifteenth-century Europe women's embodied travail—her *labor*—had become an apt metaphor and a generalized word for all kinds of strenuous physical work.

The labor that began with nineteenth-century industrialization, populated by young women in textile and match manufacturing, had changed by the mid-twentieth century to a testosterone-powered body, one organized to fight the male capitalist corpus that was squeezing it for profit. Labor was called blue-collar work by then because, like childbirth, blue-collar work was physical and brutish.

Women in my family were unafraid of physical work. But labor attitudes were dictated by gender, with women's labor more like joining a secret club, her childbirth kept discreet and disabling, behind closed doors. By contrast, working men's labor was hard, sweaty, and strutted about publicly. Oh, and one gender's labor was paid.

Working women felt torn and still do today, wanting domestic pleasures even when they have to go to work same as men. Both spheres of time, the supposedly tranquil domestic one and the ruthless business one, become harder the more we try to enforce outmoded models. So today, labor is becoming less gendered in old, stereotypical ways, becoming trans-gendered—and more diversely incorporated.

Yes, I'm talking about men sharing housework and parenting, as women build careers and earn money. But I also mean that laborers in the job market are having more say in their work life and are even becoming business owners, a trend I'll describe more later. Before we go there, though, let's take another look at the laboring human bodies of the past.

That Was Then

Historian Gerda Lerner in *The Creation of Patriarchy* draws attention to women being the first slaves and their reproductive powers being the first property. No doubt male bodies were harder to control. The Greeks generally killed male adversaries, but carried off the wives and daughters of vanquished men as sexual property, proof of their enemies' humiliation.

Some slaves, especially those taken from the upper classes, might make it to their owners' beds and become concubines, acquiring a toehold in status. Should a concubine be sexually successful and deliver an heir, she had some hope of inheritance, one step up from slavery. The concubine's slippery status was widespread in cultures as diverse as the Incas, the Chinese, and the tribes and kingdoms of the Middle East. She is truly a tribute to our species' adaptability.

One of our foundational concubine stories comes from the Old Testament. Unable to bear a son, Sarah, wife of Abraham, gave her young servant Hagar to lie with her husband. But when Hagar became pregnant and a bit uppity, jealous Sarah banished her. In the desert, an angel advised Hagar to humble herself and return, and when Hagar gave birth on the lap of Sarah, Abraham became the father of the Arabs, and later of the Israelites when Sarah had a menopausal baby.

In the last chapter, I called corporate workers "concubines" because of that underlying sexual drama of hierarchical mounting, a male tradition. You may have thought I was putting concubines down, not suspecting I was actually paying a compliment to them. What do I mean?

You've seen the reign of male culture in corporate America. Wall Street's wealthiest men will cross-dress and make jokes about homosexuals and women in order to be initiated into the highest male ranks—and women, too, will impersonate men to gain status in all-male corporate bodies.

Verbal mounting and pseudosexing routinely goes on in this male corpus, whatever one's actual gender. Corporate culture feminizes and makes mountable all those lower ranked in the hierarchy, keeping all but the man at the top in fear of being screwed. In that way, today's workers can be seen as wonderfully adaptable concubines.

Some of the earliest known records of paid wages are five thousand years old. Coins hadn't been invented yet, so payment was in rations and a uniform measure of some commodity. A concubine worked for this reward, but not for herself. She earned them for her male owner.

Likewise, when a patriarch became indebted or was found guilty of a crime, he could use his concubines or slaves to pay off his debt or substitute for his punishment. Concubines worked or took the lash for her master and owner, who in exchange kept her alive—or not. His call. While working, she might be called upon to sexually service her master's creditor, whether she liked him or not. Sexual harassment, I suppose, is part of that employee heritage.

Long Shadow

There are other striking parallels with our present day. Employee concubines still exist, but cultural norms blind us to their status. At best, all workers take on that role when living within the sexual ambiguity of hierarchical organizations. Figuring out whom best to serve, who in fact is on top, is part of every worker's job in a shifting environment.

We're encouraged to think of wage and salary earners as those renting out their time by choice, acting as free and independent agents. We don't consider workers the property of shareholders, yet corporate concubines are sold regularly and have nothing to say about it. When a corporation is sold, its workers are part of that sale, having little choice in what may drastically affect their lives.

We feel badly when someone's job is moved, eliminated, or downsized, but it seems only normal to us, repeated often enough that we can't imagine it being otherwise.

Should an employee give birth to fresh ideas or original language, invent a new methodology, a more efficient widget, or win a patent while on the job—same as Hagar, she will deliver it on the lap of the corporation. The heir of that patent, its future profits, belong to the patriarchal corpus, not to the concubine—though as Abraham reportedly was, the corporation may be generous. Or not. His call.

It is harder to be indifferent to worker needs when you work with people you get to know. In earlier US corporations, when owners were often on site, the expectation for some profits to go to employees and the community was still present. Today, decisions affecting workers often happen half a globe away.

Even in large corporations, a more fully human impulse could be regenerated from the bottom up by creating more diverse corporate boards. In the United States and England, workers are typically excluded from corporate boards and policy making. Labor groups are feared and hated. But in countries as different as Germany and Japan, employees are regularly included on policy-setting boards, which changes their concubine status. Managers there expect and even welcome working with organized worker groups. Germany's laws actually require labor's ample representation on boards of German corporations. There is no report of anti-capitalism in Germany or Japan.

Employees, unlike stockholders, have no limited liability to protect them from losses and so perhaps are even more invested in seeking corporate profits. Economist Richard Wolff says more democratic corporate governance that included its workers would help prevent offshoring jobs, but also reduce lawsuits over unsafe or noisy or polluting work sites. And who but workers know more about operations and their efficiency on the ground?

A Less Painful Labor

An exciting number of women, many of whom have never been part of big labor, are beginning to organize in ways that remind me of Rose Schneiderman. Using fresher language and having wider goals, some work within existing union bodies, although union or not, their vision includes the surrounding community. Others are venturing into cooperative ownership with new corporate structures.

These twin developments can seem utopian, based on the wish to sustain bread and roses for all. Yet in the shadow of pending environmental and economic collapse, the notion of everyone sharing and everyone owning their piece may be only sensible. A new breed of woman on the labor stage could make all the difference.

This new, younger woman knows abuse when she sees it, and while an assertive individual, she also trusts the strength that comes from supporting her peers. She's unafraid of sex and believes she has the final word on where and with whom it happens. Like Rose Schneiderman, her vision spans business and home spheres, seeing how they affect each other, far from separate.

She tackles issues beyond her own wages. Rejecting impersonal business norms, she engages as many as she can in problem solving that addresses broad mutual needs. She prefers solutions over fights, and, knowing deprivation from the inside out, she refuses it for others.

So the labor market's unprecedented new numbers of women are a reason for hope. Most have never identified with capitalists or with labor. Hers is a whole new script on the economic stage, a brand-new production.

Saru Jayaraman of Restaurant Opportunity Centers (ROC) United is one example of this new kind of woman. Her restaurant industry work has created a new kind of labor organization. Her career began with helping middle school girls claim themselves and their voices and the homeless after that. Her experience of their collective power growing in their peer support groups led to her helping to found ROC United.

ROC United provides hands-on training and peer support for workers. But its education and guidance also include restaurant management and diners in its vision of safe, fair, and sustainable employment practices, as well as ethical eating and the safety of local food sources. ROC United seeks to improve the lives of restaurant workers but also of community-minded restaurant owners who are also members of ROC, along with thousands of restaurant customers who also join.

ROC United has helped increase wages, but also more broadly addresses issues of women and people of color, whether as workers or customers. One ROC United campaign was called I'm Not on the Menu, which emphasized the sexual harassment women endure. ROC United seeks to transform the restaurant industry to one sharing profits, loyalty, and good food in healthy meeting places—with worker's health care and sick days protecting not just workers, but customers also.

Their report "The Low Road Business Model of CKE Restaurants, Inc." helped sink the 2017 nomination of fast food CEO Andy Puzder to head the US Labor Department. More sexist ads, sexual harassment on the job, and starvation wages like those of Puzder's companies were not what America needs, they said.

Democracy at Work

This broader view that includes roses can be seen in some corporations with traditional structures. Cindy Turcot at Gardener's Supply in Vermont has become an expert in Employee Stock Owner-ship Plans called ESOP, which are similar to 401(k) plans, adding company stock to pension plans. Increasing employees' stake in a company's success spreads benefit, Turcot says, as does empowering workers with ongoing education about the business and more opportunities to influence decisions.

Small businesses with a similar ethic seem particularly attractive to women. New networks like Vermont Businesses for Social Responsibility (VBSR) and the Business Alliance for Local Living Economies (BALLE) promote ethical ways to broaden a sense of sharing and ownership within a business, while deepening roots and connecting with a wider community.

Worker-owned cooperatives are on the cutting edge of this business identity change, too.

Unlike consumer cooperatives, which save money through collective purchases, worker cooperatives produce a service or product for sale, and are owned, managed, and governed collectively. Still relatively rare in the United States, they too are growing in numbers, as Marjorie Kelly writes in *Owning Our Future*.

For instance, ROC United operates two worker-owned restaurant cooperatives called Colors in New York and Detroit. Not every report shows perfection. Lawsuits and an anti-ROC blog exist, but much of the news is more exciting. Reviewers on Yelp and other social media love Color's food.

Its more democratic structure appeared in the magazine *Dollars & Sense*. Eight occupational teams of line cooks, prep cooks, waiters, and others work with a head chef and managers. Importantly, each team has a representative on ROC's board of directors. All their wageworkers belong to the Hotel and Restaurant Workers Union, and every worker-owner has a benefits package and a wage well above the typical.

The best-known worker-owned cooperative today is Mondragon, founded in 1956 by five unemployed Basque workers in Spain and named for their hometown. They began with study circles to address unemployment. They learned a traditional corporation's governance was determined by investment size. Mondragon's idea was simpler: each worker-owner got one vote.

As a result, today the pay ratio of the highest- to lowest-paid worker at Mondragon is less than twenty to one. Compare that to the 2016 Fortune 500 CEO ratio of 347 to one for the average wageworker, not the lowest paid, reported by the AFL-CIO's Executive Paywatch, the most comprehensive searchable database online that measures and tracks CEO pay.

Another result? Mondragon's co-op owners may have hours reduced but not their pay. They can make up their time later when business improves or choose to work in another cooperative within the corporation.

Mondragon has grown huge, a conglomerate of over one hundred cooperatives with 147 additional subsidiaries worth over $382 billion. They manufacture goods, operate a chain of grocery stores, run health services, and incubate new innovations. They've created Mondragon University which trains workers, and their member businesses own and manage a cooperative bank.

Owning their own bank and an early worker-owner decision to reinvest profits in the corporation are considered two keys to their expansion. Mondragon now employs eighty thousand people. Yet that largeness has also made cooperative democracy harder. Less than 40 percent of workers are voting members today. Workers have to prove themselves before being invited to join, and must invest the equivalent to a year's salary. So worker representation is incomplete, and in such a huge organization, decisions are often made far distant.

As Frank Bryan argues in his book about New England town meetings, *Real Democracy*, votes will get diluted as governing bodies grow larger. There's an advantage to keeping it small, an idea we'll return to in Chapter 19 about how we can build economic trust.

Cooperative businesses that stay small, rooted to a particular place, can be powerfully networked with others. Hundreds of examples exist in Japan, such as Zen-Noh, a federation of agricultural cooperatives with revenues of $56 billion, and in Germany, the German Sparkassen savings bank network has over eleven thousand branches. Cooperatives exist in the United States, too, linked in federations of credit unions, mutual insurance, and dairy and farm co-ops. But most of these co-ops are not worker-owned businesses.

Incorporating a New Body

A brand-new legal body, the worker-owned cooperative, is recognized in only twenty-three states in the United States. A few worker-owned co-ops exist as nonprofits or limited liability corporations. Because of this legal limbo, financing for growth is harder to win than a typical small business loan. But that's changing in two places that have already seen remarkable worker cooperative successes. In 2015, California updated its law books, and New York City invested $1.2 million into expanding cooperative businesses.

The first survey of US worker-owned cooperatives was published by Democracy at Work Institute in 2015, based on US surveys done two years earlier on 256 known worker-owned cooperatives. Though a few employ upward of 250 workers and bring in more than $10 million annually, many cooperatives were just startups in 2013. All told, the survey accounted for 6,311 worker-owners with estimated revenues of $367 million. About 42 percent started out as conventional businesses and then transitioned to cooperatives. A surprising half reported having no board of directors at all.

Like the stories of women and labor, the history of a cooperative economy has been suppressed here in the United States where worker security is widely held to make companies less efficient. Despite 2008's gargantuan inefficiencies, Wall Street capital alone is still widely viewed as our sole corporate savior. But friendlier self-help is possible.

When Jessica Gordon Nembhard, an African American economist, began her studies in international development and finance capital, she gradually came to view big finance and development as a source of inequality. She looked for alternative economic models and was surprised to find some very close to home.

She says few of her colleagues were aware of different options either, and so she wrote *Collective Courage: A History of African American Cooperative Economic Thought and Practice*. She told *YES! Magazine* recently that although the wealthiest winners have generally created what is called history, "there's this other activity under the radar that's still happening because human beings are human beings, meaning they work together, and they help each other and care about each other."

Nembhard says instead of letting the conquerors tell the story, if we listened to the people involved in collective survival strategies, we would learn that we already have alternative economic models.

Look Around You

Instead of accepting Wall Street's EconoMansplaining that tells us women have no choice but austerity, we can look to women writers like Nembhard and Kelly, but also to our own experience—because women are ingenious survivors. My easy alliance with girlfriend Sue during the Vietnam War is one tiny example of an alternative model. But perhaps you, too, can remember stories of relationships that helped deliver a livelihood, like the following story of mine.

Years later, after Sue and I both were busy mothers, I began to write and occasionally publish. I needed a good typewriter to be professional but complained I was too broke to come up with the needed down payment. Sue and another girlfriend combined funds to loan me the money. I invested it, repaid it—but really, it was their faith in me that did the most, their vote of confidence empowering me to keep going.

Nembhard discovered similar empowering strategies within black communities. Cooperation began during slavery, she says, as they gardened together, shared produce, and even sold it, purchasing freedom for some. As long ago as 1907, US sociologist and black intellectual W. E. B. Du Bois had written a book on the subject of economic cooperation among "Negro Americans." He called such cooperation the *group economy*, something Nembhard says has most often been created by oppressed people. The Basques of Spain who created Mondragon are another example. And surely women around the world are, too.

"We really can't make political or social progress without economic justice. And that's where Fannie Lou Hamer comes in," says Nembhard.

A key player in the civil rights movement, Hamer saw African Americans who voted in the south could suffer from economic retaliation, so she created the Freedom Farm Cooperative. With money cobbled together, her cooperative grew food, raised livestock, built affordable housing, and secured mortgages on seven hundred acres in Sunflower County, Mississippi.

One of Hamer's lasting legacies is the recently established Southern Rural Black Women's Initiative that aims at social and economic justice for women and girls. They have many programs, among them the Women in Agriculture cooperative of women-owned and women-run farms that operate in five Mississippi counties.

Like many cooperatives, Women in Agriculture has a passionate dedication to sharing good food and land stewardship. They train farmers in sustainable practices that reduce the use of pesticides and prevent soil erosion. They educate consumers about what they are eating. It's clear these women understand the value of remembering cooperative stories that answered oppression.

On the Ground Groups

The urge to include a broader picture of *we* is that same one I identified in the last chapter, the one Marilyn French and Riane Eisler both describe in their analysis of power—power *with*, not power *over*. It is the inclusive power of Eros deep within us that longs for a joining with something larger than self-interest alone.

Unlike the urge for power over, which likes to go to war and to win, this greater subversive survival power drives a passionate urge for sharing survival and life. It unites Gaia's *yang* creativity with the *yin* of Eros, love and will, in hot pursuit of a pleasure-full, peopled future to love.

The first-person *I* speaks of individualism. *We* is the erotic pronoun of joining.

I'm struck by a cooperative tendency toward eco-wisdom in these women's groups, even in big cities where you wouldn't expect it. The Latinas who organized Women's Action to Gain Economic Security (WAGES) started in Oakland, California. Their study circle eventually led low-income immigrant women to collaborate in worker-owned businesses.

By 2013, ninety-two jobs had been created, says their website. Their enterprises were "green" cleaning services, Emma's Eco-Care and Eco-Care Professional Housecleaning, and most recently LaCochina, a new food manufacturing company interested in local, safe food sources rooted in their culture's cooking.

WAGES has renamed itself Prospera: Co-ops: The Business of Empowerment. While members' wages have increased significantly, and they report better housing and transportation, what appears to matter most to these worker-owners is that vote of collective confidence that changed their lives. Transformed, they are eager to share their empowerment and enlarge their "group economy" in the communities where they live.

Similarly, Si Se Puede! (We Can Do It!) Women's Cooperative, begun in the Bronx in 2006, now has fifty-one members and in 2012 began its own line of environmentally safe cleaning products, reports Laura Flanders in *YES! Magazine*. One owner-member, Yadira Ragosa, testified at the New York City Council recently that her hourly wage of $6.25 had gone up to $25 per hour since joining Si Se Puede!

But it isn't just wages. Zaida Ramos, who had been raising a family on public assistance, told Flanders how her life was transformed when she connected with Cooperative Home Care Associates (CHCA), the largest worker-owned co-op in the United States. Ramos, who had been a home health aide with CHCA for seventeen years, was just celebrating her daughter's college graduation.

She's not rich, Ramos says, but she is financially independent. She's a worker-owner who enjoys flexible hours, steady earnings, health and dental insurance, plus an annual share in the profits. "I belong to a union, and I have a chance to make a difference," she said in the interview.

In other words, Ramos is no economic individualist, nor is reason her only tool or competition her single method. She loves her life with a will and a passion, the only meaningful purpose for any economy, don't you think?

Quick Rehash

- Women's reproductive property has not been owned by her until recently, but her ingenious survival came from cooperation and problem solving, not war.
- Organized labor began with women short on money and time—and is being reinvigorated by women today.
- Worker-owned cooperative businesses are on the rise and, like other more democratic business structures, engage as many as possible in their "we."

EconoGirlfriend Conversation Starter

If you were the boss at your workplace, what changes might you make for workers?

PART V

BANKS AND BIG FIXES

Systemic Financial Changes for
Widespread Property

Chapter 16: All About Money—And Yes, It *Does* Grow on Trees

How EconoMan's paper currency made only from debt bankrupts nature and us.

What do you think—that money grows on trees?"

That was my mom's comment whenever I spent more than she thought I should, which was most of the time. Repeated often enough, her voice guided me into adulthood, insisting on bargains even when she was nowhere nearby. I heard her in my head, the way daughters hear mothers.

The last time I took her out for dinner, Mom didn't repeat that tree phrase, but the look on her face when she asked me, "*How* much did you pay for that glass of wine?" stuck in a sore spot. I had paid ten dollars and was shocked that she was shocked.

We were women in a world where money *did* grow on trees—at least the paper dollar bills we used for tipping in restaurants did. Money's value was floaty as air, hovering on waves of opinion chattered by EconoMansplaining worldwide. His banks created currency out of debts, loaning money out of thin air.

If that sounds crazy to you, all I can say is that Mom would have been as disbelieving as you, and as I was, too, when I first learned how our dollars are created. I didn't have a chance to talk with her about it that last visit, so this chapter is really for her—and for all the mothers on earth who still teach their children about thrift.

Thrift is what we need now, but our money literally makes it impossible. The true nature of our money demands growth, always a push for more. Understanding why will finally answer the question I first posed in Chapter 1. What actually causes inflation, the loss of your dollars' buying power? Money's story is not the usual one EconoMansplains, but like everything in his realm, our currency—that paper token of exchange we use today—is not what it appears to be.

The Real Nature of Our Money

I first learned where dollars came from when my high school class visited Washington, DC. We learned how the US government stamps our coins at its Mint and prints the bills at its Bureau of Engraving and Printing, and this probably matches your ideas and those of most Americans. I watched as the paper dollars freshly rolled off the government's printing press in big paper sheets, later cut into bills.

Each bill carries two signatures, both the treasurer of the United States and the secretary of the Treasury. Since 1949, the treasurer, not the secretary of the Treasury, has been a woman. It is her job to oversee the operations of the Mint. But that position should not be confused with the more elite one within the president's cabinet. Still exclusively male, the secretary's office requires something few women have, which is serious Wall Street banking connections. Here is why Wall Street matters.

Everything about the dollar trumpets the United States, proclaiming our nation's money. It is, but the devil is in the details. Our national eagle and the Great Seal, that giant eyeball atop a pyramid, have both been on the dollar since Benjamin Franklin helped design the original bills. Only when you look at the very top in the border do you see what's really going on in small type, the words *Federal Reserve Note.*

A note is a paper designating an amount owed, a debit. We also call debits *bills.* The US Mint prints our dollar bills, but these notes or bills belong to our creditor, the Federal Reserve. The Fed, as it's known, oversees how many dollars get printed—and the two signatures are on behalf of the Fed's debtors, we the people, meaning you and me. We are the debtors, and the currency we carry around in our wallet is actually an IOU we've taken for a loan on the Fed's account books.

So who exactly is the Federal Reserve that has loaned us our national dollars as bills—and how exactly did we borrow it?

The Fed and Your Money

Books abound on this complex subject, and several guide my account here. Ellen Brown's *Web of Debt* is my favorite, accessibly told through the story of Dorothy in *The Wizard of Oz,* and listed in my Recommended Reading. Created in 1919, the Federal Reserve calls itself the US central bank in charge of monetary policy, although its website also describes it as "a system, not a bank," more rightfully so.

It is a system of privately owned bank members, and its reserve is not a vault somewhere as you might imagine from the name. Its reserves are electronic accounts that rapidly move money among our banks, clearing our checks, and making discounted short-term loans to any banks short of cash, if needed.

Janet Yellen became the first female chairperson of the Fed's governing board in 2014, her nomination by President Obama approved by Congress. The Fed thus appears to be a government agency, but it isn't. This facade is carefully maintained while also making sure the Fed functions, in its own words, as "an independent entity within the government." It's a little like a tapeworm.

All seven of the board's governors are installed for terms of fourteen years, tenures oddly out of step with elected members of Congress who supposedly are their boss. Twice a year, the board's chair must report to Congress. Yet by statute, no decision of the Fed can be countered by the president or by Congress.

As independent overseers of the free market, the Fed's system of privately owned banks are not in business to serve the public, but rather to stay solvent and make profits for their stockholders. They do this by loaning money for an interest fee. While the Fed is required to pay attention to US employment rates, their greater concern is keeping inflation controlled.

Assuming you believed that the government issued your money, you probably also thought that banks loan out money from their accounts, the money that you and I have put in as savings. But this also is an illusion. In fact, your money on deposit registers on the banks' own accounting books as a liability—a minus—not the plus you may have thought it did. It is considered a bank debit, because banks must pay interest to you, the depositor.

Because deposits are a cost to the bank, banks try never to keep deposits on hand beyond a required reserve. They invest it, use it to leverage, or loan it out to other banks for an interest fee through the Fed's system that interconnects privately held banks. If all of any one bank's depositors decided to take their money out, that bank would have to borrow funds from the Fed to cover its shortfall.

The Fed has not prevented routine economic crashes and recessions that hurt workers, but it has prevented most banks from failing. Still, when too many demands come in all at once, as happened in 2008's panic, the system can still freeze or collapse.

Now here is where you begin to feel like Alice in Wonderland gone through the looking glass. The banks' ledger books count loans as a credit, a plus, because you will pay back what's owed, with interest added on. That's income and profit for the bank, a plus. To you, the debtor on the receiving end, a loan remains a minus. Remember Pacioli's duality principle.

But here's the weird part. A bank does not take money out of the bank's vault to make their loans of Federal Reserve Notes. It doesn't loan its deposits. The Fed simply enters plus numbers on the bank loan accounts, creating what is called *fiat currency*.

Fiat means something akin to Captain Picard's command on *Star Trek*. Banks possess no holodeck or Star Trek replicator, only the power that Congress has granted them to loan us a future built on what amounts to their air and our hopes. Like soothsayers, banks predict your ability to pay them back with interest added on, and then wave their wand to make fiat money that the Federal Reserve Act of 1919 made possible.

So private bank loans—not our savings, not the US Mint, and not the gold bricks you imagined were stored in a vault—create our nation's currency. We are literally passing around our collective IOU notes, all tracked electronically by the Fed.

Paper Money's Backstory

At times in the past, our government did directly produce its paper money. The first Continental Congress printed money to pay for the American Revolution, Abraham Lincoln created US Greenbacks to pay for the Civil War, and John F. Kennedy bypassed the Fed to create Silver Certificates directly from our Treasury. The story of how we got so muddled on the nature of our money, and who exactly should issue it and how, is again a mostly male tale, largely about power and control. But it's helpful to know it.

Historian Jack Weatherford in his book *The History of Money* says that paper currency first appeared in China in 1273 when the Mongol ruler Kublai Khan forced everyone to turn in their silver and gold for new paper bills for all business transactions. This made robbery rare. Concubines and sexual services sweetened their business deals, an old-boy tradition still pursued in halls of power, and the government returned any gold or silver due when a foreign merchant like Marco Polo left.

Weatherford says Kublai Khan's monopoly tended to slow commerce. By contrast, he says the early paper systems of the West were issued by multiple banks, increasing the flow of goods among merchants, all using the Venetian accounting method of double-entry bookkeeping. He calls the results of this system "magic," though to my eye it seems more a bamboozle that unintentionally spread wider prosperity to people who knew nothing about its source.

> ## ✔ EXTERNALITY
>
> This economic word describes an effect experienced by someone who did not actively participate in that effect's cause. An externality is viewed as either negative or positive. Kublai Khan's concubine slave suffered a *negative externality*. She had no say in the cause of her reduction to sexual commodity, but paid the opportunity cost of her other options. Today our water and air suffer from a negative externality from some people's use of fossil-fuel energy, a cost that registers on other people far removed, experiencing floods and storms they did not cause.
>
> A *positive externality* benefits you without your effort. A partner who cooks grants you more free time—but take it for granted for too long and social benefit may erode. The positive externality of the Fed multiplying money out of bank loans has the positive effect of increasing the supply of money for people who had no part in its creation. But over time, as this single kind of money multiplies, so do the debts—and eventually numbers become unsustainable.

Magic Bamboozle

Money is a token or symbol. No practical reason makes gold or silver more valuable than paper or wampum or conch shells or cows. Rather, any currency's worth depends on what people agree or imagine is fair to exchange as a signal of trust. Tally sticks, coins, and paper generally represented something of tangible, touchable value, like gold, sterling, or land—at least until fairly recently.

During the Renaissance in Marco Polo's time, the royalty of Italian city-states and their merchants traded in coins, often stored in the safes of goldsmiths and money changers. These men tracked the value of different coins and could exchange, for example, *florins* for *ducats* when needed for business. Sometimes they went further and rented out money for a fee, called *interest*, on the sly.

Weatherford describes how the old limits of those kinds of concrete exchanges were transformed by the Renaissance moneylenders' *bills of exchange*. While a royal bag of coins might have sat idle, hidden away for years, bills of exchange enabled moneylenders to loan that money out several times over, so that merchants in several cities exchanged the paper bills—while the king still had his gold florins, untouched, on deposit. When paper bills circulated as money, there was more of it than ever.

This "magic" of bank-created "air" money was eventually named *fractional reserve banking,* the kind we use now. As a result, our bank reserves held in the Fed's system have grown smaller in relation to all loans leveraged. Our largest banks multiply money exponentially through financial tools we have talked about already, the over-the-counter radicchio-derivatives that Brooksley Born said were dangerous when kept secret.

Loans, Interest, and Morals

Loans that charged interest were kept secret in banking's early days because during the Middle Ages and the Renaissance, charging extra for loaning money was a crime called *usury*. Bonds and debts of all kinds are now the backbone of our economic system, but dozens of texts in the Bible and the Koran clearly condemn profiting from loans. Charlemagne found it a criminal offense, and Pope Clement V declared it a mortal sin since giving to those less fortunate was expected charity.

By contrast, today's banking practices increase the debts of the poorest. The toxic mortgages of 2008 charged the poorest more interest, not less. It was one reason investors were eager to get in on Wall Street's highly profitable mortgage securities. No one talked about morality.

Those US politicians who quote Bible verses condemning abortion and homosexuality forget the far greater number of verses damning usury as oppression. Newer Bible translations redefine usury as "excessive interest," toning down the King James Version that named usury an "abomination." But even the watered-down version offered by the Living Bible's Ezekiel 3:18 is a comfort to quote out loud when opening a credit card bill: "He lends at excessive interest. Should such a sinful man live? No! He must die and must take full blame!" Try it sometime for therapy.

Modern finance is rooted in the idea that money should work for you, although only people and the planet can actually do work. People labor to provide services or extract or refine raw materials. Materials exist because the planet and its systems first worked to produce them. Because paper money cannot perform labor, or increase productivity itself, I put money's interest "earnings" in quotes, much as John Stuart Mills called this effortless money "unearned income."

It requires no blood, sweat, or real productivity. Overvaluing such income, allowing it outsized expansion, depreciates the concrete time and real life of most people and the planet.

Earth's healthy growth and our own are bound by seasons and time, birth rates, and mortality. As early classical economist Malthus saw, and as I've often repeated, land can only add and subtract resources. When people multiply over time, and outgrow the simpler math of the environment, they starve, said Malthus.

Money, like people, can multiply. But its ingeniously abstract numbers lack the earthbound limits that you and I must live within. Money is immortal. Its multiplying numbers have no negative feedback loops. It won't starve and its power increases the greater its numbers.

Now billionaires are multiplying and overpopulating the earth. At the beginning of the twentieth century, we had one billionaire, worth about $300 billion. By 2016, *Forbes Magazine* counted 1,810 billionaires, still nearly all male, with a net worth of $6.5 trillion. As we've seen, billionaires survive any collapses they cause and seldom pity those who don't.

Added-on interest is an incentive that helps keep money circulating, but it's also a cost. Margrit Kennedy, another amateur economist like me, who first trained as a German architect, environmentalist, and professor, confronted the inevitable results in her book *Occupy Money: Creating an Economy Where Everybody Wins*. She found that about 40 percent of Germany's current prices paid by consumers were generated by interest payments.

Like Germans, you and I pay interest on our personal credit cards and mortgages, but so does every American business, municipality, all state governments, institutions, landlords, and transporters. They all borrow money, reflected in their prices. Every financed economic truck on our indebted highways carries a load of debt and delivers debt, passing more debt on the way to arriving at an indebted loading dock.

EconoMan's Fertility

Not only do we all pay interest, we pay compounded interest. Just to review, the amount of money borrowed and lent is called the *principal*. The rental fee moneylenders first invented is called *interest*. To *compound* means to calculate together both the principal amount and the interest owed, as if the two were chemically joined. They are not, of course, but *compounding interest* reliably doubles the lender's unearned "earnings" from the rented-out principal.

How often compounding is done affects how long it takes to double numbers. Mortgage lenders most often compound balances monthly, but some credit cards compound amounts daily. More frequent compounding benefits the lender while less frequent compounding means the borrower pays less over time.

Compounding interest creates those interest "money babies" we met in Chapter 14, called a *kid*, a *fetus*. Compounded annually, a loan's numbers will double at regular intervals. How quickly this happens, the length of gestation, also depends on the interest amount charged. The math is irrefutable: at 1 percent interest, money doubles in seventy-two years, at 6 percent it doubles in twelve years, and at 24 percent it doubles in three years.

Such reproduction or doubling through interest "earnings" is simply a property of mathematics. A number's doubling, its ability to create money-newborns, cannot be prevented with a pill. The numbers of dollars (and amounts of debt) must grow greater to meet the demand for paying that added-on interest, like another new mouth to feed.

With greater numbers of dollars, each dollar gets a smaller share of what's on the table. Each dollar's value is decreased. It takes more dollars to pay for prices that have risen to meet demand for that added-on interest. Although other factors may inflate prices as well, interest payments must inevitably lead to inflation and the loss of buying power for the dollars in our wallets.

It seems fair to assume American interest payments are at least as large a part of our spending as Germany's, about 40 percent. This is why some say inflation is like an invisible tax, as money moves from those with less to those with surpluses to loan out—and even to multiply if they happen to own a bank—but always with that push for a little something more.

All Together Now

In previous chapters, you saw the doubling effect of interest in the example of mortgage payments and on the creditor side, the doubling fortunes of Bill Gates. Neither money-baby population increase had to do with real labor, real productivity, or an increased concrete value. However tiny their amounts, EconoMan numbers will not only inevitably double, but will double *exponentially*, the way only numbers can multiply in the abstract over time.

✔ EXPONENTIAL GROWTH

Just as the vastness of trillions is hard to grasp, so is the magic of mathematics and the dangers of geometric out-of-this-linear-world growth. It defies human reason and intuition. As an example, if you had to choose between two pay raises, would you pick $10,000 per week for a year, or one cent in the first week, doubled every week from then on for fifty-two weeks?

Most choose the first option, easily calculated at $10,000 per week, or a raise of $52,000. Were you to choose the second option, fifty-two weeks of compounding, your money would "earn" a total of $45 trillion, or about two-thirds of the world's GDP. By year-end, your final week's "earnings" would be $900 billion.

Money's exponential growth has never before grown so huge. The bigger our billionaires' wealth of abstract numbers, now celebrated as progress, the greater the hulking concrete debts we carry, owed to a relatively small number of men. Flesh and blood, water and earth, cannot keep on inflating *ad infinitum* like abstract-growth numbers can. Growth mirrors debt, and the mismatch of debt money's intellectual construct pits us against our tangible, earthbound edges.

The swelling weight of money created only from debt presses on our ant-sized lives. Worse, it crowds the planet's smallest, remotest microbes and plankton, affecting the basest source of our real wealth, the food chains of soil and water. Like you, their living systems can be exhausted and depleted beyond repair.

Pursuit of unearthly sums may literally kill our golden goose. EconoMan's growth of those interest-babies is not the pregnancy he promised. It's a tumor. It is time to remember that money is only paper. It is only what we agree to.

Ongoing Currency Debate

The printing of paper currency was not described in the US Constitution. Thomas Jefferson and Benjamin Franklin, who both had strong opinions about paper's democratic value, did not play a role in the drafting of Article 1, which claims government authority for the nation's money creation and minting. It discusses only coins, not paper. Still the nature of both coins and paper currency was of terrific interest to the US public in our first hundred years.

Was fiat currency good for the nation's prosperity? And if so, what should back it and who should issue it? The government? Land? Wealthy bankers? Monetary arguments were long and complicated but essentially pitted old royalist ideas of debt, compounded to the advantage of the wealthiest, against the idea that a democracy could produce many currencies, to avoid the concentrated power of bonds of debt.

The debate about the nation's currency continued until 1919, the year that President Wilson signed the Federal Reserve Act. After that, the public seemingly went to sleep about monetary matters, perhaps lulled by the fire hose of verbiage presented by the Fed's chair twice a year. Now there are signs that public debate is beginning again, with women helping to lead new challenges. Margrit Kennedy and Ellen Brown are only two of the female monetary thinkers in *Screwnomics*. There are others. You are now one of them.

Dollars, Dollars, Everywhere

Women think about dollars every day. We weigh prices in dollars, pay for goods and services with them, and try to earn as many as we can. Without them, we couldn't pay taxes, purchase food, pick up prescriptions, or shop for new clothes. Yet if women, considered the lynchpin of consumer-based economies, fail to look more closely at how dollars get created as units of exchange, we might find our purses filled with worthless paper.

This has happened in many countries—in Germany, as you'll remember. Most economists say a failed dollar will never happen in the United States, but then most economists didn't anticipate the 2008 crash, either. The International Monetary Fund (IMF) was established by Bretton Woods to foster monetary stability. Yet its database, according to Margrit Kennedy, revealed "124 banking crises, 326 currency crises and 64 public debt crises at the national level between 1970 and 2007." Then the real crisis happened in 2008.

In a global economy, currency trust matters. Our dollar still enjoys *reserve currency* status, one of five such currencies considered safe for world trade. But it is not so exclusively trusted as in 1944, when Franklin Delano Roosevelt hosted the Bretton Woods conference that created the IMF. The United States then represented nearly half of all global economic activity.

Nations agreed to the dollar's reserve status because central banks of nations could return their dollars to the US government for gold at an agreed upon thirty-five dollars per ounce. (During the Great Depression, Roosevelt had ended individual banks' redemption of dollars for gold and made gold a controlled substance.)

In 1974, President Nixon removed the US dollar from the gold standard. France suspected we were printing more dollars to pay for the Vietnam War than our national gold could possibly back up. Worried, they had begun cashing in their dollars, threatening an international bank run.

The closing of the US gold window went nearly unnoticed by most Americans, more concerned with their paper wages than international currency trading. But now the dollar's value would "float," relative to other currencies. This was probably realistic, but new private market forces now grew more important. Currency trading had been rare, but neoliberal players put it on hyperdrive. Today, hedge funds trade currencies like modern-day money changers.

> ## ✓ HEDGE FUNDS
>
> Like much of the language of Wall Street, this term means the opposite of what the dictionary would lead you to expect. *To hedge* means to protect and reduce risk, but the goal of hedge funds is to maximize profits, not reduce risks. Hedge funds take great risks and occasionally get caught committing blatant fraud. Sam Israel's Bayou Fund and Bernie Madoff's Ascot Partners are merely the hedge funds we know cheated.

No-Woman Woods

No woman official attended the financial conference at Bretton Woods. It's astonishing how little women have had to do with any definitions of currency. This remains true despite Christine Lagarde's appointment as head of the IMF in 2011 and Janet Yellen's naming to the Fed in 2014, both firsts. They front what remains a highly privileged nobleman's club.

Margrit Kennedy is much nicer than I am, but admits that gender still drives monetary matters. She notes it is limited to about two hundred thousand "guys" under forty who trade currencies to the tune of 4.5 trillion US dollars a day, chasing after profits with zero concrete value. These are the macro-players using algorithms and software programs called *quants* for high-frequency trading, already mentioned. I said their nutty speeds didn't benefit most of us—but in truth they often hurt many, a nation's people undone, without knowing what negative externality just hit them.

Hedge funds are credited with creating growing numbers of US billionaires. Only accredited investors can participate in hedge funds. Accredited investors haven't earned some license or passed some test. In the United States, this term only means that an investor's net worth is more than $1 million. Most often, hedge funds work by leveraging investors' money, using it to borrow like mad.

Unlike the bond and stock markets, hedge funds are a free market dream, all but unregulated. Sometimes called *vultures*, hedgers manipulate currency values by using derivatives. International currency is now traded as if it were itself a commodity.

Today that commodity isn't even paper. It's a green blip on a computer screen, multiplying unearned "earnings" at an unprecedented rate. Hedge funds can impact national economies more quickly than the money changers of the Renaissance affected the fates of kings.

Mad Hatters of Money

Learning about this, you may feel like you're attending the Mad Hatter's tea party in Alice's Wonderland. Paper notes float like teacakes with signs saying *Trade Me*. Their numbers and values glide up and down—only sometimes down is up, depending on what is being bet upon. And who are the maddest hatters? I'll try to explain more.

Currency manipulation is our "free market" at its most ruthless work. In practice, the devaluation of the US dollar has allowed us to bully less powerful countries. Despite the dollar's shrinking value (your money's inflation), foreign nations' central banks must stock up on US dollars for their reserves.

Why, since our gold window was shut? The "oily dollar" replaced it. The Organization of Petroleum Exporting Countries, known as OPEC, prices all its oil sales exclusively in US currency. It's another of those EconoMan secrets hidden right under our noses. Even if you had heard of the oily dollar, you'd be unlikely to understand its importance.

In 2000, Iraq's Saddam Hussein broke with OPEC and refused to accept dollars. He demanded the new currency, Euros, for Iraq's oil. Both Bush presidents, with ties to oil companies and Saudi Arabian OPEC royalty, tried currency warfare and boycotts. When that didn't work, both Bush presidents chose to invade.

Muammar Gaddafi of Libya, another oil-independent tyrant, was actively challenging the oily dollar, seeking a gold-backed regional currency. The first act of US-backed Libyans after Gaddafi was murdered was establishing a new central bank—orchestrated and assisted by the US Federal Reserve of New York, the most powerful bank in the private-bank Federal Reserve system.

Our oily dollar also helps explain US resistance to alternative, earth-friendly energy solutions.

Heart of Darkness

The boards of Wall Street's biggest banks, those Federal Reserve stockholders, and the US Treasury are all populated by alpha males waging a masculine war game. By contrast, very nice women populate your small local banks and credit unions, and most often take your money at the window.

Occasionally, a woman heads a local bank's operation, but guys in suits head the majority. The stockholders of most banks remain mostly male, and men usually head state bank associations. These are family guys who coach their daughters' baseball teams. They should be, and sometimes are, as worried about Wall Street's EconoMan as I am.

State banks and credit unions are supervised and regulated by the Federal Reserve System, and with the Fed, size matters. By statute, the Fed's twelve regional banks are owned by the country's 2,900 biggest national banks that are, in turn, required to purchase stock in their region's Federal Reserve Bank. For a century, this practice has paid them an annual 6 percent dividend (a pretty nice requirement). Normally, you don't see profit-making businesses owning stock in the agency that regulates it, but that is the exceptional nature of the Federal Reserve System.

Local banks are regulated by the Fed. Since passage of Dodd-Frank's reform in 2010, small banks numbers have grown smaller. In late 2015, the *American Banker* reported there were 1,524 fewer small banks with assets under $1 billion. Fewer small banks make it harder for local small businesses and home buyers to get the financing they need.

Meanwhile, big banks have gotten bigger. No banks are richer or bigger than those Wall Street banks on the board of the New York Federal Reserve. The Fed's own website acknowledges that the New York Fed plays "a unique role." It oversees all "open market" operations, which determine national costs and investor returns that influence currency and credit conditions worldwide. Only the New York Fed is involved with foreign currency "interventions," like Libya's. Only the New York Fed sells and buys US government securities and Treasury bonds that fund government operations.

To do the latter, the New York Fed conducts daily conference calls with "primary dealers" in bonds and securities (think Goldman Sachs) about interest rates. Only after that insider conversation, do they then call the US Treasury in Washington, which next authorizes the New York Fed's daily ten-minute auction so that the same primary dealers can bid and purchase our national bonds, described in Chapter 6.

The New York Fed sells short- and long-term notes, bills, and bonds to finance government operations. The auction winners of our debt, always primary dealers, then resell these to other dealers to sell to other investors around the world. A bond can be sold and resold, and in that way a virtual chain of bonds functions like a second reserve currency gone global.

It's important to understand that both our dollars and our bonds operate only as instruments of debt. The National Priorities Project (NPP), which gets its numbers from the Office of Management and Budget, reported that 6 percent of our tax dollars went to pay $218 billion in interest from deals brokered by the New York Fed in 2016.

The next year, it was up to 7 percent, or $303 billion. They note the debt ratio to GDP is down from its 10 percent after the crash, to 2.6 percent in 2017, the pattern for the past fifty years. But the Congressional Budget Office expects debt service to increase dramatically as interest rates go up. The Federal Reserve, independent of government, controls that externality.

No wonder there is never "enough" money. Interest demands more always be paid in the future. Its reliable doubling is the rich man's secret.

Could We Own the Fed?

The US government is not now a stockholder in the Fed. It could be with a change in its statute. Congress could play a more active role in our monetary policy, and there are signs some want this. The Fed was never audited in its first one hundred years until US Senators Bernie Sanders on the left and Jim DeMint on the right insisted on an audit's inclusion in the 2010 Dodd-Frank reform bill.

The Government Accountability Office (GAO) completed the Fed's first audit in 2011 and reported its discovery of $1.6 trillion of secret, cheap bank loans to all the biggest banks. These loans were hidden behind mysterious terms like *quantitative easing* and foreign interventions, like the one in Libya. All had been done without Congress even knowing of it. As Senator Bernie Sanders famously put it, "This is a case of socialism for the rich and rugged you're-on-your-own individualism for everyone else." The Fed and allies, including Democrats, have actively resisted another GAO audit, though thirty-two senators cosponsored a Fed transparency bill in 2015, proposing it.

Taxpayers are ultimately responsible and live with the monetary results, but the Fed excuses its apparent exclusion from the usual fiscal rules by describing itself on its website as that "independent entity within the government, having both public purposes and private aspects." One of the vaguest words in the dictionary, *aspect* can mean a facet, a piece, or an even more elusive appearance. Those aspects of the Fed need to be seen rather than hidden.

My initial disbelief, my shock at these discoveries, was confirmed by an earlier but similar reaction from a man elected to Congress in 1929, the year of the Great Depression's crash. Ellen Brown first introduced me to the late Texas Representative Wright Patman in her book *Web of Debt*. For forty years, Patman chaired the US House Committee on Banking and Currency, and for twenty of those years he sought to repeal the Federal Reserve System.

The *Congressional Record* of September 29, 1941, is worth comparing to the mumble-speak of Fed chairs. That day Patman, aiming his remarks at the Fed's operations, put it simply to Congress: "I have never yet had anyone who could, through the use of logic and reason, justify the Federal Government borrowing the use of its own money."

As the times changed, the long-serving Patman and his committee continued to hold hearings. Patman became less radical, no longer seeking to overthrow what had clearly become entrenched. Marking the Fed's fiftieth year, however, Patman's committee in 1964 issued a report proposing changes for the Fed's improvement.

Their top suggestions emphasized the public character of the Fed, and called for retiring all of the Fed's bank-owned stock. They sought to shorten the Board's terms of office to match up with the Congress that oversaw them, and to widen the expertise of its board to include "men of integrity devoted to the public interest," not just money experts. If Patman were alive today, I'd like to think he'd include women in that public call.

His committee also thought those open market auctions performed by the New York Fed exclusively should be performed by the Fed's Board to provide wider representation. The committee recommended annual audits and that Fed operations be funded by Congress, not the banks—apparently seeing the dangers of clubby connections among unelected big bankers. This report is a good place for women reformers to begin.

Now It's Our Turn

The question Patman raised about why our government must borrow money to use our own currency remains unanswered. I can hear my mom's reaction, if she'd had a chance to learn about this: We paid how much interest for issuing our own national money? Do you think it grows on trees?

Well, as we've seen, paper money *does* grow as freely, but not only because its bills are made from wood pulp.

Given the American ideal of no taxation without representation, at least half the players on Capitol Hill—and surely half on the Federal Reserve Board itself—who oversee all things monetary should be women. Possibly all of them should be women if we were to be granted our fair turn. Not all of them should be bankers either.

Women's faces alone will not change things if their brains have only been trained in neoliberal free market individualism. Janet Yellen's ability to get out the verbal fire hose shows us the dangers of female overexposure to EconoMansplaining. More verbosity will only continue general confusion.

So let new womanish leaders, whatever their genitals, sing us simpler songs of what we need. Let us write limericks about our suffering and our hilarious hypocrisies.

We needn't do away with interest and banks to create healthier economic exchanges. Sexier solutions are out there, along with more fun, still ahead.

Quick Rehash:

- Our dollar is actually an IOU for a loan on the Fed's account books. The government does not own our money, although it prints it at the US Mint.
- The Fed, an independent, for-profit entity, creates *fiat* money when it wants to but only through loans, increasing our collective debt.
- Compounded interest increases prices over time.
- Infinite growth and expansion is driving us and our planet into bankruptcy.

EconoGirlfriend Conversation Starter

Why do you think the topic of money remains so taboo? Does our silence help us or hurt us?

All About the Money—And Yes, It *Does* Grow on Trees   213

Chapter 17: More Than One Way to Skin a Cat

Banking in the public interest already is working—
a secret cat more women can let out of the bag.

Life often calls for quick fixes with materials at hand. When it works, even if it isn't pretty, you settle for a problem solved for the short term at least, and it can sometimes be pretty ingenious.

My mom, for example, never threw ruined nylons away. She used them to stuff throw pillows, or tied big knots for the dog to tug on. Once she cut off the foot end of one leg and duct-taped it to the washing machine hose. When the washer emptied, the nylon mesh caught lint before it clogged the drain. Her stitch in time saved nine, and best of all, it hadn't cost a dime.

She was a believer in proverbs, including there's more than one way to skin a cat. It's a grisly saying, but intriguingly, it first appeared in 1840 in "The Money Diggers," a satirical piece. At the time, American snake oil potions, not all above board, were creating fortunes. A woman in those days had to be as careful of medicines as she was of fur collars; none were cure-alls, and some collars looked strangely calico in sunlight.

Wall Street's complex financial inventions of the past thirty years are the money diggers of our time. We've seen that the United States has become a financial-ized economy. Inflated bubbles of value, for much that is guessed or imagined or pretended, yield little for most. Instead, as economist Michael Hudson puts it in *Killing the Host*: "The financial sector has the same objective as military conquest: to gain control of land and basic infrastructure, and collect tribute. . . . Finance has become war by other means. What formerly took blood and arms is now obtained by debt leverage."

We have always had inequality, but its excesses today undermine the trust that societies need to function. Les Leopold's *Runaway Inequality* shows us a shift that Americans already sense, and that I've shown you in cherry pies and parfaits. In 1970, the financial sector was just 5 percent of the US workforce and yet claimed 10 percent of our national profits. Today, its mere 6 percent of workers claims 25 percent, he writes.

We've also seen how money that would have been plowed back into maintaining US-based corporations a generation ago now gets swept up to CEOs and Wall Street bankers. Leveraged buyouts help devalue real corporate production. You've also learned some solutions, like membership of labor on corporate boards and cooperative ownership of business. But we also need changes in finance itself to help fund more cooperation.

Women can do more here than you might have thought possible. When I was poor and struggling with my budget, paying overdraft fees, I never imagined I would take an interest in banking. Banking is boring and dull. It has horrible associations of always coming up short. But after confronting the mathematical impossibilities of compound interest, after learning US currency only represents bank debt, I've had to take another closer look.

I can either learn about money, and discover and work for alternative ideas, or continue to be invisibly screwed by a system that disadvantages me and refuses accountability. There has never been such a need for fresh repurposing and jerry-rigged runarounds. In this chapter are just a few that are already working and could be replicated in your part of the world.

✓ WOMEN'S BANKING

Until the Equal Credit Opportunity Act (ECOA) in 1974, married women needed a husband's signature to open a separate bank account or get a credit card. Unmarried women often had to have cosigners as well. In 1975, Judy H. Mello, a former investment banker and businesswoman, opened the First Women's Bank in Manhattan to address discrimination.

Women's history was just being born, so its founders appear unaware of an earlier predecessor, Brenda Runyon, who in 1919 had founded a First Women's Bank, but in Clarksville, Tennessee. Its staff and board were female, but capitalization came from male stockholders, and it closed two years later when Runyon grew ill

Between 1975 and 1980, nine US women's banks were formed with similar aspirations, including the First Woman's Bank of California. In all cases, raising capital became difficult. The ECOA ended the worst discrimination, increasing competition. All ten banks were relatively short-lived.

Yet even earlier than Runyon's forgotten bank, in 1903, African American Maggie L. Walker had opened the St. Luke Penny Savings Bank of Richmond, Virginia. Aware of financial bias against her race, she organized a majority-female board by selling stock to members of the Independent Order of St. Luke, a mutual insurance and burial cooperative. Maggie Walker headed the bank until her death in 1934, having by then successfully merged it with two other black-owned banks.

Banking the Public Interest

Ellen Brown wrote a number of books about health care before she wrote *Web of Debt* about our currency system. An attorney, she says her research into a corporate health care industry introduced her to economic realities. "There can't be anything more inefficient," she said in an interview. "We're going to private hospitals, private doctors, using profit-seeking drug corporations, and they all have a vested interest in sickness."

Something similar goes on with the vested interests of private banking fortunes that profit from renting out money as debt. Brown's book and its illustrations from Frank Baum's *Wizard of Oz* help make monetary history and theory both readable and inspiring. She seeks reform for the Fed, but above all she is after efficiency.

Changing the Fed will be protested and fought by the biggest money in Washington. So meanwhile, Brown's research has revealed a more immediate way to counterbalance a vested interest in debt.

If we can't beat private banks at their game, maybe we should join them. What difference might it make if we the people also owned a public bank? Or better, perhaps, if a network of public banks could help finance public ends, like education and infrastructure?

The nation now has only one such bank. The Bank of North Dakota (BND) was founded in 1919, the same year as the Fed, when the *Wizard of Oz* and monetary issues were both popular. Brown discovered the BND's existence has made all the difference to red state North Dakotans who are solid, conservative Republicans.

She decided to write a book about public banking and in the course of her research identified many other examples. By then I'd gotten to know her while I was writing a series of articles called "An Economy of Our Own" that won a National Newspaper Award in 2012. She asked me to be one of her readers for her book, *The Public Bank Solution*.

By the time I had finished the book, I was convinced that public banks, which I had never heard of before, could make a huge economic difference for most of us. As a disclaimer, I have served on the national board of the Public Banking Institute, founded by Brown, and continue as an advisor. I have traveled a far distance from seeing systemic problems of poverty to seeing systemic solutions.

If You Only Owned a Bank

You may have seen "state" banks in other parts of the country. The BND (Bank of North Dakota) doesn't have the term *state* in its name, but it is owned by the state. That's important to understand. The bank's business is public, not private, and is intended for enriching the common welfare. North Dakota's democracy, not just its wealthiest class, determines who sits on its board, sets the bank's goals, and manages its funds by hiring banking professionals.

The BND is backed by state revenues, tax money. Individual North Dakotans are not depositors in this bank, but indirectly and collectively they put all the people's tax receipts and the state's public money into the BND. What difference does state ownership of such a bank make?

North Dakota was the only state in the union to maintain a continuous budget surplus, despite the 2008 Wall Street crisis. While other states like Minnesota and California suffered near-bankrupt crises in 2008, and forty-eight states suffered budget shortfalls, dividends from North Dakota's bank returned to its people.

Over the past twenty-one years, the BND has made nearly $1 billion in profits, and contributed more than $400 million to North Dakota's state revenue. That's a sizeable amount for a state with only seven hundred thousand people. The Institute for Local Self-Reliance ILSR estimates $3,300 per household over that period has gone into the state's budget, reducing their taxes by that much.

The BND also operates as a bank for local banks with an aim to help them do their on-the-ground business, namely financing farms, local small businesses, home ownership, and affordable education for North Dakotans. BND networks and works in partnership with over one hundred local banks and credit unions for those public purposes. Its equity and loan portfolios have only grown and set record profits since 2008.

ILSR also found that local banks and credit unions are six times more plentiful in North Dakota than the national average. They control 83 percent of deposits in the state, not the 29 percent of state deposits typical of local small banks elsewhere.

Keeping It Local Works

It might not be obvious that the health of your local, small bank matters. Like the nylon footie on a washing machine hose keeps water running freely, a network of local banks keeps money circulating at home by extending credit in state. As a result of BND's public mission and their partnership with local banks, small business owners in North Dakota keep their money local. Even large loans can be made locally because the BND helps back them.

In the years leading up to 2008, when many small banks were selling their mortgages to Wall Street banks for mortgage securities, the BND stepped into the secondary mortgage market. They bought and serviced mortgages in state, avoiding the mess that nearly sank Wall Street's financial system and so many state budgets. Servicing those loans means more local jobs and more money circulating locally instead of being siphoned off to banks leveraging more risky global deals.

Banking experts operate the BND, but their salaries and overhead remain local and earthbound. Same as other banks, the BND's profits benefit its stockholders, but in their case these happen to be the united people of North Dakota. Nowhere is their advantage more evident than in North Dakota's educational loans. In 2015 these were offered at rates from 2 to 5 percent, compared to 10 to 15 percent elsewhere, while a special program helped students consolidate their loans to escape exorbitant interest.

BND's student loan default rate is low, which their spokesperson attributes to the bank's financial education efforts. It also sponsors loan-forgiveness programs in exchange for graduates' public service as teachers and health professionals—another great way to foster the state's local economy.

Brown often reports on public banking in the *Huffington Post*. In 2016, she wrote: "[North Dakota's] balance sheet is so strong that it recently reduced individual income taxes and property taxes . . . and is debating further cuts." Some argue that North Dakota's good fortune is due to oil production, but Brown says a study done by the Center for State Innovation from 2007 to 2009 revealed the BND added nearly as much money to the state's general fund as oil and gas tax revenues did. Its model creates partnership, rather than competition, and helps preserve the state's independence.

The Washington Public Bank Coalition has compared their state's cost of public education construction through loans from Wells Fargo to North Dakota's state-owned bank; they found interest payments nearly half theirs, with a lower cost per pupil despite North Dakota's greater investment in school construction. And unlike the credit lines of private banks that most states have in case of emergency, North Dakota's is effectively interest-free. A publicly funded credit line allows state and local governments to avoid pricey rates for bonds on Wall Street, and answers today's cry to reduce public services in order to keep a good bond rating, Brown explains.

Wall Street and Main Street

Assuming you don't live in North Dakota, do you know where your state or your city deposits its public funds and tax money? Most states deposit state funds with super large banks judged big enough to risk a state's enormous deposits, which, remember, represent a bank liability. But since 2008, it seems fair to ask your public officials: What exactly makes you think Wall Street can better handle this risk? A related question is: What amount does your city or state pay to their big banks for services?

Pamela Powers Hannley of Tucson, Arizona, had become a proponent of public banking in her financially troubled state. She joined the national board of PBI (Public Banking Institute) where I met her. Through her advocacy work, she had learned about the Comprehensive Annual Financial Report (CAFR), a uniform accounting system required by the US federal government for states and cities. By law, CAFRs are available to any citizen, part of the public record.

She looked at Arizona's CAFR reports, searching in particular for the budget line labeled *debt service*, or *interest and fees*. She was shocked to discover that in 2014 her state had sent $312 million to Wall Street banks for interest payments alone. The number struck her as particularly ironic, since just that year, Arizona's state school system had taken Arizona's state government to court for its failure to fund public education adequately—to the tune of $300 million.

Nothing political is ever simple, but it looked to her like state officials had caved into budget pressures increased by Wall Street fees and deals. Further research revealed that over a longer period, from 2007 to 2014, and at a time when the Fed's interest rates to US banks were set at historic lows, Arizona's debt service numbers had doubled. Shades of compound interest! Pamela decided to run for a seat in the Arizona legislature in 2016. And she won!

Her research and that of other activists from Pennsylvania, New Jersey, Colorado, California, New Hampshire, Washington, Maine, and Vermont helped lead to a new project at the Public Banking Institute, entitled What Wall Street Costs America. It will seek to aggregate now largely hidden costs of finance to states, cities, their schools, and public services like water (Think: Flint, Michigan).

Imagine a network of fifty-plus state- and city-owned banks multiplying affordable credit and a sustainable counterbalance to the current high-risk, centralized private banking system dominated by Wall Street. Such a network, Brown and many others now argue, would act in the public interest to stabilize any crisis. It could resist asset price inflation and devaluations, build infrastructure, and fund expansion of productive capacity and jobs. States and cities could adopt their own most pressing mandates for what they decide most needs financing.

Old Ideas Return

Brown's research in her latest book, *The Public Bank Solution,* revealed many international examples of publicly owned banks. For instance, nearly every developed nation has had a public postal banking system that deposited people's savings directly to public treasuries. England was the first to open such a postal savings bank in 1861 to encourage people to save for a rainy day. Other countries like France, Belgium, and Japan soon followed. The savings of a nation's people were seen as an inexpensive way to finance public debt.

The United States adopted a savings bank system at its postal offices in 1911 and used it successfully for decades, selling government Liberty Bonds during World War II. Its low interest rates on savings after the war made it less attractive than new money markets. The postmaster general quietly discontinued it in 1966 as part of Lyndon Johnson's government streamlining. There was little public discussion. Only recently has it again been put forward as an alternative to check-cashing services' exorbitant fees.

More than sixty-five countries have used public banking. Those of former colonies sometimes failed and a wave of privatization of publicly owned banks began, some described in Naomi Klein's *The Shock Doctrine*. For the past thirty years, the Washington consensus has operated on the assumption that privatization of banks is always more efficient. Greater growth and larger profits define this efficiency—but as we learned to ask earlier, efficient for whom?

Michael Andrews argued in an IMF working paper in 2005 that research has never really identified a bank's public nature as its cause for failure. The reasons for public bank failures are as multifarious and varied as private failures, which are much more numerous.

By 2008, we had surely learned that no bank is an island. When sound public institutions like an independent press and a functioning government with an impartial judicial system don't exist or are corrupted, public *and* private bank failures will occur, says Andrews. Then, we have to ask, who picks up the bill?

England's postal bank was privatized in 1990, sold to an investment bank, the last bit of Margaret Thatcher's privatization of government services done in the name of efficiency. It has yielded results similar to what Ellen Brown saw at work in the United States and its vested interests in the health care system. England's postal bank has been plagued by arguments similar to health care ones in the United States over who is bigger and better: Are the people better served by private or public means?

It's the wrong question and the wrong warring methodology. Neither of these sectors, the public and the private, uses a majority of women to make its biggest management decisions. Women, from experience, know that " big" matters far less than to whom any growth is attached, and "better" depends on your mutual purpose. Is it a short fling or a longer commitment? Are we growing national cooperation and trust? Who will efficiency serve? There is no reason we cannot be served by both public and private banks and services.

A Workable Stocking

If you suspect a communist plot behind public banking, consider Germany's network of state and municipal banks called the *Sparkassen* or *Landesbank*. Begun in 1801 to fight poverty, municipal savings banks to serve a public purpose multiplied. Unlike the national postal service banks, these banks are required by statute to invest locally, seating townspeople on their boards. Ellen Brown has reported that while the rest of Europe staggered from the [2008] global crisis, in 2010, Germany reported a 3.6 percent increase in its economic growth.

In fact, German exports led the world until 2009 when China (with a population of 1.3 billion) narrowly overtook Germany (with a population of only 82 *million*). How was Germany able to do this? Brown wrote in an *OpEd News* piece in 2011, "One overlooked key to the country's economic dynamism is its strong public banking system, which focuses on serving the public interest rather than on maximizing private profits. After World War II, it was the publicly owned Landesbanks that helped family-run provincial companies get a foothold in world markets."

Such local investment is at the heart of recent US effort, too. Fifteen US states have submitted legislation from both sides of the aisle to consider a state-owned bank like the BND or the Landesbanks, including Ellen Brown's state of California and my own state of Vermont. Vermont's bill was defeated in 2012, winning as compromise a transfer of 10 percent of public receipts by the state treasurer, to create millions in direct local lending. This financed solar energy and increased housing efficiency that wouldn't have happened otherwise, a step in the right direction. But it misses the long-term fix that a public bank can provide.

A treasurer is elected for the short term while a bank is an ingenious money multiplier with an institutional lifetime greater than its founders. A state-owned bank will outlive shifting political winds once it is up and operating. Its creation of credit grows money for the future—so the advocacy group Vermonters for a New Economy will have to keep trying.

Government, while it can be the problem, can also serve as a good roll of duct tape when democracy is working well. Financial networks well populated by savvy women could keep the gush of global finance, with its overleveraged lint, from clogging up our local works. A public bank owned by the people gives empowered voice to local community needs and common goals, whatever the politics of the day.

✓ CREDIT UNIONS

A more egalitarian financial environment where women managers appear to thrive, credit unions grew out of Europe's cooperative movement of the 1850s, first appearing in the United States in 1909. As nonprofit organizations, credit unions are owned by their members who elect their board. Today, credit unions lead the US financial industry in women's leadership, numbering fully 57 percent of their CEOs and 70 percent of employees.

During the 1970s when women's banks were forming, feminist credit unions were, too, with a special mission to serve and educate underserved women. By 1976, there were eighteen such credit unions. Men could join, too, but only when they were also members of the League of Women Voters or the National Organization for Women. The Equal Opportunities Credit Act that helped end discrimination in the mid-1970s affected women's credit unions as they did women's banks. It became harder to compete.

In 2012, when the National Credit Union Administration (NCUA) closed down the Women's Southwest Credit Union in Dallas, it blamed "too idealistic loaning practices," the same reason others had closed. Women's undercapitalization is a problem that will take a lot of creative thinking.

A small-sized loan to a woman with a micro-business costs just as much to assess for risk and to service as does a large loan to a millionaire businessman. The latter brings in bigger profits. The NCUA has found the larger the assets of the credit union, the scarcer the number of women CEOs and upper management. Only 24 percent are women in the top tier of $100–$500 million, compared to the average 57 percent.

Bigger still matters for EconoMan. And bigger doesn't often fit women. Despite credit union advantages, serving women and their interests in credit and loans remains a tiny part of banking's business. The 2012 US Census Survey of Business Owners reveals that while women own 35 percent of US businesses, they generate only 4.23 percent of business revenues.

Most owners are self-employed and make less than $25,000. Only 10 percent have paid employees, and average revenue between 2007 and 2012 for women business owners decreased. We have to ask: Could more access to credit help them grow?

In 2016, the US Women's Chamber of Commerce, reacting to these numbers, requested proposals for partnership with an existing credit union to form what they named a Seed Federal Credit Union. While this could answer women's wildest desires for a financial body that serves and educates women business owners and mortgage seekers, its name is unfortunate. *Seed* plays on that outmoded trope of woman as ground to be plowed, while debt-money semen is the supposed homunculus of economic life, delivering those interest-born babies.

Women need to continue to stretch how we think about small businesses, cooperative exchanges, and that dual mirror of credits and debits—growth, risk, and limits—so closely attached to gender and life decisions.

A Bank Without Interest

Money works brilliantly as a medium of exchange. Local banks and credit unions serve a useful purpose, storing and lending it. Even interest works well as an incentive for circulating our surplus money instead of hoarding it. Compounding interest is unsustainable in the long run, but debt renegotiation, sliding scales, and even debt forgiveness could help us reshape familiar financial tools with jerry-rigged solutions. Who knows what ingenuity might happen when more of us begin to think of the economy as our own?

Margrit Kennedy describes one cunning solution in *Occupy Money*. Sweden's JAK bank (its acronym stands for Land-Work-Capital in Swedish) was founded in 1965. It uses the national currency but provides an interest-free template. Begun by a group of farmers—those grounded folks who most often feel downturns first—the JAK bank requires membership like a credit union does. However, instead of paying interest on the savings of depositor members, JAK awards them *savings points*. This enables them to charge members no interest for its loans.

Can that work? It apparently does. By 2008, JAK had grown to thirty-five thousand members with deposits of $97 million and loans of $86 million.

Legally, JAK is a cooperative, but Kennedy says they prefer to call themselves a *member bank* to emphasize their social solidarity. Members are expected to help one another in trouble. Education, volunteering, and local member socializing are part of their ongoing work.

Joining the bank means having a vote, as in a credit union, but it also carries responsibilities for making decisions as a custodian for the bank's development. "Shareholder value becomes careholder value," Kennedy writes. "Rather than earning profits in the conventional sense, these shareholders are custodians of profits for everyone."

The JAK bank's remarkable interest-free difference sets it apart from typical savings banks—even public ones like North Dakota's. Let's say you need $200,000 to buy a home. Like any bank, JAK requires you to save $20,000 as 10 percent of the loan amount, the down payment up front. Each month's mortgage payment will be only slightly less than conventional banks: $1,511 a month for a JAK mortgage, compared to $1,568 at the average 8 percent interest of conventional banks. So why join JAK?

The astonishing difference is that nearly half of what you pay, about $654 a month, will be credited to your savings account. By the time your mortgage is paid, you will have in the bank $196,200 in savings, a plus for the bank and all its members. Imagine the assets that women could grow with such a bank!

You can cash out up to 90 percent of your savings for your needs, using portions for home improvements or to purchase another home, or to buy equipment for your business. You can also give it away. Perhaps your kids need to buy a home, or you want a nonprofit or an unfortunate fellow member to receive a gift. But you are not allowed to sell or rent out these savings for interest-usury, or conventional interest-born unearned income.

While interest rates for loans at conventional banks and credit unions will change, adjusted to meet the fluctuating global market, JAK cannot increase loan fees without a vote from its membership. So it provides greater long-term security by keeping fees extremely low and steady.

Kennedy writes that conventional banks must cover four costs by charging us interest. First, is the cost of liquidity. Banks pay interest on customer deposits and on any short-term loans they may need to clear their daily checks. Second, they buy insurance for risking debts that might not be paid, and to hedge inflation. Third, they pay for staff salaries, supplies, and office overhead. And finally, they return a profit to stockholders, the people who first capitalized the bank.

The JAK bank removes most of these costs: the payment of interest to depositors; the shareholder's dividend; and much of the personnel and overhead cost. When a loan is first taken out, borrowers must pay a 6 percent *risk premium* as insurance, but after a period of on-time payments, JAK returns this money.

Importantly, there is no inflation because there is no interest, the deposits and loans kept nearly equal, balancing each other out. As a result, fees are kept to just 2 percent of the loan, not the comparative 8 percent, compounded.

Might your local co-op or credit union consider starting such an asset-building program for women, or a separate cooperative member bank?

How Indian Women Can Lead Us

After thirty years of free market thinking, Americans are on the way to catching up with India. Newly competing in what is euphemistically referred to as a flexible global workforce, with fewer jobs because of technology, fully 40 percent of US workers today are independent contractors, or what the US Department of Labor calls *contingent workers*, meaning they have no guarantees. In India, only about 10 percent of workers have full-time jobs with benefits, the majority working for subsistence on the land or hired for short-term jobs, essentially self-employed as contract workers.

These are the workers that English economist Guy Standing writes about in *The Precariat: The Dangerous New Class*, a growing world phenomenon. Even when well-educated, these workers' short-term contracts with newspapers, universities, and businesses grant no more economic stability than other migrant workers, no benefits or pensions. Interestingly, Standing expresses hope in the example of Indian women who have slapped together impressive practical fixes of financial do-it-yourself, rather similar to Maggie L. Walker's cooperative Penny Savings Bank and my enterprising mom.

In 1917, Indian textile workers, inspired by Mahatma Gandhi and led by Anasuya Sarabhai, a pioneer in the women's labor movement, formed a trade union. The Textile Labour Association (TLA) was not interested in warring or defeating an enemy from the beginning. Their core value was nonviolence, and they sought to raise women's consciousness and unity through meetings and education.

In 1971, a group of women who were living on the street came to the TLA looking for housing. They talked to Ela Bhatt, another woman organizer, about their work carrying fabrics on their heads or in carts from warehouse to factory. Their wages were low and erratic, won only by waiting on the steps of merchant warehouses, hoping to be chosen.

Bhatt wrote their story for the local paper, and the fabric merchants, very upset, countered with a story of their own about their fair policies and decent contract practices. Bhatt's next move was wily. She copied the merchants' high-principled story and gave it to the women to use in their negotiations with the merchants.

This was so successful that TLA and Bhatt launched a new Self-Employed Women's Association, or SEWA. Theirs was a brand-new notion, because SEWA's workers were not employees but their own bosses. They were entrepreneurs and business owners. At first the government's labor department refused to let them register. With no opposing employer, against whom would this union battle?

Rather than thinking in old ways about winning a war against an employer enemy, SEWA foresaw the empowerment possible when women organized to help each other with social protection. Over the past forty years, SEWA's four hundred thousand members have grown to seven hundred thousand women.

I particularly love the organizational chart on their website. They see themselves as a great banyan tree—an organism, not an organization, and certainly not a pyramid of unfeeling stone. That makes their economic world less abstract and theoretical, more concrete and alive—and I could even say *sexy*.

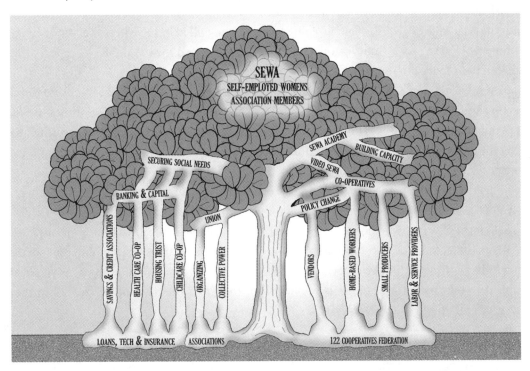

We've redrawn it here. The banyan tree's trunk is SEWA's union; its leaves are its many members. Its great branches define needs and structures they devised to serve rural development, social security, and fair social policy. Similar to Mondragon's collective diversity, their dozens of trade groups include all kinds of economic players, including agricultural workers, garment stitchers, cart pullers, and scrap collectors.

But SEWA's banyan tree also sends its branches down into the ground to nourish the whole. Its services include childcare, training, and legal aid. Its cooperatives access networked markets for raw materials, contracts, and management training. Seeing the need for more formal education, SEWA organized its own academy.

And seeing a need for extending credit and loans at reasonable rates, SEWA created its own bank. It has been staffed and serviced by women for forty years now. The bank has grown from a team of five women, working out of the union office lobby, to seven branches and 250 women on staff.

SEWA's bank provides services for those unused to banks. They educate those who have never had a personal or business account. SEWA's education services encourage poor women to avoid debt, understand interest, and practice thrift and savings. Every penny counts.

The bank provides life insurance, asset titles, and mortgage recovery; and importantly for women in business, credit for the purchase of needed equipment and repairs, and for connecting with green energy sources. Their website says green loans have helped two hundred thousand women purchase efficient cooking stoves and solar lanterns. They also encourage pensions.

Instead of the standard bank practice of charging more interest for loans to this extremely high-risk group of poor women, SEWA's tiny loans are made at very low interest rates—and always in the context of a peer group of encouraging women who will help solve personal problems when they inevitably arise. As a result of their making economics so personal, SEWA reports that 95 percent of their loans are repaid fully.

SEWA knows and cares about the women they loan to, maintaining a relationship aimed at educating and empowering her at every stage of her life. This wider vision of a common welfare is part of public banking as well. The JAK bank operates this way, too, and so do the best small banks and credit unions. All are as humble and useful as pantyhose and duct tape, providing that one financial stitch in time that saves nine.

So there's more than one way to skin a cat. Fat-cat bankers are not the only ones out there and surely not the smartest or the safest bet. Look for women-led banks and credit unions to see if you can't help form new pathways for women's wider financial livelihoods in your community.

If banks create money, why shouldn't women create more banks, or even different species of money? That, I think, is the sexiest economic idea of all. Some already are doing it, as you'll see in Chapter 19—but first let me talk to you about that other invisible hand of our economy, the one much greater than self interest. It's *love*.

Quick Rehash:

- She who owns a bank, whether private or public, multiplies money. The question of how to use it remains.
- Adding a network of well-run public banks to America's century-old private banking system would end a monopoly.
- Whether public or private, banking becomes risky whenever and wherever corruption is tolerated, and public trust is violated.

EconoGirlfriend Conversation Starter

What's your most embarrassing banking moment? Your happiest one?

Chapter 18: Ending the Old Double Standard

Huge changes underway make dominance and war obsolete.
It's time for a dancing revolution—and fast!

After she became a widow, Mom took up with a gaggle of spinster girlfriends who, despite my mom's conservative politics, seemed pretty feminist to me. She read my feminist novel and told me it was pretty good, and when she died, years and years after a bad time of falling out, it was disorienting, like losing a brick wall I'd spent my life pushing up against. She was steadfast and stubborn. I still miss her.

My dad had already died, and I knew by then how much my father's attentions had shaped my girlhood. His sitting me on his lap and reading me the funny papers during our Sunday visits to the family farm had taught me the value of story, and the ways language and tone shape purpose. Becoming Dick Tracy, he'd confide raspy secrets to his wrist radio and me, tracking gangster Fly-Face—and next he was Prince Valiant, swooshing nobility with the Singing Sword. He'd check in with me, translating when needed, making sure I was following.

He didn't just disappear, as often happened with divorced dads in those days. He took me hiking at the farm, and taught me about the toolshed and the coal-burning furnace. Even after he remarried and had five more kids, Dad regularly drove hours to bring me home, pitching balls into my new catcher's mitt, taking my picture every chance he got, embarrassing me with declarations of love when he tucked me in at night.

I was lucky to have such an expressive parent, more affectionate than my mom could be. But then Dad had heaps of social permission for showing confidence and becoming my hero. No one had expected much from Peggy Mae.

While still a girl, she'd been worked hard and badly frightened, scared to wear her heart on her sleeve. Same as I did, she identified with males, but differently. She thought if you were lucky, one would protect you. In return, she protected every male prerogative, whether in the church, in the company she worked for, or in her politics. She sided with the standing order that said males equaled power and money. She chose, as I imagine our foremothers did for thousands of years, to align with her best hope for safety.

Constructed Norms

EconoMan is not the individual and varied men that you and I love, even should your individual guy happen to work on Wall Street. When I object to EconoMan, I am speaking of masculine social constructs and cultural norms, which mothers no doubt helped to hammer and nail. Probably you have seen what I have, that those hierarchical structures that feminize and humiliate lower ranks are no kinder to the majority of men than to those of us with labia.

The rigid pyramid structure of command that men climb and enforce does work for the short term, protecting us in battles or disasters. But it does not serve our essential, joined exchanges in the long run. Individual men are as varied as we women, but they typically have not had a reason to think much about masculinity's meaning. For five thousand years, mankind has tried to disown the female, in us and in themselves.

We've already seen, in Chapter 11: Egg Money, a fuller human biological tale at least a million years old. Sex and connection drove our story's plot. In the beginning, women's reproductive powers were obvious when she bled monthly without dying. She gave birth in bloody dramas of new life miracles. Her seemingly independent life-giving powers gave her status, reflected in those carved figures, thirty thousand years old.

Historian Robert McElvaine and other researchers posit that before men knew their role in reproduction, they compensated. They didn't menstruate. So they defined themselves with blood shed in puberty rituals, hunting, and sacrifices. Man did not give life. He took it.

When hunter-gatherer groups stopped migrating about ten thousand years ago to grow food in settled places, they depleted hunting stock. Men then had "an unemployment problem," as McElvaine puts it in *Eve's Seed*. They resorted to women's work, namely planting seeds and herding tame animals instead of hunting wild ones. This must have caused disruption, confusion, and free-floating resentment.

Over time, herding made clearer the billy goat's ability to pass down traits. McElvaine believes a second mistaken idea about conception then "reversed the apparent positions of the sexes. . . . What had always appeared to be a principally female power was transformed into an entirely male power." Language newly associated males planting *semen* in females with farmers planting seeds in the ground. (*Semen* literally means seed in Latin.)

Death and Taxes

These reversed ideas about the source of human life eventually brought us pharaohs, kings, male gods, and armies with the power of life-and-death. Man took land and woman for labor-intensive farming, but competing raiders could steal both. So taxes, a form of tribute, began to be paid to the nearest warrior king in return for his pledge of protection.

✓ TAXES

The Latin root, *taxare*, means "to assess." Eventually, the word *tax* added a sense of burden and threat. Violence and protection money go together. Early taxes were paid in labor, to build pyramids and temples, or paid in staples like grain that could be stored for emergencies. As government grew more complex, taxes did, too.

The obligation of paying money to a government takes many forms, but tends to shift the burden to those least able to object. The tea tax of England underestimated New World colonies' readiness to revolt. Since its founding, the United States has debated who pays tax and how much. In a democracy, taxes still pit *us* against *them,* on the way to claiming a shared *we.*

About five hundred years ago, male explorers, merchants, and traders began reconceptualizing our world as a marketplace, says McElvaine. More of us became mobile again, untied from agriculture by sweeping industrial and transportation changes. But now, it is we women who face an unemployment problem for our traditional role.

An oversupply of population threatens our environment. Less human labor is needed when high-tech robotics compete in global markets. As a result, birth rates are falling worldwide, and women find themselves doing "men's work."

Capitalists get a bargain in women today, but things are still pretty muddled, as it must have been back in those early times of agriculture. Fundamentalists assert the old order, while the near religion of economics attempts to explain a new marketplace order. There's confusion, disruption, and a lot of free-floating resentment, judging from the 2015 global purchases of $1,676 billion on weapons.

✓ NATIONAL SPENDING & NATIONAL DEBT

Like people, nations have income, called revenue. US revenues in 2015 were $3.18 trillion, sourced from income tax (47 percent), FICA payroll taxes (34 percent), and corporate income tax (11 percent). Eight percent came from other fees and tariffs, and interest gained from investments.

Unlike people, nations can borrow from themselves. US payroll taxes go into trust funds, including Medicare and Social Security. Trust fund money is invested in treasury bonds for government operations to gain interest. National governments can spend at higher levels than individuals can. Some economists think up to 90 percent of GDP is safe. FY 2015 federal budget spending was $3.8 trillion, or about 21 percent of GDP.

For forty-five of the past fifty years, US spending has exceeded revenues, and the nation worries about debt. But we need to look at our war costs, both past and present. National Priorities finds that just since 2001, a male-majority Congress has enacted over forty-five appropriations for war expenses. US war costs incurred from 2001 to 2015 amount to nearly $18 trillion.

Past and Future

War's bloodshed has been the theme of the collective history we've most often heard the past five thousand years. Only this past century has its unquestioned heroism itself come into question. John Lennon's haunting musical refrain called it out for my generation, sick of Vietnam: All we are saying is give peace a chance.

Part of every life is the history behind it. But the other part is a longing for what is not yet known. Living individual decisions combine what we learn from experience with a hankering to try what we don't know for sure, or haven't yet done. A sensual curiosity marks Eros at work in biology's dynamism, whether you're a microbe or a primate. It's the core of adaptation.

Your personal passion right now might be for a red-hot lover or a hoped-for degree, a career, a family, or maybe a journey, a particular project on your bucket list. Once that desire is won, or perhaps lost, over time your passions change. They surely can be deadened. But a purpose larger than you unlocks the will to accomplish things you never dreamed you could.

Our language lights up with phrases that recognize this erotic impetus at work in the big and the little things. That's exciting, we say. Or, I love, I adore, that purse, dress, movie! This idea turns me on. That lights my fire. Longing for what is more beautiful than deserved, more magnificent than can be hoped without trembling, we court our future and work tirelessly for its realization. Without Eros, we lose our way.

This drive keeps on provoking humans to risk love and make commitments, as humans have done for eons, or else none of us would be here now. Your own families, whatever your culture, hold tales of a crazy kind of devotion, of wholehearted persistence against all odds. The jet stream wobbles, the reefs bleach and die, the Arctic melts. Will humans be able to adapt again to make sure future generations survive? Few other species have adapted so diversely to changing environments of every type. Judging from unprecedented protests worldwide against corrupt governments and war, people feel a growing imperative for change. What can unite us?

✓ WOMEN'S ECONOMIC STATUS

The International Finance Corporation with the World Bank estimates that women perform 66 percent of the world's work, produce 50 percent of its food, but earn just 10 percent of global income. Women comprise two-thirds of the world's illiterate people, and one-third of the world's girls are married before age eighteen. Women own 30 percent of registered businesses worldwide, but only 1 percent of property.

How Now?

We're already beginning to adapt. Human work roles shift in the light of our unprecedented longevity. We know now about the dual sources of life. Mom *and* Dad are both required for sustaining life. Menstrual blood and patriarchal semen sorted us into the original *us* and *them*, which enabled all others. But now such divided thinking only gets in our way.

Revising old ideas about male dominance and female subordination goes way beyond the treatment of individual women. It goes to the root of how we organize ourselves and the way we look at the world. It requires new metaphors and redefinition of what we call productive work, and what we choose to most value.

Riane Eisler describes wider marketplace potential in her book, *The Real Wealth of Nations*. She writes, "Our capacity for caring is just as wired into us by evolution as our capacity for cruelty—perhaps even more so. . . . We humans are equipped with a neurochemistry that gives us pleasure when we care for others." Why then shortchange it?

Our homes, once supposedly women's separate domain, stand emptier today. More of us have rented out our lives to the market, gone mobile, gone global. We compete, we race to win, we live with terror and war. But the old, imaginary wall separating the home sphere from the market sphere is crumbling, brick by brick. As usual, Eros has driven the story's plot.

Practical Erotic

"The past is prologue," Shakespeare wrote. The comfortable but bored middle-class women of Betty Friedan's *Feminine Mystique* were expressing their awakening Eros in the early 1960s. They sought to outgrow the given. Just a few years later, 1969, Rollo May wrote *Love and Will,* warning of apathy, addictions, and violence that came from losing Eros.

Then in 1978, Audre Lorde wrote a remarkable essay called "Uses of the Erotic: The Erotic as Power." In it, Lorde, like May, first warned of the dangers of avoiding self-knowledge: "We have been raised to fear the 'yes' within ourselves, our deepest cravings." She called this "living outside ourselves."

When we are directed by external marketing messages, not living "from within outward," she said, we lose what we most need: a sense of deep responsibility to ourselves and to our inmost longings and abilities. We confuse the erotic with the pornographic because "the erotic has often been misnamed by men and used against women. . . . But pornography is a direct denial of the power of the erotic, for it represents the suppression of true feeling."

She described Eros's absence from an economic system that defined good in terms of profit, rather than good in terms of meeting human need. That economic design defined our human needs without including its psychic or emotional parts: "The principal horror of such a system is tantamount to blinding a painter and then telling her to improve her work, and to enjoy the act of painting. It is not only next to impossible; it is also profoundly cruel."

An African American lesbian poet, author of *Sister Outsider*, Lorde came out of the closet into a world that hated her color, had no time for poets, and was freaked by lesbian love. Yet she still aspired to a future, free-and-welcoming world it was foolish to dream of embracing. Lorde didn't live to see Edith Windsor's triumph of love and marriage in the US Supreme Court in 2013, but the late Audre and Thea Spyer must have opened their arms to encircle our changing world.

By then Beatle John Lennon was dead too, but his song lyrics still ring out, above a chatter of verbiage, insisting on change: All we are saying is give peace a chance. Even straight men are examining themselves and masculinity's warring intersections with racism, sexism, and LGBTQ (Lesbian, Gay, Bisexual, Trans, Queer/Questioning) issues. A conference my husband attended featured a keynote by Eve Ensler of *The Vagina Monologues*. She asked: "What greater tragedy is there than for a man to be separated from his own heart?"

Men, too, can learn to "live from within," though money still talks in a male voice to police them to live outside themselves. The day after Trump's inauguration in 2017, unprecedented crowds spoke out for our right to be united in our desire to love more, not less. I saw fathers, husbands, and brothers unafraid to march with wives, daughters, and sisters, all claiming a nation freer of sexism, racism, hatred, and exclusion. We don't have time for it, if we mean to survive.

To confront one's most tender and vulnerable fears and hopes—as my father dared in a time when dads stayed distant from caring, and as my mother risked, venturing into moneymaking worlds—takes nerve. I can recognize that now that I'm older. Their active, loving role modeling enabled us kids to adapt and recognize joy, a self-defined love and laughter.

Most often, that joyful love and laughter is regularly blocked by problems and frustrations, totally out of any one person's control. And yet it persists inside, finding pleasure there, finding pleasure with others. In a confusing, blaring era of markets that reduces everything and everyone to commodities, that inner energy named Eros becomes a shared human imperative.

More Caring Markets

The tumult of our families these days includes beautiful and complicated male caregivers, high-powered and formidable women careerists, brothers and sisters coming out of the closet, and many who intentionally make homes with and without children.

Highly intelligent and caring, few members in our families aspire to dominate an imaginary pyramid. McElvaine and May both say that the sexually insecure seem most motivated to prove themselves that way.

Questions of power, whether public or private, quickly get personal. What does one do with the erotic power one has? Cultural paradigms come in handy when you ask that question. Caring adults model behavior, helping children and each other to make sense of the world. Is it power *over*? Or power *with*?

It has been both. Our human need to belong to a distinctive group has resulted in wars but also in the sharing of family and community that forges identity, no trivial function. An identity is first shaped from outside by cultural values, then honed from inside. But in the new world of the marketplace, paying attention to this once natural process gets harder.

Selected for Survival

Milton Friedman, the economist you met in Part I of this book, proposed that markets act as *selection vehicles*. It is a strange phrase, mixing a constructed conveyance with Darwin's idea of natural selection. Picture a pickup truck filled with lions and lambs. Darwin's phrase described the long genetic process by which adaptive traits enabled survival. Friedman explained that as businesses compete, unsuccessful rivals (the lambs, I'm guessing) fail to capture the needed market share, go bankrupt, and have to exit. In shorthand, market vehicles rationalize the belief that the strongest and best just naturally win the market's profit game, selected for survival of the fittest.

The market's money *keeps score*, a phrase that carries whiffs of threat and sexual braggadocio. But market capitalism's selection chooses not what biology needs, but what works for producing the biggest piles of money. The market's selection vehicles overlook Darwin's most important point.

The species that are Darwin's fittest are the ones best able to adapt environmentally suitable methods for the survival of their young. Ingenious parenting and symbiotic alliances, flexibility, and sexy connections are the real essence of evolutionary fitness. For social animals, like us humans doing business and growing a market economy, any child's boredom and apathy, addiction or violence—any child's hunger, fear, or loneliness—holds costs to our species and the ecosystems where we live. So does the desperation of microbes and tiny life forms we don't even understand yet, but depend upon.

If we were to take Darwin's evolutionary standard for a market's measure as a selection vehicle, we would expect the bottom lines of nations and companies to be more concerned about the stability of children's families where they do business. Is the offspring of a town, a state, or a nation drinking clean water? Eating healthy food? Are all the children learning and above average? Do they play well with others? That data can be generated, if we want to help communities adapt for long-term survival.

Relationship Numbers

The Gaia Theory of James Lovelock, mentioned in Chapter 15, and the ideas of Marilyn Waring, who first wrote about the shortsightedness of the GDP described in Chapter 13, have birthed a new generation of environmental economic thinkers. They attempt to value nature's systems. Its methods could be used to better value human care systems, too.

In my state of Vermont, a recent report to our legislature accounted for our forests' removal of carbon in the air equal to that emitted by fourteen thousand cars, plus another 1,610 metric tons of other pollutants each year. For every dollar spent on forests, we saved twenty-seven dollars on the cost of purifying water. Such numbers make it easier to defend forest preservation. It gives a fuller accounting. Vermont's attention had been heightened by a terrible flood, worsened by treeless riverbanks.

Economists still largely depend on masculine narratives, however, thinking ultrarationally about a data-based science that masters all. Numbers cannot quantify the invaluable as completely as poetry might, but no doubt legislative readers of that report brought their own heartfelt experience of forests and flooding to their funding decisions and those numbers.

Vermont's life at home provides biological services that shape Vermont lives, too. Yet its services remain mostly uncalculated, the will to know human care's value not so great an immediate pressure. Such services are still provided freely, and most families are not yet out in the street, yelling. Not yet. Green economists give us an example of what could be calculated.

What is the value of Vermont families preparing and eating meals together? How much time do we spend talking together? How much money do we spend on dinners out? What is the cost of multiple TVs, phones, and cars? How thin do family members feel they are stretched, on a scale of one to ten?

Macro Walls

In 1967, I smacked up against that old economic wall separating nest making from moneymaking. Frankly, I loved caring for my nest and my babies. They brought out my best. While they napped, I had time for reading, cooking, creating art, and thinking. Forty years ago more of us could still afford to volunteer for such caring, at least for a few years.

EconoMan's market selection vehicles drove my consumer choices. Money spent was counted in the GDP, but not my vital production of three intelligent dynamos, my children—who more than tripled my output of human ingenuity. Omitting living production from our economic accounts makes it easier to steal the wealth of women's time and pleasure—as well as eons of soil, forests, and oceans—and convert it into those piles of paper money.

Though our species' economic future depends on our offspring thriving, a third of American pregnant workers take no maternity leave, reported MomsRising in late 2015. The BLS and its National Compensation Survey (NCS) found in 2016 that only 14 percent of civilian workers had access to paid family leave. Only California and New Jersey have financed six weeks of leave for mothers, and Rhode Island two weeks, all through employee-paid insurance programs that cost workers as little as forty-five cents a week. New York (2018), the District of Columbia (2020), and Washington (2020) are scheduled in the years indicated. Benefits vary, and only Washington shares the cost with employers.

Unfortunately, even this new insurance applies only to companies with twenty workers or more. A caregiver who works with a family, a clerk in a small store, or a self-employed consultant remains out of luck should she get pregnant.

The richest nation on earth could fund far more than six weeks of leave through social insurance for every parent, or better yet, a universal insurance paid by everyone, since everyone's future counts on the next generation. Norway, for instance, provides thirty-five weeks of maternity leave at 100 percent pay, and an additional ten weeks at 80 percent pay if a mother chooses. Dads get fourteen weeks at 90 percent of pay. New mothers also qualify for a child benefit that helps pay the cost of parenting. Little Finland provides twenty-three weeks of paid maternity leave and eight weeks of paternity leave.

Most developed and developing countries also have reliable and accessible daycare programs and enough sick time and vacation time to allow parents to work without the stress so common here in the United States.

Vermont's former governor, Madeleine Kunin, wrote *The New Feminist Agenda: Defining the Next Revolution for Women, Work, and Family* to encourage young women ready to organize and accomplish what a few states have already managed. But she says the family values of some politicians need to be radically redefined. We need family-work policies that help sustain strong families and a strong economy—for today, not for a bygone ideal that was always unfair.

She considers childcare a national security issue. Why? Because the best childcare system in the United States is funded by the Department of Defense, she says, showing us the way to a system that would make every family safer and more secure. Her arguments "that the cost to the nation of our inaction is greater than the cost of action; that investment in family/work policies fosters economic growth, and that we must share this investment for our children, our grandchildren, and the nation" bear repeating in your state.

Such policies would require that US money go where so little US money has gone before—over the crumbling wall that divides the public from the private, a masculine construction that withholds filthy lucre from our homes, the real selection vehicles of our survival.

Layer Cakes and Frosting

It would take me years of working and writing, following the money and always personally falling short, before I met up with a graph of economic reality that finally made sense to me. It's the brainchild of Hazel Henderson, a futurist and economic iconoclast who thought ethical markets were smart business. You'll remember Pareto believers think ethics irrelevant to efficiency and profit. But Henderson became a world leader in responsible investing. Today, she is no amateur in anyone's view.

Henderson's graph sets the sweetest, richest part of the cake—the monetized frosting of corporations, business, and finance—up on top of four layers. That confection of ownership, as in private enterprise and private property, could not be enjoyed without the other layers in place, holding it up, she argued, in this graphic and many books.

The public sector, the next-highest layer where government and nonprofits prevent chaos, is also maintained by money; it helps to keep social order and protects the position of the frosting

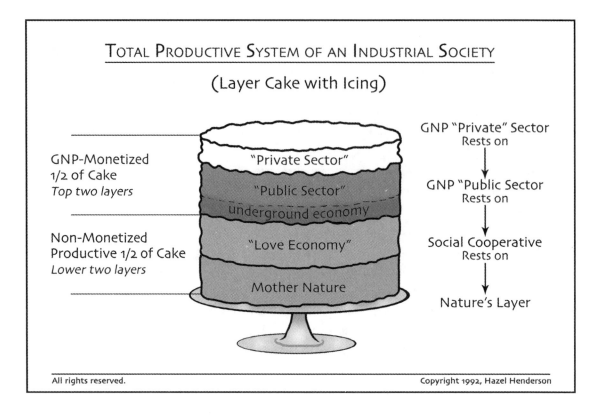

TOTAL PRODUCTIVE SYSTEM OF AN INDUSTRIAL SOCIETY

(Layer Cake with Icing)

GNP-Monetized
1/2 of Cake
Top two layers

"Private Sector"

"Public Sector"

underground economy

Non-Monetized
Productive 1/2 of Cake
Lower two layers

"Love Economy"

Mother Nature

GNP "Private" Sector
Rests on

↓

GNP "Public Sector
Rests on

↓

Social Cooperative
Rests on

↓

Nature's Layer

Copyright 1992, Hazel Henderson

up top. A nearly hidden layer, the illegal underground economy, gets a slice of stolen money too, a kind of custard filling our government carefully tracks. All three top layers are monetized, their dollars counting in our nation's GDP, and the BEA going to great trouble to define their data and analyze their dollar numbers.

GDP leaves out the two biggest layers of economic cake that the three monetized layers rely upon, whether they acknowledge it or not. Her cake is a clear picture of who depends upon whom. What Henderson names *the love economy* is the same sector that you'll remember Simon Kuznets, Marilyn Waring, and Duncan Ironmonger all sought to count, too.

Like the illegal realm, the love layer's valuation would require some educated guesswork, but it has been done in many nations. Green economists have valued nature's production, too. But Henderson's cake still pictures the status quo here in the United States, with love and nature ineffable and uncounted here.

✓ ETHICAL INVESTING

When Hazel Henderson began, she discovered data needed to invest more wisely did not exist. She worked with the Calvert Group, an investment group, to gather more comprehensive statistics beyond the typical dollar measures. In 2000, these were named Calvert-Henderson Quality of Life Indicators.

> With this new data, investors could put their hard-earned dollars where a healthy environment and society were more likely to sustain businesses with lasting returns. It even exposed damaging business practices and human rights violations.

Twenty-five years ago, only fifty-five mutual funds engaged in socially responsible investing and its more comprehensive data; they held $12 billion in assets. By 2012, there were 493 such funds with assets of $569 billion. Their global dollars have now reached the trillions.

Today, nearly every corporate website lays claim to socially responsible efforts. Getting past their gloss requires research. Many mutual funds provide this data, as does US-SIF and the Forum for Sustainable and Responsible Investment. Of special interest is their report, Investing to Advance Women. It cites several studies that show businesses with women on their boards outperform all-male boards.

Investors today can make better-informed choices than they could when Henderson began to question money-only measures. Most telling, however, are these funds' solid returns. It makes good business sense to pay attention to a bigger picture. Henderson's generative thinking brought us a greater awareness of the wider ecosystems needed for healthy business exchanges, and the economic harm that comes with perpetual war-think.

Unpaid Labor Persists

Even socially responsible investors never, ever invest money in that most private enterprise of home, the great un-profit—unless it is their own. Our homes may be where the maintenance of our human life, its brains, and its nerve goes on, but no one wants to profit from home or family. It gets ethically sticky.

A livable wage helps homes indirectly, and a market selection vehicle does exist for homemaking and care. It's Cruella's Cadillac, I'm afraid, driving only in one direction, away from your own home. Caring for another woman's children or another woman's aging parents will pay you wages. Caring for your own will not.

At times market vehicles separate a whole culture's mothers from her children, as with Filipino mothers, working as nannies in the United States, sending cash back home. Rachel Aviv in a 2016 article from the *New Yorker* quotes their president calling them "the heroes of our economy." But at what cost? Does it have to be that way? See more ahead.

Henderson's cake shows the economic world's hierarchical arrangement, its elements and relationships made visible. The energy of Eros baked this economic cake and not just the love layer. Love is more one-dimensional than the erotic, as I'm using it here. The erotic includes all our genetic information and urges—even the ones for competition and violence.

Henderson's cake brilliantly shows current old thinking, which endangers us, viewing nature and emotion as separate and lower. Yet within all these cake layers of our economic ecosystem, biology's erotic dynamics, its transformative exchanges, preserve conditions for life—and never simply.

Without molecule-sized exchanges in each layer, there'd be no cake. Heat makes baking powder form little bubbles of gas, and changes egg from liquid to solid. Without similar tiny exchanges in daily lives, there'd be no living energy, no heat.

Rollo May describes the complex generative dynamic at work within our psyche that enables us to change and adapt within any of these layers: "We are in Eros not only when we experience our biological, lustful energies, but also when we are able to open ourselves and participate, via imagination and emotional and spiritual sensitivity, in forms and meanings beyond ourselves in the interpersonal world and the world of nature around us."

Living social networks and interconnected ecosystems include all sorts of investors and many kinds of investments, but only a few are moneyed. The economy's total production, bought and sold in markets, relies first upon generous and forgiving production in nature and at home. If we add women's concrete reality into a joint economic history, we find that we have not only warred and competed, but also collaborated and made big love.

Together, all these elements create a generative economic ecology, highly complex, and always moving, adjusting, and selecting—no mechanical vehicle needed.

Nested Survival

Another amateur economist, political scientist Elinor Ostrom, actually won the not-quite Nobel Prize in Economics in 2009. Her research focused on shared public resources, such as water sources and their living production. She is the only woman ever to have been so honored.

Like Milton Friedman, Ostrom was no believer in big government solutions, but her winning this cherished prize challenged purely mathematical economics. It opened the auto-locked doors on those neoliberal vehicles of market selection that only drive in one direction.

Biologist David Sloan Wilson reported these reactions to her Nobel win, written on a blog frequented by job-seeking economic faculty, still mostly male:

- What kind of bullshit is this? This year is the worst.
- Well, they had to give it to a woman at some point. Why not just throw a dart at a board.
- Never heard of Ostrom in my life. Lame.
- This girl seems to be a political scientist. I don't think she has published original research in any major economics journal.
- Multidisciplinary?? Other disciplines are all rubblish [sic]. Why let them conteminate [sic] our purity?

A few writers were more respectful of Ostrom's political and social ideas widening economic thought, Wilson reminded us, but mathematicians remain the majority of economists. "Be afraid," he wrote.

Ostrom grew up in poverty and came to her education post-divorce. Her eclectic career adapted to a time that discounted a woman working in an elite man's world, the university. Ostrom had asked the question: How do humans manage what is not owned by anyone? Her discoveries about successful governing of the commons could help us to manage our common and un-own-able erotic contributions to the economy.

Her work began with water management. She bucked the notion that free, competitive markets alone would save us. California's sinking water table, overgrazing, and overfishing were all proof that no invisible hand of the market would guide everyone's pursuit of self-interest to collective well-being. But as she said of herself, she was an optimist.

Some cultures had long inhabited an area with shared resources, sustaining them. How had they come to whatever agreements that had succeeded? When cooperation failed, how exactly did it fail? Ostrom researched and analyzed ways that small self-regulating groups of people could and did share vital resources in the commons.

Her research revealed a diversity of smaller groups nested within larger ones, her word *nested* letting in just a tad of feeling and care. She found groups that sheltered the commons within a neighborhood, a town, a state, a nation, a whole rookery of nest makers. For instance, shareholders in a river's health organized in nested ways, with intersections of circling exchanges cooperating locally, regionally, and for a variety of purposes, including for fishing, for health, for manufacturing, for local water use.

She came up with a list of traits or principles that researchers use today for policy analysis. These might strike you as common sense, but she named our common sense parts, and she measured them. First, everyone had to know who they were, and what the function of their group was. Identity mattered. Second, small groups worked better than big ones. Next, all members had to be involved in the rulemaking. A failure to build consensus harmed trust. Ostrom found that trust was most essential.

When trust was built, then fairness had to be imposed by a group's self-monitoring, and enforcement of agreed-upon rules. Quick and fair resolution of conflicts enabled people to keep on trusting each other. Shaming and honoring were both important group trust-building tools.

Ostrom found a great diversity of systems used around the world that enabled sharing of common resources and a great many different forms of cooperative agreements. Some were informal. Households come to mind, sharing common space and common time, with all members making diverse, informal agreements.

At my house, a rule that struck all of us as fair was: the one who cooks dinner should not have to also clean up. This has to be enforced; the hope of freeloading is universal. Sometimes there are adjustments: I *promise*! First thing in the morning. We shame; we honor. We renegotiate.

Ostrom's research revealed that public, more formal groups require similar openness, transparency, and fair enforcement of rules—or else they don't work for long. Imposing rules from high above or by force only delays an agreement's demise and leads to new, ingenious methods for subterfuge. Think of children who perceive an injustice.

Each group intersection, she found, demanded more collaboration and negotiation, rulemaking and conflict resolution that was accessible to all, and made quickly and inexpensively. Any human group can never be anything but complex, but Ostrom writes in her best-known book, *Governing the Commons*: "As long as a single center has a monopoly on the use of coercion, one has a state rather than a self-governed society." Like protection money and violence, monopolies and coercion go hand in hand.

The Erotic Commons

Herodotus first named economics during the agricultural era. Land and households produced our earliest wealth. Over time, men who owned property organized to conduct trade and make war, an ultimate coercion. The urge for manly largeness brought us monopolies of kingdoms and corporations, their laws, nations, and armies.

The founding fathers distrusted monopolized coercion, too. They separated government powers into judicial, legislative, and administrative branches, to avoid abuse. The constitutional debate—a gathering of men, remember—included arguments against forming a professional military. Elbridge Gerry of Massachusetts compared a standing army to a standing penis, calling it "an excellent assurance of domestic tranquility, but a dangerous temptation to foreign adventure."

From US beginnings the wealthiest men distrusted too much democracy and too little force. Coercion was needed for slavery, including wage slavery. Industry and economic thinking further separated home and nature from production. Corporations resisted efforts to democratize work.

All was built on assumptions of limitless renewal via women and earth. During this same era, women won enormous changes. Without weapons. Without violence. We know now that a wider democracy is far from dangerous. We begin to suspect that coerced, endless extraction and growth may well kill us.

A grounded, more generative economy would give a fuller accounting of our larger ecology. Ostrom showed how humans successfully shared the commons. A clear identity, purpose, collaboration, and democratic process enable ways to self-monitor sharing and enforce fairness.

Like air and water, biology's drive in our own lives can never be owned or monopolized. It can only be shared. But it is harder to share what remains unnamed. So I here propose a new word, *EroNomics* (pronounced ero-nomics), to help us notice and collectively govern that driver of our economy that sustains our staying alive. James Lovelock's brief Gaia theory serves as my model for an erotic theory of economic ecology.

> ## ✓ ERONOMICS
>
> *EroNomics* proposes that human organisms interact with the organic and inorganic systems of Earth to form a synergistic, self-regulating, complex system of exchanges that helps to maintain and perpetuate the conditions for life on the planet.

I know. It's a dry mouthful. But by giving a name, *EroNomics*, to this foundational system of exchanges, we can begin to see and quantify—and legitimate—those urges that madly insist we pursue our happiness. It could help us end old double standards and adapt, yet again, for creating a new future. The Persian poet Rumi long ago celebrated that crazy wisdom that has always empowered us:

> Love is reckless; not reason.
> Reason seeks a profit.
> Love comes on strong,
> consuming herself, unabashed.

EroNomics is the renewable fuel of market selection vehicles still being redesigned. It is already creating new ideas, new money, and new trust, badly needed. More about that next.

Quick Rehash:

- Denying deep feelings and self-knowledge wastes the economy's motivational fuel of Eros on materialism and addiction.
- Public and private governing of what must be shared requires a clear identity, transparency, shared rulemaking, and shared enforcement, quick and affordable.
- Monopolies and coercion go hand in hand and disrupt all-important trust.

EconoGirlfriend Conversation Starter

Can you name a time when a passionate feeling influenced an economic decision of yours wrongly? Did you learn from your experience and adapt?

Chapter 19: A Real Fixer-Upper

Building trust is a DIY project, with small local changes making the economy friendlier and more livable.

Growing up, we never lived in a home where Mom wasn't rearranging furniture, making plans for an added-on room, or knocking out a wall. When it was time for me to make a home, she was there admiring my changes, suggesting remodels. Once when my stepdad couldn't help, and a new baby made an attic conversion imperative, she and I half killed ourselves hauling drywall upstairs. When we ripped boards with a circular saw and cut drywall with a jigsaw, I understood why men call them power tools.

The smell of paint, sawdust, and wallpaper paste says home to many of us because nothing is better than saving money by doing it yourself. My youngest daughter, grown up and an experienced remodeler by now, will get a look on her face while staring at a wall, and I know she's about to widen a doorway or put in a new window. In between her own projects, she'll help her sister or revamp the offices of the organization she now runs.

Do-it-yourself ads and the pictures of the homes of the rich and famous we see everywhere intensify our wish for beauty. Back when I was working in the anti-poverty movement, I visited a woman whose home I can only call bleak. I was accompanying her tutor, who was pleased she was reading at a fourth-grade level now.

From upstairs her grown son yelled we had better be quiet, and in the kitchen, her granddaughter complained the fridge was empty. She gave the girl a glass of water mixed with a spoonful of powdered coffee creamer, a trick she'd learned to stretch groceries at month's end, she told us. Then she smiled—to ease our tension, I think, sensing our shock—and reached for another jar on the sink's windowsill. In it leaned a single, long-stemmed velvet red rose.

A neighbor had just given it to her, she said, and her detailed descriptions of the kindness, as well as her close attention to what distinguished that rose's color and shape, taught us, the teachers, the power of her pleasures against all odds.

In our common human purpose, survival, the roses of beauty, spirit, and gifts have kept us energized. Paintings on cave walls forty thousand years old show us how essential human sharing of beauty is. Long before we turned tools into weapons, we carved figures, made musical instruments, and invented sacred rites. My mother always put money in an envelope for the church's charities and taught us kids to give coins, too. There were always others less fortunate. We shared stories.

Great rooms of beauty, song, and worship express a dependable human urge for perspective. Finding awe, we can feel ourselves more rightfully a small part of the whole. It is easier, then, to be kind.

Common Rootstock

Different faiths can cause conflict, but of greater importance than differences are common wisdom traditions. These apprehend an unseen dimension of our lives, and did so long before psychologists named our drive for survival after the Greek god Eros. A faith can help you to know who you are and what the rules are, the first of Elinor Ostrom's principles.

All the oldest faith traditions attempted to grapple with bad luck, inequality, and keeping things peaceable. Faith customs operated to encourage trust within the group, the most essential element for exchanges of devoted relationships. First come kinships and partnerships, then commerce and trade.

We know from the Bible that the Israelites, for instance, built trust by forgiving debts in the year of Jubilee. There is some disagreement about which year it is—forty-ninth or fiftieth—but it hardly matters, since the custom hasn't been practiced for several hundred years. Is it out of the question today?

We've already seen that both Judaic and Muslim traditions forbade usury. Lower rates of interest would give debtors more time to pay off debts. Profits for creditors would slow down, it's true, but a longer gestation still would deliver. There are others less fortunate.

Sharia law describes *sukuk*, a committed investment relationship unlike Wall Street's quickies. The latter gobbles stock earnings, regardless of harm done. By contrast, Muslim investors expect to suffer any losses equal to those who only contribute labor and time. Shared responsibility fosters trust.

Even older Hindu tradition saw all humankind as debtors, teaching that each of us owes a debt to our Creator, to one's teachers, to one's parents, and finally to all humanity. In all the traditions I've mentioned, giving alms and food to the poor was considered a duty.

Such common beliefs have deep roots in our psyche, dug in the organics of observed life over thousands of years. Whatever its form, life requires close attention, faithful care, the more so when chances grow small and vulnerable. We all begin and end helpless, aided by others. Success only multiplies responsibilities. Even the most worthy are undone by disaster. All these common reflections no doubt resulted in debt forgiveness, grants, gifts, bequests, and other economic equalizers.

All Things Unequal

Spiritual traditions influenced Western democracies, where the wealthy have always paid a higher rate of income tax. This has been true in the United States for over 150 years. Our nation avoided aristocracy by imposing a hefty inheritance tax. Its recent renaming as the *death tax* popularized its reduction but omits this original intent. A 2015 Congressional Joint Committee on Taxation report found it affects only two percent of Americans. Taxes on the wealthy keep the economy's lifeblood, its currency, circulating.

✓ US INCOME TAX

First imposed during the Civil War, US income tax was a *flat tax* of 3 percent for all those with annual incomes over $800. The average laborer earned $297 a year and so was exempt. The flat tax was later modified to a *graduated tax*, sometimes called a *progressive tax,* meaning that higher incomes paid greater percentages.

Still, wealthy industrialists continued to get wealthier, and so they convinced Congress to repeal the tax in 1872. Meanwhile, farmers struggled and formed the populist movement. They advocated renewing the income tax, originally paid only by the wealthiest.

Hoping to kill it, wealthy opponents proposed it as a Constitutional amendment in 1909 because the process was difficult, requiring Congressional passage and then approval by two-thirds of US states. To their horror, states quickly ratified it, and the Sixteenth Amendment of 1913 established the right of Congress to impose an income tax. The devil remains in the details with the rates, deductions, exemptions, and tax credits in flux. But interestingly, the term *tax deduction* did not enter the dictionary until 1940, and *tax shelters* not until 1961.

Today's EconoMan individualism ignores older wisdom, replacing it with favor for the upper tranche only. This has been tried before by many a king and emperor, and it always ends badly. The latest episode of self-serving EconoMansplaining, detailed in the *Panama Papers*, widely reported, found twelve world leaders and twenty-nine of Forbes' 500 Richest hiding billions of dollars offshore to avoid paying taxes. It hardly surprises, except for how few Americans were named, with Panama a relatively small player. A worldwide shell game helps the richest avoid sharing in national responsibilities.

Opponents to a progressive income tax argued, and still argue, that it is an undue burden on those who make the economy strong. During the 1950s, under President Eisenhower, the tax rate for the top tier was 91 percent. Under George W. Bush, who spent trillions for new wars and bank bailouts, the top rate fell to just 35 percent.

Don't forget, though, that income for the richest today most often comes in the form of short- or long-term capital gains that pay an even lower rate of tax. Tax specialists have created an industry, finding loopholes, deductions, and capital losses to reduce upper income tax bills.

> ### ✔ US CAPITAL GAINS TAX
>
> Most working Americans pay income tax rates on their wages at 28–40 percent, while the tax rate for owners of capital assets that gain profits is 15–20 percent. Only the wealthiest Americans get to pay this lower tax on short- and long-term buys. John Stuart Mill originally called these mathematically occurring profits *unearned income*; they include the doubling interest-babies Michael Hudson identified. Congress lowered capital gains tax rates in 1997, 2001, and again in 2003.

Lowering capital gains taxation had political opposition, but it is probably fair to say that not many Americans understood the stakes on the table. The wealthiest Americans who own most of US assets typically argue their lower tax rate encourages entrepreneurism, freeing capital for business investment. But critics point to the resulting glut of untaxed, free-floating capital, resulting in greater global speculation and asset inflation. How free to roam should American capital be?

While wage income is time limited, grounded, and a matter of addition and subtraction, capital gains income can multiply wealth anywhere in the world. Women, at a disadvantage again, own far fewer capital assets than do men. Women investors also tend to be conservative, opting for security, a good thing anywhere but on Wall Street. There EconoMan's riskier gambles earn higher returns. That doesn't make them smart.

The US tax code is another prime example of EconoMansplaining, but women have never been better organized to confront tax issues that affect them. Tax policy is created at the city, state, and federal level, and women are populating legislatures in increasingly greater numbers.

Small Is Beautiful

I sometimes feel overwhelmed, using my small teaspoon to bail an economic ocean. But if each of us does a teaspoon's worth, we could raise a small wave of change together. We needn't travel the globe to do it, either. I know that from fellow Vermonter Gwendolyn Hallsmith, yet another amateur economist. She writes practical tomes on very local solutions, one small piece at a time.

Her books include the workbook *Taking Action for Sustainability*, and two written in partnership. She and former central banker Bernard Lietaer wrote *Creating Wealth: Growing Local Economies with Local Currencies*. Most recently she and economist Michael Shuman produced *Vermont Dollars, Vermont Sense*. All three publications draw on her twenty-five years of local and international experience that has been focused on finding practical solutions. Begin where you are, her books say.

Hallsmith worked in Kazakhstan during that country's currency crash. She witnessed her elderly neighbor's devastation when the woman's pension, which once supported her, became enough for only a loaf of bread. She began to understand the effects of a removed global financial system.

You may not think of yourself as an investor, but you are one, explains Hallsmith. Banking at a local bank or credit union and shopping at local businesses makes you part of an investment revolution just beginning, says her latest book. Businesses with far-removed owners "leak" money to other states or nations. Keeping more of your dollars at home helps you and your neighbors multiply its circulation. Locally owned businesses spend more money locally, too.

Consumer investments are two words not typically put together, but spending is taking more innovative local forms, too. Community Supported Agriculture (CSA) raises money in early spring, for instance, when farms most need cash to plant. A growing number of people pay money upfront for shares of their local farm's crops.

Local Delivery

Last year, I prepaid in March for a half share in a local CSA. I got to know George, my farmer, and other shareholding neighbors. I got fruit and vegetable deliveries all summer and fall, much fresher than my grocery store's produce, and so bountiful I could give some away.

Presales can help raise capital locally for restaurants to source locally. Presales finance other businesses, too. One theater in my hometown presold movie tickets to raise funds for needed repairs after that Vermont flood I mentioned. A bank loan would have been more costly.

Hallsmith and economist Shuman estimate in *Vermont Dollars, Vermont Sense* that our small state's share of the approximate $30 trillion now held in Wall Street stocks, bonds, and pensions amounts to about $50 billion. If even a small portion of Vermont investors' $50 billion on Wall Street were moved to Main Street, the business climate at home would change dramatically. Small and mid-sized banks typically make more than half of all local small business loans, but today they have only about one-fifth of bank capital. Since 2008, small businesses have struggled to find capital, among them growing numbers of women business owners.

You are represented in that money held by Wall Street, even if you don't have investments yourself. Your bank, your state government, your town, and local businesses all have deposits and investments there. This is why public banking, which moves some tax revenues of your state to a bank administered in the public interest, makes sense. It multiplies money and pays back dividends. It strengthens local banks and credit unions.

Small business owners and local banks are not the only ones affected by underinvestment where we live, Hallsmith and Shuman found. A new generation of young workers could find more jobs at local small businesses. After the 2008 crash, while big corporations cut their workforce by 4.3 percent, local businesses led growth by creating 1.2 percent more. A 2010 *Harvard Business Review* article's title put it simply: "More Small Firms Mean More Jobs."

Bucking Assumptions

Globalization is widely promoted today by national trade agreements, government subsidies for fossil fuel, and tax policies that keep multinational corporations' costs relatively low. Global distribution prices will increase as coal and oil supplies diminish, Hallsmith and Shuman point out. Wages will inevitably go up in China and India. Global import and export will cost more over time.

Moving overseas to find cheap labor, US multinational corporations manufacture durable goods, such as appliances, automobiles, and computers. But durable goods represent only a quarter of US purchases. Most consumer dollars go to local services and pay for nondurable goods. Food, clothing, health care, and office products must all be produced or distributed locally. There is room for local expansion.

Local investors can help. Hallsmith and Shuman show how small Vermont businesses have found local financing through direct private offerings, public offerings, crowdfunding, long-term convertible notes that protect equity, peer-to-peer lending, municipal bonds, and land trusts. More local investment matchups are expected from the 2012 Jumpstart Our Business Startups (JOBS) Act, too.

Hallsmith and Shuman make the whole process of local businesses finding a good investment fit inspiring to learn about. Their book's real people and real stories explain in detail how these financial tools work, or in some cases don't. They include some remodeling dreams for the future, too. They wish for a public bank not yet realized for multiplying Vermont's public revenue deposits in local investments. They'd love to see local banks offer certificates of deposit dedicated to local investments. Why not develop a local mutual fund for investors, too?

Any of these changes could happen where you live. One might make your town, your state, your own concrete situation more prosperous and friendly.

Local Credit R Us

Debt money is Hallsmith's name for the dollars we take for granted as Federal Reserve Notes. She coined the term with coauthor Bernard Lietaer, a former European central banker. I have used their term freely because I think it so essential for understanding why the built-in systems of current money creation cannot help but result in inequality. As long as the Fed issues US dollars only through bank and bond debt, the demand for interest added on will dependably move money away from those who have less, to those who already have more.

You'll remember Margrit Kennedy discussed the debt toll of compound interest in Chapter 17. Without interest accumulated from everyone's loans, prices might be 40 percent less and housing half the cost. Using interest-free savings points like the JAK Bank does for its local lending is one solution. Debt-free local currencies and exchanges are another.

Any local currency is not technically *legal tender*. The US dollar by law must be accepted for all payments in our nation. But that doesn't mean we cannot also accept other sorts. We do already.

The electronic blips that move money from bank to bank, clearing our checks and deposits, are not technically legal tender, but this electronic practice is routine.

A software revolution has opened the door to other new sorts of electronic money exchanges. One such new currency is called a Commercial Credit Circuit, or C3. It confronts small business owners' most pressing problem, cash flow. Small businesses invest in products or services, and then sell them. But there's always a time lag between putting out money for production and receiving payment.

C3 currency addresses this by enabling businesses to use their invoices, insured and tracked by a bank, as cash. C3 invoice-money can be converted to legal tender whenever needed but meanwhile speed up payment in the supply chain. Small businesses can avoid the cost of a bank line of credit. Uruguay and Brazil are already successfully using C3 currency, says Lietaer, who reports that Uruguay even moved to accept C3s as payment of taxes.

Hallsmith and Lietaer also discuss the eighty-year-old Swiss WIR, a currency that is part of a business cooperative founded in 1935. In German, *wir* means "we," and the currency's founders, Werner Zimmerman and Paul Enz, expressed a Swiss ideal (and a US one) that a community united better protects the individual. Proponents of women's rights, the two men were also early environmental defenders.

Today, the WIR currency is exchanged by sixty-two thousand member businesses that enter an agreement called *mutual credit*. It creates a shared financial commons. Only members can exchange goods and services using WIRs, which are equal to the Swiss franc, and most often used in combination with national Swiss francs. By 2012, WIR trades amounted to 2 billion Swiss Francs

Mutual credit associations or cooperatives that use alternative digital currencies like the WIR are catching on around the world. People involved with them connect online and at conferences. Most systems tend to be small and populated by idealists, but one advantage any-sized system shares with the WIR is its self-regulating money supply. There's no danger of inflation.

Unlike debt money's inevitable increase to meet interest demands, the supply of mutual credit dollars expands or shrinks depending on its use. All that's required is a willingness to accept the credit currency in payment for your goods or services, plus administrative time and software to track exchanges. In 2013, a group called Vermont Businesses for Social Responsibility began its own Marketplace Trade Dollars program, for instance. Like the WIR, its software summarizes trade exchanges, and sends member businesses monthly reports and a tax statement annually.

That the IRS counts Marketplace Trade Dollars equal to US debt dollars for tax purposes shows the real financial value of mutual credit exchanges. But importantly these are dollars multiplied and circulated without debt. They also knit local business relationships closer.

Growing Local Money

Though mutual credit requires membership, virtually anyone can create paper money. Coupons and rewards and store rebates are all forms of paper currency, a payback for loyal shopping. Such paper works whenever you can build trust enough that people are willing to use it. It can't work for everything, however, not being legal tender. You can't pay your taxes with coupons or with local paper currency.

But much like WIR or Marketplace Trade Dollars, which exchange IOUs within membership organizations, a local paper currency can work geographically—among groups that have agreed to an exchange in trust. More flexible than local barter, such currencies also multiply debt-free money.

Paul Glover is another of the leaders of the local currency movement, first issuing currency called Ithaca HOURS in 1991 in upstate New York. Ithaca has printed only $110,000 worth of HOURS, but because these are regularly circulating in debt-free exchanges, they represent millions of local dollars in use.

The HOUR's motto is *In Ithaca We Trust*. Each HOUR, worth ten dollars, can be used wherever five hundred businesses and over one hundred nonprofits have agreed to accept them.

Expanding the money supply by multiplying local exchanges is catching on, too. Another local currency appeared in Philadelphia in 2012, called Equal Dollars Community Currency. That same year, CNN reported on eleven similar local paper currencies in the United States, including Traverse City's Bay Bucks, Portland's Cascadia Hour Exchange, Seattle's Life Dollars, and Washington, DC's new Potomacs.

One of most ingenious examples of a local currency, BerkShares, circulates in the Berkshire region of Massachusetts. Like other local currencies, BerkShares currency notes depict beautiful local sites and portray local heroes far more diverse than the US dollar's presidents. From the beginning, the currency's promoters forged an alliance with local banks, and like the Good Housekeeping Seal of Approval, this built public trust.

You can get BerkShares at eight bank branches. You can get one hundred dollars worth of BerkShares for ninety-five dollars in Federal Reserve Notes. In local stores, BerkShares are traded at face value, so you automatically enjoy the currency's discount. Should US dollars be needed again, BerkShares are easily redeemed at the same exchange rate. This exchange flexibility is important, especially for merchants who need legal tender to pay taxes and pay out-of-state suppliers.

We rent out our time to earn wages, but our hours can also become a literal currency, and not only in Ithaca. Edgar Cahn first proposed Time Banks in 2000, in his book *No More Throw-Away People*. Community nonprofits especially value his idea of time's mutual credit, which enables the underemployed, the elderly, the disabled or ill to exchange tax-free, dollar-free services and resources.

Time Banks assume everyone has something valuable to offer. My hometown of Montpelier created the Onion River Time Bank where everyone's hour is an equal swap. Its web page posts services offered and tracks exchanges between members. Since 2008, four hundred members have traded forty-three thousand hours. Services ranged from legal advice to sewing, from house painting to childcare.

I joined and got some no-cost friendly help with patching the drywall on my ceiling. No one has needed my editing help yet, so I've still got a time debit in my account—but no one seems to mind. Making sure you pay up is not a Time Bank goal. Building trust and community networks is. A time currency supplies human connections that people need to be healthy and happy. As one woman named Diane put it on the exchange's web page, "I gained not just the hours I banked, but I also met two wonderful people."

All mutual credit associations and local currencies multiply local trade and exchanges. They also guard against the unthinkable—the dollar's crash that everyone says can never happen here. Depending on how you feel about the equally unthinkable crash in 2008 or Hallsmith's frightening story of her Kazakhstan neighbor's pension shrinking, a stash of local currency steeped in relationships that credit community mutuality could well help you sleep better at night.

Time Is Money

Time banks do not address another very real issue: the time poverty of many working families. Sociologists interested in the intersection of work and family today, most notably Arlie Hochschild in *The Second Shift* and *The Time Bind*, describe today's competition between needed workplace rewards and diminishing pleasures at home.

Time is money, Benjamin Franklin once said. But time used for care and connection remains very much a freebie. EconoMan's excluding money from realms where care happens increases profits for a few but bankrupts the majority of us who care. It is not as if caring and the maintenance of our lives is an option.

If we look at things as EconoMan does for a minute, the biggest problem is that kids no longer work in factories for wages. Instead they go to public schools that cost us. Some slackers get food stamps and free lunches. Kids don't even pay taxes for the first two decades of their lives! The disabled, the elderly are more of the same, freeloading off the free market by getting public benefits or by working part time, or whining they can't find a job. You can see EconoMan's point, can't you?

I hope not. But if you drive a market selection vehicle that only goes in one direction, toward more debt dollars and profit, then things like homes, schools, health care, civic life and town halls, piped-in clean water, roads without potholes, public health—all appear costly in money and time.

We in the four lower quintiles can barely afford volunteerism on the school board, or on town councils. More and more of our hours must be rented out on the labor market to keep up with the interest-driven inflation of prices and lopsided taxes. Our new 24/7 role as self-employed innovators tasks us not only with the usual care but also with keeping abreast of the glut of information in that digital world that creates billionaires by eliminating jobs with software and robots.

No major government official but US Senator Bernie Sanders dares confront the wealthiest, but even his demands for decent wages don't address the great un-profit of our homes, our time poverty, or the elimination of jobs by more efficient technology.

There must be a better way to bake our economic cake. In the spirit of EroNomic wordplay, let's think cupcakes rather than that old-fashioned layer cake of our past. Make them marbled cupcakes, their diverse flavors swirled, not layered. Each cupcake's frosting can be different, too, spread by local trust and consensus. We can nest them in Ostrom's small baskets of purposeful groups.

Mixing metaphors along with our batter, let's set these baskets of cupcakes on a table in the newly remodeled entryway of EconoMan's palatial estate. I've unlocked his front door with my ocean-moving teaspoon, added on rooms for the homeless, and remodeled wages that cannot keep up with prices inflated by debt.

There are two other new ideas I want you to consider, but these will require you to join with me in an EroNomic urge for reimagining our economy, to quote Rollo May: "To open ourselves and participate, via imagination and emotional and spiritual sensitivity, in forms and meanings beyond ourselves."

Wage Efficiency

We're getting radical now. The *basic income guarantee* and the *national dividend* are two possible solutions that look similar but are quite different approaches for a common problem. As national economies develop, technology meets human needs with far fewer hours of labor. Production rises, but jobs diminish. Wages no longer provide security. Hours worked as a measure of production doesn't work any better these days than does money as a measure of worth.

Our sisters in India and Africa spend as much as five hours a day just gathering water and fuel, while technology enables us more privileged women to turn on a light switch, a faucet, in an instant. In such an unequal world, maybe wages as the only reward for labor are outmoded. They never were very fair.

Basic income guarantee or BIG, sometimes referred to as *universal basic income*, or UBI, is a government-issued sum paid regularly to everyone. Social Security payments are universal, for everyone, and made a real dent in the poverty of aging. What if everyone got a basic income just for being born?

If you think this a nutty, far-left idea, consider that President Richard Nixon and economist Milton Friedman both liked the notion. They anticipated lower public costs for administering a single government program, instead of scores. UBI might lessen resentment of the poor, now suspected of freeloading by those nearly as poor. If everyone got it, there would be no need for means testing. Such a government-issued income could also finally include that realm of productive work in our homes that EconoMan has disinherited, the time of our lives and its maintenance.

In 2016, Switzerland's Federal Council shocked the world by proposing every Swiss adult receive $2,500 income a month, and each child $650. The Swiss people voted against this in 2017, but with software and robotics doing more in a digitized world, the conversation about the nature of productive human work is far from over.

Finland piloted a similar program granting $1,100 a month to about one hundred thousand people in 2016, and four Dutch cities are weighing pilot programs as well. Those who say this costs too much tend to see the world as EconoMan does—narrowly. If you look more broadly, its greater efficiency becomes visible.

In the 1970s, the Canadians actually experimented with a health services basic income project in Dauphin, Manitoba. Called Mincome, it was a little different than basic income, aimed only at bringing every citizen up to the poverty line. Manitoba had Mincome program results from 1974 to 1979, but the data was never analyzed until recently by Dr. Evelyn Forget. She found a 8.5 percent drop in hospital visits, fewer mental health crises, fewer work-related injuries, and fewer visits to emergency rooms from car accidents and domestic abuse. Women stayed home with their babies longer, and children remained in school and graduated at higher rates. Men worked only a little less; the job market remained stable.

In 2016, the Canadian Parliament debated a similar program for the nation. The cost was not a small one, estimated to be about $12 billion. But based on results in Dauphin, the bill's proponents argued the $12 billion investment would also save money. More importantly, it would save human dignity.

That bill didn't pass either, but the province of Ontario is now planning an even more ambitious pilot to test out a universal basic income. A conservative legislator saw its value for cutting back on bureaucracy while at the same time addressing precarious wages and irregular contract work in a global economy. Expected to cost $25 million, it was slated to begin in 2017.

Pros, Cons, and More

In the United States, Silicon Valley entrepreneurs have undertaken a UBI research project with a hundred Oakland, California, households. Why would private billionaire businessmen take up such research? Some think a basic income could potentially make it easier to ignore the institutionalized power of wealth and its huge inequalities. A state-provided income could help rationalize Uber's underpaying its drivers, for instance.

Libertarian free market billionaires, similarly to Friedman and Nixon, might also expect UBI money to come from disassembling our welfare programs for the poorest. UBI is not "free money," as US media tends to call it. The money has to come from somewhere, and it now seems unlikely to come from increased taxes on Silicon Valley billionaires. If these men suggest it come from dismantling programs for poor or homeless children, women should look twice.

Here's a picture of what welfare in the United States looks like in 2017: A mother with two children qualifies for Temporary Cash Assistance for Needy Families (TANF) when her income is below the poverty line, less than $1,702 a month for a family of three. Mothers must work or volunteer service to receive TANF and cannot own assets worth more than $2,000. Cash benefits vary from state to state, but can never go beyond five years.

Which states grant mothers in poverty enough cash to meet the poverty guideline? That's a trick question. All fifty states welfare programs leave mothers and children well below the poverty line. The most generous states grant no more than 60 percent of cash needed, while the stingiest go as low as 13 percent. With food stamps added in, families in fifty states still fall far below the poverty guideline.

So what else might work better? The *national dividend* idea looks similar to UBI, but is very different, and quite a bit older. During the era of our gentleman Lord Keynes, a social credit economic reform movement emerged from the writing of C. H. Douglas, a British civil engineer. Another amateur economist become expert, Douglas clearly saw the problem of banks alone creating currency from debt. It inflated prices, typically always outpacing wages.

Such debt money only shifts costs into the future. Its demand for interest creates exponential growth of the debt, ultimately impossible to pay. To help counter the banks' monopoly, Douglas called for a universal national dividend issued debt-free from the government. Unlike UBI, paid for by taxes, these debt-free dividend dollars issued by the Treasury would be calculated as a return on our collaborative national production.

Unlike UBI, national dividend dollars might fluctuate from year to year. Its amount would be tied to GDP dollars but could also include those other healthy indicators we need to give us a more complete account of our real wealth production. A national dividend could increase our sense of unity and direction. Its dependability would also remove pressures on our precariat workforce.

Accounting for Living

Being freed to lift our noses from the wage-earning grindstone for a moment might lift our hearts, as well as unleashing EroNomic urges and ingenuity. I love Douglas's idea of a Social Credit Commonwealth that counts all of an economy's dynamic parts as important. Many play a valuable role in our economy without ever earning money themselves.

When you think about it, every infant counted as a cost in most family and government budgets actually provides a great many people with jobs and a living. How many teachers and doctors would be laid off if parents stopped supplying them with their youngsters?

What would doctors, hospitals, food producers, and toymakers do if women agreed to go on strike and not have babies for one whole year in 2020? Imagine the jolt to business and military demographics, anticipating a year without new enrollments, new consumers, new hires. They'd pay attention to women after that.

The same can be said about the addicted, the handicapped, the imprisoned, the frail elderly—are they only costly and a budget drag on society? Are they worthless if they don't earn wages?

They, too, provide Americans with a good many livelihoods. Every dying breath generates a great deal of money in this economy, a shameful amount actually.

So why is there no compensation for the hard human work of breathing, of growing up and then growing old, all the while sleeping, waking, eating, digesting, thinking, and pooping? Don't laugh—the latter is a big source of income for plumbers, pipe makers, and earth-moving machines.

Household technology was sold to the modern woman as a way to save her precious time. Meeting basic needs is easier now, our housework more efficient. But pictures of our future ease and leisure shown in old ads do not match up with today's increased stress and a pressure to work more hours on the job.

The Economic Policy Institute found our productivity more than doubled from 1948 to 2013. We've examined women's response when wages began to stagnate in 1973. According to Gallup, adults employed full time worked an average of forty-seven hours a week in 2015, an hour and half more than they reported the decade before.

Nearly four in ten workers report working fifty-plus hours a week, and these overworked managers, mostly male, depend on others for care—as if wives and mothers remained at home, as if managers were never parents or had aging parents.

In the same way that our measures of poverty no longer make sense, neither do our measures of work. US Department of Labor statistics count any worker with a tax-paying job as part of their reports, without distinguishing between part-time and full-time. Some economists think tracking the total numbers of hours worked in relationship to the Gross National Product would be more informative. But even that would be misleading without including the hours of the informal economy.

Everyone agrees unemployment statistics hide working reality. The numbers of discouraged workers, out of benefits and still unable to find jobs, drop off the reports and disappear. They join invisible at-home workers—laboring for free, for barter or cash, unaccounted for. Work in the military and our prisons is unseen by the Labor Department, though both work groups clearly have a relationship to discouraged workers in poverty.

A Time Raise

Given women's unparalleled entry into the job market in such great numbers, not only do we need a national dividend, or a universal basic income—we need to resuscitate the old dream of a thirty-hour workweek. We can't stop those managers who work fifty hours at the office from setting an inhuman example, but we can remodel our job space to let in some air and daylight.

We cannot get by on less money, but we can demand the raise that has been postponed for American workers the past thirty years. This needn't cost employers a cent. Only give workers a rebate in time. *Forty-hours pay for a thirty-hour workweek* should be our new motto.

Perhaps then, the more flexible work hours we've sought will be offered as a countermeasure.

Perhaps a national dividend or a UBI can help fill in gaps. This isn't warring between the owners and the owned. It is negotiation and agreement to shared lives lived productively, and by rules we women help set and enforce ourselves.

Some of our market work is already being done from home digitally, further crumbling EconoMan's old wall between our "feminine" domain and our "masculine" markets. Appreciating the commons of our caring—the beauty of its gifts, the excitement of work remodels, and new learning—inspires the kindest possibilities, as that woman who showed me her red velvet rose so many years ago taught me.

Quick Rehash

- Time is money, except in our homes and communities. Excluding caring time from the economy profits a few but dearly costs the majority of us who care.
- Solutions exist for finally including now unpaid caring in the economy, such as the UBI or a universal national dividend issued as debt-free legal tender.
- Local currencies and mutual credit cooperatives can further diversify our money supply and build Main Street's resiliency.

EconoGirlfriend Conversation Starter

Do ethics or spiritual traditions ever affect your personal financial decisions? If so, in what way? If not, who or what do you trust to advise you?

A Real Fixer-Upper 259

Chapter 20: The Personal Is Powerful and Plentiful

EroNomics cannot be owned, only shared—in an eco-economy fired by devotion, not rape, founded on trust, not fear.

I've taken you through a rookery of nested ideas. The economy has so many parts, it needs many solutions, a million small changes.

Small pieces are all any one person can do. Marjorie Kelly's piece was redefining business ownership and intentions. Ellen Brown unearthed public banking for a shared public good. Margrit Kennedy took on the doubling numbers of compound interest. Hazel Henderson changed investing by adding up more than dollars and Riane Eisler defined Social Wealth and caring's vital connections. The women of ROC United, Prospera, Si Se Puede!, and SEWA showed us how to organize ownership more organically, while Madeleine Kunin and Elinor Ostrom showed us how to organize politically to protect our families and natural resources—by self-regulating what we must share or else deplete.

Together, these women have created a blueprint for *EroNomics*, my word for the living self-regulation of the sexy, biologic power at the root of any economic ecology. EroNomics cannot be bought and sold, or stolen. Its value is undermined in hideous ways whenever someone attempts to sell or force it. Without naming this biologic power and valuing it, we cannot fully address an internalized sexism that now permeates economic thinking.

Besides, the pursuit of our happiness, whatever our gender or preferences, simply makes us more interesting, more dynamic, alive, and hopeful. Without it, we become bored and cruel.

My other new word, *Screwnomics*, is more easily recognized and usually brings a laugh; everyone has a story of being screwed by today's economic system. A taxing government marches in step with corporations that seek to own the world. Royal money fiefdoms continue "private law," the literal translation of the word *privilege*, a medieval term for the granting of territory to an individual. In feudal times, that individual was his lordship.

Personally Speaking

In 1988, Peggy McIntosh, a professor of women's studies at Wellesley, wrote a controversial paper that named white privilege and male privilege. It was a very personal essay that explained how perfectly well-intentioned people, including McIntosh herself, enjoyed unearned advantages.

Her white male professor colleagues had been taught that they were the makers of knowledge. They always considered her seminars "the soft stuff," not the foundation blocks of civilization. Male scholars were perfectly nice about this, she wrote, but it felt oppressive, leaving out the ideas and experiences of half the population.

Then she remembered her reaction years before to some essays by black women describing white women's oppressive behavior. She heard her thoughts responding, *Well*—I *think we're very nice—and especially nice, working with* them. It was a wake-up. Writing about this so personally helped her and the people who read her to recognize the possibility of being oppressive without knowing it. No one felt accused, just awakened.

In a recent interview in the *New Yorker,* McIntosh said that if you look closely enough and get very personal, we are all born with unearned advantages and unearned disadvantages: your gender, your birth place in the family order, your physical stature, your trait of being verbal or not, or good with your hands or not. She thinks we all need to make ourselves a personal study, which is different from therapy:

"But it has to do with working on your inner history to understand that you were in systems, and that they are in you," she says. "It has to do with looking around yourself the way sociologists do and seeing the big patterns in the rest of society, while keeping a balance and really respecting your experience. Seeing the oppression of others is, of course, very important work. But so is seeing how the systems oppress oneself."

I've been saying that economics is personal, urging you to think more about your own story in it, and to share it, if you can; it is part of that important project of self-study and a study of social systems.

To be screwed is to be made female and humiliated, whatever your color or your gender. Nearly everyone experiences it. Females and people of color are economically screwed far more often. A woman of color gets screwed the most, left with fewest material assets and more unearned disadvantages than anyone. To be screwed is also to be coerced and forced against your will. To be screwed is to reveal the power of someone who cares nothing about you.

In some deeply troubling way, that kind of exchange diminishes the humanity of the victim and of the screwer. Economic rape is not equivalent to physical rape, but it is more routine and widely accepted as a norm. People laugh out of recognition when I use the term *Screwnomics.*

Men nod and look wry, not as eager as women to share details of their shame, unless a female boss was the perp—which then seems highly unjust. Otherwise, his shrug accepts it's how the real world works, that's all. Some women who've been screwed will use vivid sexual language to describe their learning to "grow balls." They sound tough and put on a manly scowl. Whatever the speaker's gender, the hope is to no longer be mounted.

Male mounting of females makes the animal world go around, but it needn't typify human economic exchanges. Somewhere in our far distant past, human females began to turn around and look their partner in the eyes. The bonobo monkey, a rare pygmy chimpanzee, is the only other animal to do this. The female bonobo did this so often, her clitoris evolved to move forward and share in the pleasure. So did ours.

We share 99 percent of our genome with the bonobo and chimpanzees, but a small variation between the two chimp groups also helps account for increased social signaling among the bonobos and us. The bonobos use sex for easing all kinds of social tensions, crossing gender lines.

I imagine that first female turned around because she was curious and found her partner interesting and desirable. She wanted to know: Was he just going through the motions? Was he trying to impress other monkeys? Or did he prefer her in particular? To turn and see her partner's desire was to know him intimately as an individual, and reciprocate.

Somewhere in that hot monkey mix a million years ago, human pair bonding began and helped everyone survive. Its trust extended into family groups, into tribes and coalitions, and enabled all those exchanges and social arrangements we have talked about that created such diverse cultures and environmentally adapted economies.

This Is Now

I've tried to make EconoMan more visible as a social construction, housing the last remains of an old belief system that expects excessively rich male royalty to rule by Divine Right. It took England until the fifteenth century to commend a woman named Elizabeth to that royal status as queen, but she had to remain a virgin to keep her power. Why?

In that old outgrown paradigm, the female, you and I and even royal Elizabeth, once married became the subject, a person owing obedience. Interestingly, the Latin root of *subject* literally means "to throw under," which is only missing *the bus*, to convey its modern meaning, like screwing. That social construction is part of why it took American democracy 240 years to seriously consider electing a woman for president.

I hope by now you are angry about some small personal piece of this economic system but are also inspired by someone's resistance or ideas for remodeling. I hope that you have remembered pieces of your own money history and can talk about it with friends or family. For amateur economists who happen to be women, the place to begin to win confidence is among those whose concrete situation is similar to your own.

That's the reason I encourage EconoGirlfriend conversations. Share a chapter or two of *Screwnomics*, and ask some questions. Start there. Consider getting my workbook for your group at www.Screwnomics.com.

No, it isn't close-minded and sexist to leave your boyfriend, your husband, or your brother off your invitation list. Even bright women have a tendency to be quieter as soon as a man begins to expound. Our culture still operates by expectations that males know about the public realm of government and business, and how things really work. We expect money to talk in a male-voice.

Observe mixed-group dynamics and see what you notice. When two men begin a debate, most women and men become spectators. Usually only another man will jump in to challenge. Most women will hang back, their conversation style preferring connection. If a woman does join the joust, she is less likely to be admired, especially if she wins.

Cognitive studies have found that women will lose "expressive IQ" in gender-mixed problem-solving groups, especially in fields where stereotypes help privilege male communication styles. Women are particularly sensitive to signals of social status, and most surprisingly women's prefrontal cortex measurably slows down and the part of the brain that sorts conflicts becomes activated.

Some scientists concluded that teaching methods encouraging competition wouldn't work for everyone, especially for women. Coed conversations by participants that compete and jockey for position, as men are expected to do even when they don't enjoy it, will not help build your economic "expressive IQ" if you don't feel confident.

In all-female study groups, I have often been astonished by the quick intimacy that can form. Finding connections and similarities tends to create affection and familiarity. Sometimes it reveals a jarring difference that unnerves. But frankness and tolerance among women who disagree can deepen conversations in surprising ways.

A good ground rule I've practiced as a professor grants everyone the right to her own point of view. Asking questions and listening more closely can help bridge differences in perspective and increase understanding for all involved.

As women begin to talk with each other about economics—generally a new experience—we can encourage each other and overcome shy fears. With practice, group fantasies, born of an orgy of girly thoughts and laughter, can grow and change and branch out to meet others. Screwnomics expresses the unspoken economic theory that women should always work for less, or better, for free—but I expect you to laugh at it. You may have to be more polite when approaching the loyal opposition, those perfectly nice folks who see things the old mainstream way. They will need to be persuaded.

And when presenting alive and jumpy paradigms, having girlfriends at your back can add confidence. We are evolved to be social, to cooperate as a group, and that happens more now, especially with the Internet connecting us globally. Groups meet on Facebook or Google, or gather in living rooms to help transform ideas into action. My *Screwnomics* workbook: *Where Can I Get Some*

Change? provides five sections entitled ATMs (Allies That Matter) that match this book's five parts, as well as providing to-do lists with leads on where to learn more, so you don't feel alone or crazy.

First identify your own burning questions and interests. You cannot fix it all, but you can do something and you'll feel better when you do.

Solutions Galore

The real sticking point in a cupcake democracy that proposes every citizen gets a share of frosting is this: How do we pay for it? How can we afford childcare, more vacation time, higher wages, and a national dividend for all breathing citizens? A look at our Gross National Product and the Fed's money supply reveals plenty of dough.

To start with, we could stop money's weaponizing. We could look more closely at the price tags on government war-machines and guns, and the people who operate them. We could spend more on diplomacy and make a study of peacekeeping. Saving money is efficient.

Many options for raising revenues exist, too, and most of them involve that word that Americans hate most, *taxes*. Some we've already mentioned. We could tax income, sales, or capital gains more fairly. We could tax buildings, inheritances, and luxuries. We could close the loops of tax deductions. We could tax land, natural resources, pollution, and fossil fuel use. We could tax Wall Street transactions, first proposed by economist James Tobin in 1972 to slow down speculative trading.

We could charge more reasonable fees for the use of our public lands for profit, as well as for our public airways' broadcast spectrum used for huge profit. We could stop those money leaks offshore that hide billions in taxes already overdue.

We could also insist all the wealthy pay mandatory social security insurance and widen social benefits, including maternal and infant health, good for everyone's future. We could cooperate to build a single-payer health care insurance to stop the waste of multiple billing, eligibility testing, nonsensical drug prices, and overlarge co-pays.

But while a great many solutions exist, the political will does not, undermined by the Supreme Court's equating money with free speech. In a single ruling, Citizens United transformed the meaning of free speech into an oxymoron as huge as the so-called free market. Both phrases, *free speech* and *free market*, pretend that you and I are not subjects to today's money royalty.

We are a democracy, they tell us. The guys in Washington and on Wall Street just happen to have $billions each, $trillions as a group, and if you girly slackers would just work harder, you, too, might join them. This is America, after all.

The 2016 political season revealed a troubled country that no longer believes that, sucked dry by business as usual. Sexy solutions must now enter the public discussion of economics. Who is most motivated to see care and community as economic and profitable? Who is most likely to knit us together, or at least prevent further rips in a thinning social fabric?

Get Crazy with Caring

Let me share my personal wildest fantasy, the one I've been nursing for years. If our politicians cannot bring themselves to make EconoMan pay his fair share of taxes, if we cannot give up debt dollars and profits won at the expense of everything else, if we cannot end our war-think and the idea that the rich man must grow manly largeness—then let the US Treasury issue a new complementary currency, one that is colored pink not green, issued debt-free to reward and honor the EroNomic riches around us everywhere.

It would picture faces of compassionate courage, of moving devotion to others—say, Maggie L. Walker who started the St. Luke Penny Savings Bank. Or Dr. Jonas Salk who, when asked by Edward R. Murrow in 1952 who owned the patent for his work on the Polio vaccine, answered, "The people, I suppose. Would you patent the sun?"

Our new pink currency would partner with the green. Backed by our land and our trust and our people, it would put the real source of our wealth on the table. And here is the best part. Just for fun, the amounts of my imagined new pink Caring Commons currency issued to each of us would be authorized by the IRS, that most hated of government agencies.

Do you remember how tally sticks served to record taxes paid and then circulated as a currency in merry old England? It was trusted as proof of riches and fealty. Just so, our demonstration of loyalty to the Republic and democracy's ideals could be documented in taxes paid and care delivered, and partly returned to us in pink currency as part of our tax transaction.

The rich pay the biggest share of taxes because they own so much and have incomes so much higher, but the rhetoric of numbers alone will no longer be all that counts at the IRS. You'll also have to document your care in money and time. Did you raise a family this year? How many hours did you spend? Did you vote? Did you forgive a loan? Did you grow an organic garden? Remember your mother's birthday? How much did you pay for phone calls to family? Did you serve as a volunteer?

Businesses could be asked, Did you provide a new customer or community a real benefit? Did you pay your employees a living wage? Did you make your customers' lives more convenient and happy? What did it cost you in company debt money, in company time? In personal time? How much time did you and your employees contribute by volunteering?

Balance Credits and Debits

We can set the bar low for caring. Check a few of these, and you qualify for the top tranche of caring. You'll be honored with pink dollar rewards. But this is the IRS, and so there's also a Section XX on your tax form's Caring Addendum, where you get caring deductions that lessen a pink payback, such as:

- Did you put big gobs of money into a PAC to influence elections? How much?
- Did you pollute your neighbors' wells? What did it cost them?

- Did you fail to specify toxins on your product labels and get sued? For how much?
- Did you choose to settle a lawsuit out of court for more than $1 million? How many millions? Deduct those amounts from your benefits above.

That part on your tax form will help even things out. Still, just about everyone will get a big return on their caring because you cannot have too much care.

Some may have to cheat to get the pink caring currency, but the meanest will have high-priced accountants to help them look kinder. We won't mind, because seeing caring heroes on this new pink dollar and answering those questions about care will begin to influence our American business thinking.

Maybe there *are* caring things we could do, entrepreneurs will say, especially since they're giving us pink currency to spend. Suddenly, corporations and the wealthy, promised pink bills in hand, would have an incentive to pay their fair share of taxes. We would all suddenly love paying our taxes!

Documenting all these caring specifics of concrete situations, taking an annual inventory of our time and our money for care, could strengthen our national unity and identity. Perhaps we'd start out using our debtless pink currency only for caring. But the definitions of caring would expand as the pink money supply grew.

Parents could afford to pay pink dollars for a babysitter on Wednesday nights, so they could volunteer for the school board. The poor could give donations to a favorite nonprofit. Kids could pay their own way to the dentist. Childcare centers would offer employee pensions and would pay high-priced architects to increase children's delight in their play spaces, no longer rundown.

Corporations and the wealthy, loaded with pink cash, could readily sponsor childcare and pet care at every branch office. They'd improve libraries, old-age homes, and hospitals dedicated to their generosity with big brass plaques up front, the sort the richest like to have on display. A care currency could pay for generous maternity leaves, vacation times, and sabbaticals for employees. It could help pay for any costs associated for switching to a thirty-hour week. Pink scholarships, pink fellowships, and pink cultural exchanges, named in EconoMan's honor, would help soothe his insecurities.

He would need a continued pressure to think of someone other than himself, however. So we'd also practice *demurrage*—a charge shippers pay for storage in a ship's hold to encourage its prompt unloading, keeping ships moving and profitable. The pink bills when stashed in banks would cost a small carrying charge each month. Spending pink money, even giving it away, is the wisest course.

✓ DEMURRAGE

Pronounced *dem-ur-raj*, this incentive keeps money circulating without the usual inflation of prices. It is a small carrying charge for money not in use—the opposite counterbalance of our current interest charges paid to those who store surplus money now.

Interest functions to keep money moving, a good thing. Without its incentive, we might horde money in the sugar bowl, our mattress, or keep it in a private vault. But interest helps the rich more than you and me because they have much more money to start with. It's nice they let us borrow some, but interest charges lead to inflation of prices that affects everyone, and no one more than those women and their families without money to spare.

A pink caring currency that costs you money if you don't spend it would be another incentive to keep pink caring money active. Its use would not affect prices. You'd have to give up any fond dream of becoming rich from all your pink cash—but you'd be happier spending it freely for a safer, more prosperous Main Street.

Here's to You

I feel better just for having written this, letting my cat out of the bag, being a fool, risking your laughter, your judgment. A pink caring currency is a pretty silly idea, I suppose. But then, I think again. Exchanging, valuing, and trading our care is not all that much sillier than the idea that a king is not God-appointed, or that all people of every color, and even women, are created equal.

People scoffed at those crazy notions not so very long ago. A pink caring currency is not much sillier than the idea that an African ought to be free, not a slave, even if it is good for business. Ruin was predicted, should *that* happen, *OMG*.

When working women organized to win shorter hours and a weekend, a life with Bread *and* Roses, they were told it was crazy. It would wreck the economy! She was lucky to have a seven-day workweek, twelve-hour shifts, sexual harassment, and pay discrimination. It put food on her table. To cook. For free.

Come to think of it, a new pink currency is far *less* silly than the notion that a few, mostly white, wealthy men are entitled to price the world's lives and livelihoods at the bottom of a tranche, so that those who already own the most can claim more of what others in lower tranches have produced.

It is up to each of us to decide what we have to give in exchange for what we need. It is up to all of us to learn as much as we can and negotiate with our peers in our particular environment. Ask whatever creatures or people will listen whether we can afford what the future holds if we make no change at all.

Quick Rehash

- None of us deserves what we've got, whether riches or poverty, because nothing is that simple, except for shared luck being alive on this beautiful planet.
- Caring needs incentives of the sort that greed now receives, and women can and must help create these.
- Humans are social creatures as well as economic ones, and happiest when collaborating, cooperating, while exchanging and sharing care.

EconoGirlfriend Conversation Starter

Describe the craziest economic idea you have ever had. Share with girlfriends and compete for being the nuttiest. This will prepare you for what others will no doubt say. Let shared laughter guard your backs.

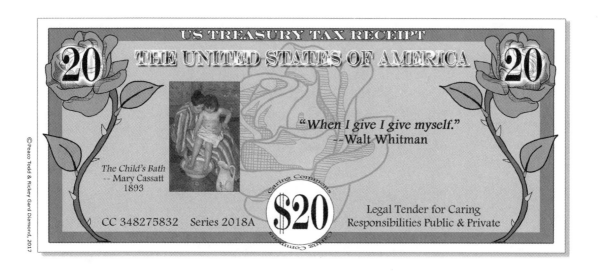

Epilogue

While *Screwnomics* was in production at the end of 2017, Washington delivered a so-called Christmas present, a colossal tax bill. Its 1,100 pages got written behind closed doors without public debate—and in an unusually big hurry even for money men. With taxes made more complex than ever, the fiscal results of this "reform" won't be fully visible until April 2019, although you may see changes in your paycheck's withholding soon.

Its largest benefits, everyone freely admits, will go to the very wealthiest individuals and their international corporations. Nor does anyone deny that these tax cuts will put our collective US governments—city, state, and federal—at risk, all now caught short of funds.

The tax vote followed party lines, though even some Republicans balked. Dems presented no clear alternative, only promising a "better deal." Too few said out loud: Tax cuts are not always good. Government is a necessity, not a problem. An American dream of expanded private fortunes alone is a forgery.

That shallow dream does not make us happier people, or better ones, the great African American writer James Baldwin observed. We are given numbers, he said, when what we need is passion: "White is not a race. It is a metaphor for power. White is The Chase Manhattan Bank."

I believe passion is why you picked up this book—because moolah's green, like race's white, is a metaphor. Our huge economic system moves so fast that no one can know all its details, but you can trust your heartfelt sense of its direction and intent. A cruel money-power guarded by sexual predation has been uncloaked by the #metoo movement of rape survivors. Time's Up fundraisers and fossil fuel divestment both reveal how quickly passionate people can change money's purpose.

In January 2017, passion drove millions of pink-hatted women of all colors and shapes into the streets with their supporters, and again in January 2018 as the government closed down, arguing meanly about budgets, money, and who gets to dream. Women's self-evident truths about these troubles connect to a wider, more diverse economic ecology—one fueled by devotion, not rape, and grounded in trust, not fear. Yes, we *can* wage life, not war.

Acknowledgments

So many have helped my attempts to unlock mysteries of America's economy now gone global. Early on, my uniquely diverse family planted early seeds of curiosity about class, ethnic cultures, and occupational differences. My experience of poverty in Michigan poked my feminism awake, as did working against poverty in Vermont, where Mary Carlson, Ben Collins, and Gus Seelig took me under their wing, teaching me politics and newspapering. Tom Slayton opened a door to my wider community, as did Joseph Gainza, Sandy Neely, Rev. John Nutting, and Veda Lyon.

Governor Madeleine Kunin encouraged *Vermont Woman*'s establishment. Her woman-peopled administration that included Gretchen Morse, Sallie Soule, Lynn Heglund, and Kathy Hoyt provided our newspaper with public stories and economic perspectives. I and the whole state owe a debt to Kunin for her empowering leadership, and also to that of *Vermont Woman* publisher Sue Gillis, and her editors Michele Patenaude, Margaret Michniewicz, and Kate Mueller, and a host of excellent women writers, whose questions and skill fostered mine.

Mentors who encouraged my voice and teaching at Vermont College include novelist Sena Jeter Naslund, poet Linda McCarriston, fellow travelers Rhoda Carroll, Maida Solomon, Bernice Mennis, and Ann Stanton, who gave me the go-ahead to mix literature and economics in seminars. More thanks are owed to many more faculty colleagues and students too numerous to mention here, whose example and engagement taught me to aspire to artful civil discourse and persuasion.

I couldn't have gone far down this economic path without the guidance and example of UVM economists Stephanie Seguino, Elaine McCrate, and the Gund Institute's Gary Flomencraft and Eric Zencey. I also appreciate Professor Timothy Taylor of Macalester College whose recorded economic classes through the Teaching Company were clear and accessible. Great monetary writers like Ellen Brown and Gwendolyn Hallsmith took me further into the currency weeds, and even befriended me—while organizers like Walt McRee, Mike Krauss, Nichoe Lichen, and Pamela Hannley Powers at the Public Banking Institute and Linda Wheatley, Paula Francis, Ginny Sassaman, and Tom Barefoot at Gross National Happiness USA modeled daring leadership and the power of big paradigms. Thank you all, though here I strictly lay claim to any errors in this work—all mine.

I was enriched by years of vigorous dialogue with students and faculty at Vermont College, and experienced a similar radical hospitality at Hedgebrook, founded by Nancy Nordhoff for "women authoring change." For weeks at a time I shared meals and challenging talk with writers whose bold voices and ideas crossed the boundaries between class, color, ethnic culture, and sexual identity.

Our intensely personal conversations about dynamic, courageous work raised my personal bar and widened my world. Special thanks to Hitaji Aziz, Olaitan Valerie, Sandra Angelita Garcia, Lisa Alvarado, Gordon Johnson, Kahlil Al-mustafa, Carole Auger-Richard, Georgetta Smith, Marc Anthony, and Neil Rico, and also to Hedgebrook writers Barbara Mhangami, Greta Schuler, Lauren Fauntozzo, Tracey Rose, Carrie Lawler Arcos, Norma Liliana Valdez, and Jewelle Gomez. Thanks too to my special German friend Antje Ricken, whose writing about her family in WWII makes history more round and as real as her hugs. Whatever continent, whatever hard-won identity—and whatever rage and wisdom and kindness that you shared with me—lives on in my imagination and my heart, and I hope in this book.

Thanks to my many, many great sources, more than are noted herein, including Rebecca Solnit, Les Leopold, Marjorie Kelly, Nomi Prins, Ela Bhatt, Guy Standing, Michael Hudson, Matt Taibbi, Jane Gleeson-White, John DeGraaf, Sabine O'Hara, Hazel Henderson, Marilyn Waring, Paul Kivel, Irene van Staveren, Elizabeth Warren, Naomi Klein and Shiela Bair, with special thanks for those who shifted my worldview, Gerda Lerner, Riane Eisler, and Robert McElvaine.

Thanks to Monica Casper, Julie Amparano, and Linda Van Leuven, who revived the great journal, *Trivia: Voices of Feminism*, and who published an early excerpt of *Screwnomics* online. Thanks to Shari Barnhart and Doni Hoffman for their website work and their much more than virtual support, and to Rebecca Davison for market mentoring.

I'm so grateful to my first EconoGirlfriend group, whose early readings and sharing of stories were immeasurably helpful. Bronwyn Fryer, you rock. So do Jo Romano, Gwendolyn Hallsmith, Diana Levine, Joanne Hardy, Heather Moz, Anika Bieg, and those rock and rollers Tiffany Bluehme and Susan Ritz, who gave me great markups. So did close readers Paul Hislop and Roberta Hislop.

My editor Nancy Marriott was indispensable, a gem, and so are the women at SheWrites Press, Pamela Long, Julie Metz, Cait Levin, and others led by the mighty Brooke Warner. I am proud to join the company of their many awesome SWP writers. Mary Fillmore and Joan Dempsey were especially kind, sharing their publishing experience.

I owe a huge debt to cartoonist Peaco Todd, who can do mind melds, and who helped me create characters that made us both laugh, illustrating ideas and jokes with professional savvy. Our regular conversations were a highlight each week of this project.

The greatest debt belongs to my family, who provided stories, examples, and inspiration. Karol Diamond joined EconoGirlfriend conversations and often put her brilliant and beautiful head together with mine. Thanks to Kristine, Justin, Keith, and Renay for our long long-distance talks and visits, and for giving me good reason to remember grandparents, and to dedicate this work to your five amazing children.

Never, never will I be able to return all the favor shown me by my dear partner, Stephen McArthur, who has read so many versions of this. He demanded my best even when it hurt my feelings, steadfastly encouraging me, not just with words but with large sacrifices in extremely concrete situations. All told, I am a very lucky duck.

Chapter Endnotes

Chapter 1: Talking Dirty about Dirty Secrets

1. See "The Rise of Extreme Poverty in the United States," Stanford's *Pathways*, Summer 2014, and also "Cities Hit Hardest by Extreme Poverty," *MSN Money*, June 14, 2017, https://www.msn.com/en-us/money/markets/cities-hit-hardest-by-extreme-poverty/ar-BBzx01m.

2. See Hillary W. Hoynes, Marianne E. Page, and Ann Huff Stevens, "Poverty in America: Trends and Explanations," *Journal of Economic Perspectives*, Vol. 20, No. 1, Winter 2006, pp. 47–68.

3. See Alemayehu Bishaw, *Poverty 2000–2012, American Community Survey Briefs*, Economics and Statistics Administration, US Census Bureau, September 2013.

4. Andrea Dworkin discusses differences in men's money and women's in her first chapter, "Power," in *Pornography: Men Possessing Women*.

5. See David Callahan, "How the GI Bill Left Out African Americans," *Demos PolicyShop*, November 11, 2013, http://www.demos.org/blog/11/11/13/how-gi-bill-left-out-african-americans.

Chapter 2: No Girly Stuff Allowed

1. See Friedman's 1976 Nobel Prize lecture, "Inflation and Employment," at www.nobelprize.org/nobel_prizes/economic-sciences/laureates/1976/friedman-lecture.pdf.

2. Yesha Levine wrote about Nobel family protest in a US article in 2013, but public controversy dates back to 2001 in Sweden. See http://www.alternet.org/economy/there-no-nobel-prize-economics.

3. Friedman's influence on Chile's General Pinochet, downplayed by him, is examined by many economists in Part 2 of the 2003 PBS series, *Commanding Heights: Battle for the World Economy*, based on the 1998 book by Daniel Yergin and Joseph Stanislaw. A sample of the PBS series, focused on Chile, is available on YouTube: https://www.youtube.com/watch?v=lw1E7pFbXoQ.

4. Naomi Klein's analysis of Friedman's ideas and that of his self-named "Chicago boys" permeates *Shock Doctrine* (2007). See her critique of his role undermining public education in New

Orleans post-Katrina at http://www.naomiklein.org/articles/2015/08/change-everything-or-face-global-katrina.

5. See Guy Standing's books, *The Precariat: The New Dangerous Class* (2011) and *A Precariat Charter: From Denizens to Citizens* (2014).

Chapter 3: Two Kinds of Men

1. The Berkshire Conference of Women Historians, founded in 1930, began reshaping their field in *Clio's Consciousness Raised: New Perspectives on the History of Women* (New York: Harper & Row, 1974).

2. See Keynes's ideas brought to life in Robert Skidelsky's three-volume biography condensed into a single volume: *John Maynard Keynes, 1883–1946; Economist, Philosopher, Statesman* (New York: Penguin, 2003).

3. The "equilibrium of natural demand and supply" was first described in Alfred Marshall's text, *Principles of Economics*, published in 1890, which established his field of study as a social science.

4. I first learned of the Italian fascist Mussolini's preference for the term *corporatist* in 2002 from Molly Ivins, the great Texan journalist. See https://www.creators.com/read/molly-ivins/11/02/molly-ivins-november-21-3683028f.

5. See Germany's Nazi Forced Labor Documentation Centre preserving Barrack 13. Their website describes companies profiting from "closed work assignments" of Berlin Jews, prisoners of war, military internees, and concentration camp inmates, including many women.

6. In 1958, economist John Kenneth Galbraith coined the phrase *conventional wisdom*, asking why the United States spent long working hours on superfluous production meeting "false needs" generated by an advertising industry. He later examined the private sector's extravagant waste and stinginess in the public realm in *The Affluent Society* (New York: Penguin Economics, 4th edition, 1999).

7. Economists Linda Bilmes and Joseph Stiglitz revealed the war costs hidden from taxpayers in their book *The Three Trillion Dollar War* (New York: W.W. Norton & Co., 2008), but have since more than doubled their figures to account for ongoing war.

Chapter 4: Played by the Players

1. WITCH's hex in protest of Asst. Professor Marlene Dixon's firing was only one of many 1969 student demonstrations at the University of Chicago. See Carrie Golus, "Which Side Are You On?" *The Core: College Magazine of University of Chicago*, Winter 2010, http://thecore.uchicago.edu/winter2010/which-side.shtml.

2. Craig Steven Wilder, MIT historian, lays bare not only Southern antebellum church justifications for slavery and "the natural order" of the races, but its institutionalization in universities, North and South, in *Ebony and Ivory: Race, Slavery, and the Troubled History of America's Universities* (New York: Bloomsbury Press, 2013).

3. Englishman Henry Spencer actually coined the term "survival of the fittest," applying value-laden interpretations of Darwin's ideas to human society to justify a laissez-faire economics, says Debby Applegate in her review of Barry Werth's *Banquet at Delmonico's: Great Minds, the Gilded Age and the Triumph of Evolution in America, New York Times Sunday Book Review,* January 29, 2009.

4. Stephen Jay Gould's *The Mismeasure of Man* (New York: W.W. Norton & Co., 1981) and *The Mismeasure of Woman* by Carol Tavris (New York: Simon & Schuster, 1992) began a discussion of the snares of science's physiological measures embodying gender and racial bias. See also *The Illusion of Free Markets: Punishment and the Myth of Natural Order* by Bernard E. Harcourt (Cambridge: Harvard University Press, 2011).

5. See a confident Milton Friedman, describing why "equal opportunity" is wrongheaded, and note the smirking male audience as one woman braves a question: https://www.youtube.com/watch?v=hsIpQ7YguGE.

6. *A Brief History of Economics: Artful Approaches to the Dismal Science* by E. Ray Canterbery (London: World Scientific Publishing Co., 2001, 2005) includes a timeline and a rare, accessible overview of argued ideas within a cultural context.

7. A slim, witty book, Katrine Marçal's *Who Cooked Adam Smith's Dinner? A Story about Women and Economics* (London: Portobello Books, 2015) focuses on what's left out and provides a fabulous bibliography of feminist economics, along with the right attitude.

8. In 1851, Harriet Taylor Mill, wife of John Stuart Mill, published "The Enfranchisement of Women" in the *Westminster and Foreign Quarterly Review*, one of England's premier journals of political opinion. Widely attributed to her husband, it enjoyed readers in the United States. Mill later credited her.

9. Susan Brownmiller wrote the introduction to a reissue of *On the Subjection of Women* (New York: Fawcett Publications, Inc, 1971), describing its dismissal by Mill's contemporaries in 1869. Only the suffragists admired it, and over a hundred years later the women's liberation movement had to rediscover it.

10. See *Pathways: The Poverty and Inequality Report 2016* from Stanford University. Economists Gabriel Zucman and Emmanuel Saez show how 160,000 US households with $20 million plus in net worth gained wealth the past forty years, while middle-class wealth diminished, contrasted by Europe's more even distribution.

11. See Mary Gabriel's *Love and Capital: Karl and Jenny Marx and the Birth of a Revolution* (New York: Little, Brown, 2011).

12. Charlotte Perkins Gilman (1860–1935) wrote two autobiographies and a raft of published writing. Forgotten until the Women's Movement resurrected her, Gilman's fiction and nonfiction writing expressed economic ideas. Her most famous story written in 1892, "The Yellow Wallpaper," still rings a *mansplaining* bell.

13. See Sharon Rudahl's *A Dangerous Woman: The Graphic Biography of Emma Goldman* (New York: The New Press, 2007).

14. Selma James writes a short history of Eleanor Rathbone's work for a mother's allowance in the *Guardian*. See https://www.theguardian.com/commentisfree/2016/aug/06/child-benefit-70-years-eleanor-rathbone.

15. See Keynes's beauty contest in Chapter 12 of *The General Theory of Employment, Interest and Money.*

16. See Rand Paul's 2010 statement (Deborah Solomon, *New York Times Magazine*) while running for the Senate from Kentucky: "I don't want to live in a nanny state where people are telling me where I can go and what I can do." He may have stomped his foot when he said it, and probably needed a nap. He won the election.

Chapter 5: Learning Consequences the Hard Way

1. You can learn how to best manage your decisions about rentals vs. mortgages, fifteen-year mortgages vs. thirty-year mortgages, and costs over time at www.mortgagecalculator.biz, created by Trey Conway. His site is lead-data free, so your visits won't result in your being hounded by mortgage brokers the way other calculators do.

2. US Senator Bernie Sanders of Vermont has persistently sponsored legislation to lift the cap on the payroll tax to secure Social Security benefits for the post–baby boomer generations, saying "Anyone who tells you Social Security is going broke is lying." In 2017 he proposed increasing benefits by about $1,300 a year for those making less than $16,000, by lifting the tax cap to $250,000 in earnings.

3. Upton Sinclair won Pulitzers for his writing, but fell out of favor for exposing foibles of economic power. After he wrote *The Jungle*, he went on to expose *Oil!*, *King Coal*, and *The Moneychangers*. Recently his series of Lanny Budd novels, set in the ultra-wealthy circles leading up to WWII, have resurged.

Chapter 6: Women's Work Is Never Done

1. Marjorie Kennedy makes the relationship between time, money, and financial tools clear in her thin, readable book, *Occupy Money,* and provided an example I use to illustrate exponential numbers in Chapter 16.

2. The Wall Street climate that led to delusions of an end to credit risk in high-risk lending is described in detail in the US Senate Investigation majority and minority staff report, 646 pages long, released in April 2011, and titled, *Wall Street and the Financial Crisis: Anatomy of a Financial Collapse.*

3. Quants that nearly destroyed Wall Street in 2008 increasingly dominate, says the *Wall Street Journal* first in 2010, "The Minds Behind the Meltdown," and most recently in 2017, "The Quants Run Wall Street Now." See www.wsj.com/articles/SB10001424052748704509704575019032416477138 and www.wsj.com/articles/the-quants-run-wall-street-now-1495389108.

4. See "Gramm and the Enron Loophole," *New York Times*, November 14, 2008, and also www.

opensecrets.org for a list of PAC contributions from Enron, JPMorgan Chase, Morgan Stanley, Bank of America, and others: https://www.opensecrets.org/politicians/summary.php?cid=N00005709&cycle=Career.

Chapter 7: A Watched Pot Never Boils

1. Sociologist Arlie Hochschild and economist Elaine McCrate have both examined the complicated lives of working women. See Hochschild's books *Second Shift* and *Time Bind,* and McCrate's articles in *Feminist Economics.*

2. Male chauvinist Ayn Rand, beloved by Republican leaders, wrote "About a Woman President," in the *Objectivist,* December 1968: "For a woman to seek or desire the presidency is, in fact, so terrible a prospect of spiritual self-immolation that the woman who would seek it is psychologically unworthy of the job."

3. See Rick Schmitt's Born interview, "Prophet and Loss," *Stanford Magazine,* March/April 2010. See also "Lessons Not Learned: The Derivatives Market and Continued Risks," *Stanford Lawyer,* Spring 2013, No. 88, and *Frontline*'s documentary film, *The Warning,* October 2009.

4. *Jackass: The Movie* came out in 2002, showing young men taking lunatic risks, also celebrated in movies like *Wall Street* (1987), *Rogue Trader* (1998), *Boiler Room* (2000), and *American Psycho* (2000).

5. See EconoMan's regular busts: a 1973–74 oil crisis, the 1987 Black Monday crisis, the 1989–1995 US savings and loan crisis, the 1997 Asian crisis, the 2001 dotcom crash, and 2008 subprime mortgage crisis. See the *Economist*: http://www.economist.com/news/essays/21600451-finance-not-merely-prone-crises-it-shaped-them-five-historical-crises-show-how-aspects-today-s-fina.

6. Deregulated in 1980, 1,043 US Savings & Loans Banks were closed by the end of 1999, costing taxpayers $132 billion, according to a 2000 report in *FDIC Banking Review,* setting a precedent. See https://www.fdic.gov/bank/analytical/banking/2000dec/brv13n2_2.pdf.

7. Born was awarded the John F. Kennedy Profiles in Courage Award in 2009. Her speech is a wake-up: https://www.jfklibrary.org/Asset-Viewer/HwcRGK-cbkeqwmeCVOlONQ.aspx.

8. Roger Lowenstein's *When Genius Failed* (New York: Random House Publishing Group, 2011) is the most intimate report on Long Term Management Capital and NY Fed's intervention, but online articles abound in major business news sources.

9. For wonky details on freeing derivative deals from regulation by the CFTC, see "What Went Wrong," *Washington Post,* October 15, 2008.

10. See Gretchen Morgenson and Louise Story, "In Financial Crisis, No Prosecutions of Top Figures," *New York Times,* April 14, 2011.

Chapter 8: No Place Like Home

1. See political scientists Martin Gilens and Benjamin I. Page's Princeton Report on US policy and the question "Who Governs?" online: https://scholar.princeton.edu/sites/default/files/

mgilens/files/gilens_and_page_2014_-testing_theories_of_american_politics.doc.pdf

2. Nomi Prins's *It Takes a Pillage: An Epic Tale of Power, Deceit, and Untold Trillions* (Hoboken: John Wiley & Sons, 2009 & 2011) saw through misleading TARP numbers early, a phenomenon since widely reported.

3. The Center for Media and Democracy and economists at the Center for Economic and Policy Research compiled a table of bailout costs, risks, and outstanding liabilities, last updated in 2011. See http://www.sourcewatch.org/index.php/Total_Wall_Street_Bailout_Cost.

4. Converting numbers into seconds better helps to clarify money differences. You can get exact with calculations on this online calculator: http://unitconverter.io/seconds/minutes/1000.

5. According to *Forbes,* 2017, Donald Trump is ranked #544 among the world's 2,043 billionaires, and #156 among the United States' 400 richest. Ranking shows a locker room purpose for proving who's the biggest.

6. See Richard Rothstein's book, *The Color of Law: A Forgotten History of How Our Government Segregated America* (New York: W.W. Norton & Co., 2017) to understand a lasting economic disadvantage.

7. See Matt Taibbi's "The $9 Billion Witness: Meet JPMorgan Chase's Worst Nightmare," *Rolling Stone*, November 6, 2014.

8. See *An Analysis of Residential Lending Patterns in Benton Harbor and St. Joseph, Michigan: A Report to the Race Relations Council of Southwestern Michigan*, Woodstock Institute, 1999. See race and age differences (though not gender) within the average 28 percent loss of American assets in the Urban Institute report, *Impact of the Great Recession and Beyond: Disparities in Wealth Building by Generation and Race*, April 21, 2014, http://www.urban.org/research/publication/impact-great-recession-and-beyond.

9. See Rev. Pinkney's release in June 2017 on the website of Black American Network Community Organization (BANCO) in Benton Harbor where he remains active: http://www.bhbanco.org.

Chapter 9: Proof of the Global Pudding

1. Our billionaire population explosion is probably greater than reported, admitted Rupert Hoogewerf, chief researcher for the 2017 Hurun Report. He told CNBC it may be closer to 5,000, "They . . . prefer operating under the radar." See http://www.cnbc.com/2017/03/09/the-worlds-billionaires-are-now-worth-8-trillion.html.

2. You'll find an illustrated explanation of how money laundering and offshore accounts work in Bob Johnson's "Money laundering? Offshore accounts? You don't say!" *Daily Kos*, June 14, 2017, https://www.dailykos.com/story/2017/6/14/1671962/-Money-laundering-Offshore-accounts-You-don-t-say. Using data from the World Bank, the IMF, the UN, and the world's central banks, economist James Henry estimates that rich individuals and families have hidden from $21 to $32 trillion in hidden assets offshore to escape tax payments, a loss to governments of about $280 billion, reported Reuters in 2012.

3. See US wealth ratios of 288:1 in https://thinkprogress.org/americas-1-percent-have-288-times-as-much-wealth-as-the-median-household-af6cfff28b73.

4. Richard Peet is professor of Geography at Clark University in Massachusetts. *Unholy Trinity* first came out in 2002 (New York: Zed Books), and led to *Geography of Power* (2007), *Theories of Development* (2008), and the updated 2009 edition of *Trinity* that I consulted.

5. See Bloomberg's 2013 archived article, "Eurobonds as Refugees from Tax Men Turn 50 in $4 Trillion Market," and their history from Bank of England here: http://www.bankofengland.co.uk/archive/Documents/historicpubs/qb/1991/qb91q4521528.pdf.

6. Greek economist and former treasurer of Greece Yanis Varoufakis has written surprisingly accessible explanations of Greece's doubled debts and global finances that result in global austerity in his books, *The Global Minotaur* (2011) and *And the Weak Suffer What They Must?* (2016).

7. See the 2013 Pew report comparing trends of falling male wages and rising female wages: http://www.pewsocialtrends.org/2013/12/11/on-pay-gap-millennial-women-near-parity-for-now/sdt-gender-and-work-12-2013-0-03/.

8. See also "As you were," *Economist,* October 13, 2012, for analysis including Jane Austen and today's crony capitalism.

9. See Frank Rich, *Scientific American*, March 31, 2015, on American unawareness of how unequal the United States has become: https://www.scientificamerican.com/article/economic-inequality-it-s-far-worse-than-you-think/.

Chapter 10: Mom's Sugar Bowl—1776-1965

1. Mitra Toossi at the US Bureau of Labor Statistics (BLS) reported in 2002 on labor trends in *A Century of Change: The U.S. Labor Force, 1950–2050.* Transformation of labor's gender structure was particularly dramatic. In 1950, 18 million women were in the US workforce. By 2000, they numbered 60 million.

2. Pin money and coverture are related marital subjects affecting women of Jane Austen's time. See Amy Louise Harrison, "Common Law vs. Common Practice: The Use of Marriage Settlements in Early Modern England," *Economic History Review*, Vol. 43, No. 1.

3. Virginia Woolf's famous Angel of the House originated in Coventry Patmore's 1854 poem about his angelic wife, burnished by William Ross Wallace's 1865 poem about mother's hand, rocking the cradle.

4. See Stephanie Coontz, *The Way We Never Were,* and also Mignon Duffy's research, "Doing the Dirty Work: Gender, Race, and Reproductive Labor in Historical Perspective," *Gender and Society*, Vol. 21, No. 3, 2007, discussing the intersection of issues that sort us women out.

5. As Rebecca J. Rosen points out in the *Atlantic*, March 2016, "Marriage Will Not Fix Poverty," only better incomes do, but dual income households are more essential than ever for most. See https://www.theatlantic.com/business/archive/2016/03/marriage-poverty/473019/.

Chapter 11: Egg Money—40,000 BCE–1965

1. See Merlin Stone's *When God Was a Woman* (1976) and also Venus figurines, breast pots, articles, and photos on Max Dashu's website, http://www.suppressedhistories.net/.

2. Women have newly reshaped archeology. See *Engendering Archeology: Women and Prehistory* (1991) and the many books on prehistoric female symbolism by American archeologist Marija Gimbutas, introduced here on YouTube: https://www.youtube.com/watch?v=yU1bEmq_pf0.

3. See a surprisingly vivid photo catalog of artifacts from Catal Huyuk, including famous female figures, at St. Louis Community College's site, http://users.stlcc.edu/mfuller/catalhuyuk.html.

4. See Jack Weatherford's *The History of Money* (1997), especially its chapter "The Golden Curse," for an explanation of the inflationary effects of the New World's gold and silver flooding Europe.

5. See Childbirth in Colonial America, Digital History, Topic ID 70, 2016. http://www.digitalhistory.uh.edu/topic_display.cfm?tcid=70

6. See NPR's 2017 report on rising US maternal death rates and comparisons to other developed nations: http://www.npr.org/2017/05/12/528098789/u-s-has-the-worst-rate-of-maternal-deaths-in-the-developed-world.

7. Mothers' economic penalty shows up by state in this map from *US News*: https://www.usnews.com/news/best-states/articles/2017-04-07/affordable-child-care-paid-family-leave-key-to-closing-gender-wage-gap.

8. See Department of Labor stats on US working moms now at 70 percent at https://blog.dol.gov/2017/03/01/12-stats-about-working-women.

Chapter 12, A Penny Saved Is a Penny Earned—1965–Now

1. See 2010 discussion of Pareto and Smith from the San Francisco Federal Reserve Bank: http://www.frbsf.org/economic-research/publications/economic-letter/2010/may/invisible-hand-relevance/.

2. See EPI Family Budget Calculator: What Families Need to Get By, a new measure to replace 1960's poverty line, which most agree needs revision.

3. See Alia E. Dastagir, "Why Does American Work Feel So Bad?" *USA Today*, June 2017, https://www.usatoday.com/story/money/2017/06/04/life-american-worker-hard-ever-get-bette/345685001/.

4. See Census numbers on housing costs: www.census.gov/topics/housing.html.

5. See *Realtor Mag* for 2017 down payment average of 11 percent: http://realtormag.realtor.org/daily-news/2017/02/15/big-down-payment-myth.

6. See the Census 2015 American Community Survey for trend of longer typical commutes.

7. See US profit center in *The Cost of Having a Baby in the United States*, Truven Health Analytics, 2013, http://transform.childbirthconnection.org/wp-content/uploads/2013/01/Cost-of-Having-a-Baby1.pdf.

8. See Pew report on numbers of children per mom trends, down from three in the 1970s: http://www.pewsocialtrends.org/2015/05/07/family-size-among-mothers/.

9. See household numbers trend of decline since 1960 (3.3 people) to 2016 (2.5): https://www.census.gov/newsroom/press-releases/2016/cb16-192.html.

10. See USDA report, *Expenditures on Children by Families*: https://www.usda.gov/media/press-releases/2014/08/18/parents-projected-spend-245340-raise-child-born-2013-according-usda.

11. See insurance premiums slowing down but deductibles going up in *Business Insider*, September 2016, http://www.businessinsider.com/out-of-pocket-healthcare-payments-skyrocketing-2016-9, and also in a 2016 *Wall Street Journal* op-ed by Kaiser Family Foundation president: https://blogs.wsj.com/washwire/2016/09/18/the-missing-debate-over-rising-health-care-deductibles/.

12. The Institute for Women's Policy Research tracks the wage gap, which appears to be all but stuck: https://iwpr.org/great-great-great-granddaughter-will-paid-much-man/.

13. Economic Policy Institute's research on 618 US communities found childcare costs of two-parent, two-child families exceeded rent costs in 500 communities. See *What Families Need to Get By*, Issue Brief #403, August 26, 2015.

14. See 2013 Census data analysis which found 47 percent of total US workforce is female, with 40 percent primary breadwinners, up from 11 percent in 1960, http://www.pewsocialtrends.org/2013/05/29/breadwinner-moms/.

15. See 2017 *US News* map for childcare status and news on state parental leave insurance plans: https://www.usnews.com/news/best-states/articles/2017-04-07/affordable-child-care-paid-family-leave-key-to-closing-gender-wage-gap.

16. See Sabine O'Hara's article "Everything Needs Care: Toward a Context-Based Economy," in the anthology edited by Margunn Bjornholt and Ailsa McKay, *Counting on Marilyn Waring: New Advances in Feminist Economics* (Ontario: Demeter Press, 2013).

17. See Irene van Staveren's "Feminist Fiction and Feminist Economics: Charlotte Perkins Gilman on Efficiency," along with other essays challenging EconoMan's point of view, in the anthology edited by Drucilla K. Barker and Edith Kuiper, *Toward a Feminist Philosophy of Economics* (New York: Routledge, 2003).

18. See the New Economy Working Group from the Next System Project, www.thenextsystem.org/resource-new-economy-working-group/, which includes the Institute for Policy Studies, *YES! Magazine*, the Living Economies Forum, New Economy Coalition, Institute for Local Self-Reliance, and the Democracy Collaborative, all groups critical of EconoMan's economic thinking.

19. See OECD for international time studies that show women spend from two to ten times more than men on unpaid care work: https://www.oecd.org/dev/development-gender/Unpaid_care_work.pdf.

20. See Bureau of Labor Statistics 2011 overview on sweeping changes in women's education, work, and range of work in the job market and at home: https://www.bls.gov/spotlight/2011/women/.

Chapter 13: Out of the Mouths of Babes

1. See archeologist Denise Schmandt-Besserat's research into development of tokens, symbols, cuneiform, numbers, and writing in *How Writing Came About* (Austin: University of Texas Press, 1996).

2. See the 1999 academic research paper, "The History and Rhetoric of Auditor Independence Concepts," written in the context of a newly formed Independence Standards Board of the American Institute of Certified Public Accountants (AICPA), which issues US auditing standards.

3. Read Robert Kennedy's eloquent speech about GDP's misdirection in full at www.jfklibrary.org/Research/Research-Aids/Ready-Reference/RFK-Speeches/Remarks-of-Robert-F-Kennedy-at-the-University-of-Kansas-March-18-1968.aspx. His remarks were informed by Hazel Henderson's Citizens for Clean Air, which was calling for correcting the GDP. His thank-you letter is framed on Henderson's wall.

4. See psychologist Daniel Goleman's *Emotional Intelligence* (1995), neurologist Antonio Damasio's *Descartes' Error: Emotion, Reason and the Human Brain* (1997), and neuroscientist Candace Pert's *Molecules of Emotion: The Science Behind Mind-Body Medicine* (1997) for accessible research reshaping old ideas.

5. See Yale's William Nordhaus on lack of US environmental measures at https://www.bea.gov/scb/account_articles/national/1199od/nordhaus.htm, and also his book, *A Question of Balance: Weighing the Options on Global Warming Policies* (Princeton: Yale University Press, 2008).

6. See a rare, sparse, and wrongheaded 2016 report from US BEA, *Accounting for Household Production in the National Accounts: An Update, 1965–2014*. Instead of measuring household production outputs, it only examines household effects on GDP, declaring its shrinking importance, while claiming household production slowed economic recovery.

7. See Gross National Happiness USA at www.gnhusa.org.

8. See Eric Zencey on GPI, quoted by John Havens in the *Guardian*, June 6, 2014: https://www.theguardian.com/sustainable-business/2014/jun/06/abolish-gdp-genuine-progress-indicator-gpi.

9. See Finland's early attempts at expanding national accounts in Johanna Varjonen and Leena M. Kirjavainen's article "Women's Unpaid Work Was Counted But . . ." in *Counting on Marilyn: Feminist Advances in Economics*.

10. See Canadian Well-Being Index at https://uwaterloo.ca/canadian-index-wellbeing/.

11. See OECD Better Life Measures at http://www.oecd.org/statistics/better-life-initiative.htm.

12. See Gallup 2014 analysis of international well-being reports at www.gallup.com/poll/175694/country-varies-greatly-worldwide.aspx.

13. See Stiglitz and Sen 2010 report on French indicators at www.stat.si/doc/drzstat/Stiglitz%20report.pdf.

14. Learn more about SWEIs (Social Wealth Economic Indicators) in Eisler, Riane (2017) "Roadmap to a Caring Economics: Beyond Capitalism and Socialism," *Interdisciplinary Journal of Partnership Studies:* Vol. 4: Iss. 1, Article 3. Available online at University of Minnesota Libraries Publications

Chapter 14: His Manly Largeness

1. My high school friend F. Roseanne Bittner has written sixty western romance titles, including the Savage Destiny series that began her writing career. See http://www.rosannebittner.com/past_titles.html.

2. The *New York Times* called Rollo May's *Love and Will* (New York: W.W. Norton & Co., 1969) "the most important book of the year," and I found it relevant thirty years later. See May's complex historical analysis of Eros in the personal and the political, in psychology and society, especially the chapter, "The Meaning of Care."

3. Gaia's namesake still wasn't in my dictionary ten years after Lovelock proposed his Gaia theory. Her memory, though, never really left us. We always refer to Mother Nature—not Father.

4. The 2003 Canadian documentary *The Corporation* made the case that if a person, corporations could be defined as psychopathic. Meanwhile Cornell research published in the *Journal of Legal and Criminological Psychology* describes predatory psychopathic language like "drinking from a firehose." EconoMansplaining? This article sees a link from the language study above to CEOs in Silicon Valley: https://www.theguardian.com/technology/2017/mar/15/silicon-valley-psychopath-ceo-sxsw-panel.

5. See Kevin Roose, "One Percent Jokes and Plutocrats in Drag: What I Saw When I Crashed a Wall Street Secret Society," *New York Magazine,* February 18, 2014, http://nymag.com/daily/intelligencer/2014/02/i-crashed-a-wall-street-secret-society.html.

6. You can still see the 1955 TV series *The Millionaire* at YouTube: https://www.youtube.com/watch?v=tL23mLBrOic.

7. The Supreme Court's first corporate landmark ruling in 1819 on *Dartmouth College v. Woodward* established that a corporate charter was a contract, "the obligation of which cannot be impaired without violating the Constitution of the United States."

8. Presidential candidate Bernie Sanders in 2016 proposed a constitutional amendment to fund elections through public, not private, means. If ever passed, such an amendment would end any need of big corporate money to run an election.

9. See "Peacocks, Porsches, and Thorstein Veblen: Conspicuous Consumption and Mating Signals," *Journal of Personality and Social Psychology*, 2011, Vol. 100, No. 4, 664–680.

10. Marilyn French's ideas about "power over" and "power with" in *Beyond Power: On Women, Men and Morals* (New York: Ballantine Books, 1986) aligned with those of Riane Eisler, who defined and contrasted two social systems in her book, *The Chalice and the Blade: Our History and Our Future* (San Francisco: HarperCollins, 1987).

11. See the symptoms of rigid domination and more equitable partnership described in a table on p. 103 of Eisler's later *The Real Wealth of Nations* (San Francisco: Berrett-Koehler, 2007).

12. See Obama's Council of Economic Advisors 2015 recommendations for "Expanding Opportunities for Women in Business," still available online at the Obama White House Archives: https://obamawhitehouse.archives.gov/sites/default/files/docs/women_in_business_issue_brief_final_nonembargoed.pdf.

13. For a PDF of "Who Owns Stock in America?" see Professor Edward N. Wolff of New York University's whole analysis at https://www.amphilsoc.org/sites/default/files/proceedings/Wolff.pdf.

14. See Chad Bown's NPR interview about the loss of 5 million manufacturing jobs since 2000 and the role robotics has played, making a comeback unlikely: http://www.npr.org/2016/08/18/490192497/bringing-back-manufacturing-jobs-would-be-harder-than-it-sounds.

15. See the details of the Panama Papers and what offshore tax evasion means to the majority at https://americansfortaxfairness.org/wp-content/uploads/Corporate-tax-chartbook_-How-corporations-rig-the-rules-to-dodge-the-taxes-they-owe-_-Economic-Policy-Institute.pdf.

Chapter 15: She's in Labor

1. For details on trends for young mothers, see economist Susan Shank's "Women and the Labor Market: The Link Grows Stronger," US Bureau of Labor Statistics (BLS): *Monthly Labor Review*, March 1988. Also Sharon R. Cohany and Emy Sok's "Trends in Labor Force Participation by Married Mothers of Infants," BLS: *Monthly Labor Review*, February 2007.

2. See the most famous contemporary account of young women's labor organizing, Lucy Larcom's *A New England Girlhood* (1889), who was eleven when she began working. It's now an ebook on Amazon.

3. The novel *Call the Darkness Light* by Nancy Zaroulis (New York: Soho Press, 1993) about the Lowell factory girls and the first turnout in 1834 also enlivens history. See http://www.lowellmillwomen.com/about.html.

4. See Kenneth B. Noble's report on shady Teamster loans, "Las Vegas Casino Loans Repaid, Teamsters Pension Fund Asserts," *New York Times*, February 5, 1986.

5. See Katherine Paterson's novel, *Bread and Roses, Too* (2006), and Vermont ties to the famous Lawrence Strike of 1912: http://www.burlingtonfreepress.com/story/news/2017/05/14/history-space-barre-bread-roses-strike/101638016/.

6. This brief overview has valuable links to labor studies: www.cnbc.com/2017/05/03/how-the-8-hour-workday-changed-how-americans-work.html.

7. See Secretary of Labor Marin Clarkberg's report, *The Time-Squeeze in American Families: From Causes to Solutions*, June 15, 1998. She cautioned that these were her opinions: https://www.dol.gov/dol/aboutdol/history/herman/reports/futurework/conference/families/couples.htm.

8. See also Pew Research Center's contrasting dual and single income households in an informative graph: http://www.pewresearch.org/ft_dual-income-households-1960-2012-2/.

9. Gallup Surveys and American Time Use Studies (ATUS) both show a steady increase in American work hours beyond the eight-hour standard.

10. See *US News* citing survey finding 63 percent thought a nine-to-five job "an outdated concept": https://www.usnews.com/news/articles/2015/07/23/traditional-workweek-has-gone-the-way-of-the-dinosaurs?int=news-rec.

11. See Richard D. Wolff's "Start with Worker Self-Directed Enterprises," part of the Next System Project of the Democracy Collaborative, August 10, 2016, available at http://thenextsystem.org/start-with-worker-self-directed-enterprises/.

12. Food workers, diners, and restaurant owners will all find useful information at ROC United. This link is to their publications and reports, but the whole organization is inspiring: http://rocunited.org/resources/publications/.

13. For more on Cindy Turcot and Employee Stock Option Plans, see http://www.vermontwoman.com/articles/2014/0414/gardenerssupply/turcot.html and also the ESOP Association at https://www.esopassociation.org.

14. Mondragon's history has not been without difficulty, especially as it has grown larger. See a 2014 survey, "Evaluating Workplace Democracy at Mondragon," by Anders Asa Christiansen at UVM Scholarworks: http://scholarworks.uvm.edu/cgi/viewcontent.cgi?article=1016&context=hcoltheses.

15. Johns Hopkins professor Vincent Navarro discusses the bankruptcy of one of Mondragon's manufacturing companies after 2008, and also analyzes difficulties of cooperatives in a competitive world. See https://www.counterpunch.org/2014/04/30/the-case-of-mondragon/.

16. The US Federation of Worker Cooperatives, representing 160 businesses and over 3,000 workers, issues an annual report, offers a Co-op Bookshelf, a referral directory, and peer-certified DAWN advisors who provide technical assistance for more democratic small businesses. See https://usworker.coop/home/.

17. See the Southern Rural Black Women's Initiative for Social and Economic Justice at http://www.srbwi.org. Their program for young women's leadership and their hall of fame both inspire with their wide vision, including artistic expression, faith, and reflection, as well as caring action.

Chapter 16: All About Money—And Yes, It *Does* Grow on Trees

1. The Federal Reserve is seeking to appear more transparent about its governance. It provides information about itself, as here explaining its mysterious "independence within the government": https://www.federalreserve.gov/faqs/about_12799.htm.

2. National Priorities Project (https://www.nationalpriorities.org) provides a user-friendly nonpartisan graphic analysis of the national budget, its money sources and expenditures, including its debts and interest payments. At 2.6 percent of the GDP, the average over the past fifty years, debts are brokered by the Federal Reserve, they note, our monetary system independent of government.

3. John W. Schoen with CNBC reports on worries about the nation's roughly $14 trillion in Treasury debt. The Congressional Budget Office estimates interest costs may triple over the next ten years. See http://www.cnbc.com/2016/12/19/interest-payments-could-become-one-of-the-federal-govts-biggest-line-items.html.

4. See the interconnections of foreign policy decisions, the oily dollar, and stock markets influenced by a weaker dollar, controlled by the Federal Reserve in http://www.zerohedge.com/news/2017-02-02/iran-just-officially-ditched-dollar.

5. See Wright Patman's whole speech about the government borrowing its own money at: The Congressional Record of September 29, 1941, pp. 7582–7583.

6. For more on bond sales and the Treasury, see my article, "The Federal Reserve and Money on the Make," which appeared in *Vermont Woman* in 2011.

7. The Federal Reserve Transparency Act joined conservative Senator Rand Paul and socialist-progressive Senator Bernie Sanders to seek regular external GAO audits in 2016, not the Fed's internal "audits." As a rule, audits are independent. See https://www.usnews.com/news/articles/2016-01-12/democrats-kill-rand-pauls-audit-the-fed-bill-though-sanders-votes-yes.

8. This news release on the Federal Reserve's statutory dividends of $711.5 million paid to member banks in 2017 includes other financial information, including increased returns to Treasury from its huge loans. Note that although the Fed remains privately owned and independent of government, it uses (dot)gov for its website address. See https://www.federalreserve.gov/news events/.

9. See a PDF of Wright Patman's 50th Anniversary report on improving the Fed online at the Government Accounting Office (GAO): http://www.gao.gov/assets/210/201713.pdf.

Chapter 17: More Than One Way to Skin a Cat

1. Seba Smith, among the earliest US political satirists, published "The Money Diggers: A Down East Story" in *Burton's Gentleman's Magazine* in 1840: "This is a money-digging world of ours; and as it is said, 'There is more than one way to skin a cat,' so is there more than one way of digging money."

2. Leopold based his numbers of financial sector profits (chart 4:4) on BEA NIPAs (National Income and Product Accounts, Table 6.16, "Corporate Profits by Industry") at www.bea.gov.

3. See Maggie Walker's St. Luke's Penny Savings Bank, the nation's longest running black bank: http://www.nps.gov/mawa/the-st-luke-penny-savings-bank.htm.

4. The St. Luke's burial cooperative that brought so many female board members to Maggie Walker's bank was founded in 1867 by former slave Mary Prout, when women still took care of the dead.

5. See Suzanne McGee and Heidi Moore's "Women's Rights and Their Money: A Timeline from Cleopatra to Lilly Ledbetter," *Guardian*, August 11, 2014, https://www.theguardian.com/money/us-money-blog/2014/aug/11/women-rights-money-timeline-history.

6. Married women could be and were denied bank accounts and credit cards without their husband's signature until 1974: http://www.cnn.com/2014/08/07/living/sixties-women-5-things/index.html.

7. The Institute for Self-Reliance, interested in building local economies, has closely analyzed the Bank of North Dakota and provides historical data and in-depth comparison to surrounding states and the nation. This link includes links to other state efforts, as well, such as the Maine Partnership Bank: https://ilsr.org/rule/bank-of-north-dakota-2/.

8. This analysis from Washington State compares Wells Fargo private operations to North Dakota's public ones: https://www.washingtonpublicbankcoalition.org/how-the-washington-public-trust-can-save-the-2017-legislature/4-comparing-public-banks-to-private-banks.

9. See also Josh Harkinson's "How the Nation's Only State-Owned Bank Became the Envy of Wall Street," *Mother Jones*, March 27, 2009, and Abby Rapoport's "The People's Bank," *The American Prospect*, April 1, 2013.

10. Reasons for lower student loan default rates in North Dakota are cited here: http://www.grandforksherald.com/news/education/3888027-und-student-loan-default-rate-stays-lower-national-average.

11. Public Banking Institute provides links and guides for doing research in your state and city here: http://www.publicbankinginstitute.org/research_guide_what_wall_street_costs_america.

12. See IMF Working Paper, "State-Owned Banks, Stability, Privatization, and Growth: Practical Policy Decisions in a World Without Empirical Proof," prepared by A. Michael Andrews, authorized for distribution by Monetary and Financial Systems Department, January 2005. While not the view of the IMF, it's a well-documented working paper.

13. Municipal banks administered by a statewide system that is not owned by anyone, but governs itself transparently, are all part of Germany's *Landesbank* system, which includes the *Sparkassen* savings banks.

14. See Ellen Brown's highlighting the German Landesbank system, along with other locally rooted financial institutes including credit unions and co-ops here in the United States, in this 2012 *Huffington Post* piece "Cooperative Banking Is the Exciting Wave of the Future": http://www.huffingtonpost.com/ellen-brown/cooperative-banking-is-th_b_1540524.html.

15. See Brown also in "The Public Option in Banking: Another Look at the German Model," *Op-Ed News*, October 14, 2011, https://www.opednews.com/articles/THE-PUBLIC-OPTION-IN-BANKI-by-Ellen-Brown-111014-55.html.

16. See Brown on Japan's postal bank's ability to bail out the Euro in 2012, also funding Britain, the United States, and the IMF. Japan uses this public bank, Brown and the *New York Times* says, for 95 percent of its debt. See http://ellenbrown.com/2012/09/05/the-myth-that-japan-is-broke-the-worlds-largest-debtor-is-now-the-worlds-largest-creditor/.

17. Under pressure, Japan Post has sold only 11 percent of stock, still holding the lion's share in 2015. See http://www.aljazeera.com/news/2015/11/japan-post-companies-net-12bn-biggest-ipo-151104073753361.html.

18. See Vermont's move to use state revenue to invest locally, a step in the right direction, but falling short of multiplying money as a public bank could: http://billmoyers.com/2015/01/14/vermonters-lobby-public-bank-win-millions-local-investment-instead/.

19. See SEWA (Self Employed Women's Association) at www.sewa.org and SEWA bank at https://www.sewabank.com,

Chapter 18: Ending the Old Double Standard

1. See historical trends, maps, and empirical evidence for falling birth rates in Fertility, Our World in Data, by Oxford economist Max Roser at https://ourworldindata.org/fertility.

2. Stockholm International Peace Research Institute tracks weapons trade by nation. The United States tops manufacturing and spent $603 billion in 2015 on a military that dwarves other nations. See www.sipri.org/.

3. National Priorities found the United States borrowed $583 billion in FY 2015, and paid $229 billion for interest on past debt, fully 6 percent of our outlay. Our national debt in FY 2015 was $18.153 trillion.

4. This late 2015 article by Megan Holohan from *Today* shows a detailed map of US policy on parental leave compared to other countries: http://www.today.com/health/problem-parental-leave-u-s-t38701.

5. Hazel Henderson's website on ethical markets that value the environment and social justice links to her many books and her many accomplishments: www.ethicalmarkets.com.

6. A 2015 Report to the Vermont legislature, *Working Lands Enterprise Initiative*, makes visible the services of the state's environment to the economy. Similar data could show the value that household and community services deliver too. See http://www.vermontwoodlands.org/documents/ReportFinal2015.pdf.

7. USSIF's *Investing to Advance Women: A Guide for Individual and Institutional Investors* measures women's global economic status from a range of 2014 economic data. See http://www.ussif.org/Files/Publications/SRI_Women_F.pdf.

8. See Rachel Aviv's remarkably personal account of "The Cost of Caring: The Lives of Immigrant Women Who Tend to the Needs of Others," *New Yorker*, April 11, 2016, http://www.newyorker.com/magazine/2016/04/11/the-sacrifices-of-an-immigrant-caregiver.

9. Audre Lorde's essay, "Uses of the Erotic: The Erotic as Power," was first presented as a paper, August 5, 1978, at the Fourth Berkshire Conference on the History of Women at Holyoke College, and is part of her collection, *Sister Outsider*, and available online here: http://www.cds.hawaii.edu/sites/default/files/downloads/resources/diversity/SisterOutside.pdf.

10. SUNY's David Sloan Wilson credits Elinor Ostrom's rescue of economics in this article describing her principles, as well as her detractors, at the website of Evonomics: The Next Evolution of Economics at http://evonomics.com/the-woman-who-saved-economics-from-disaster/.

11. You can watch Elinor Ostrom in action, delivering an eight-minute whiteboard lecture on the commons and how people have organized democratic rules that build trust here: https://www.youtube.com/watch?v=ByXM47Ri1Kc.

12. Elbridge Gerry, vice president to James Madison, warned about standing armies, available online at the James Madison Research Library and Information Center here: http://www.madisonbrigade.com/e_gerry.htm.

13. "Love Is Reckless" by Jalal al-Din Rumi, born in 1207 in Balkh, now Afghanistan, is all over the Internet along with other of Rumi's poems, but I was unable to find the translator's name.

14. Friedman's notion of markets as selection vehicles first appeared in *Essays on Positive Economics* (1953), and influenced evolutionary economics, which holds ideas similar to the "natural" free market.

Chapter 19: A Real Fixer-Upper

1. For a fairly recent 2008 report on the Swiss WIR, explanations of how it works, and a time-line of its developmental history, see: http://wiki.p2pfoundation.net/WIR_Economic_Circle_Cooperative.

2. See also this translation by Thomas Greco, author of *Money: Understanding and Creating Alternatives to Legal Tender* (White River Junction: Chelsea Green, 2001), on the origins and ideology of the WIR Economic Circle Cooperative: http://projects.exeter.ac.uk/RDavies/arian/wir.html.

3. Inheritance transfer tax, or the "death tax," is among our oldest taxes and was important to the founding fathers who sought to avoid an aristocracy. This article from the Center for Budget and Policy Priorities makes a current and practical case: https://www.cbpp.org/research/federal-tax/ten-facts-you-should-know-about-the-federal-estate-tax.

4. Mossack Fonseca of Panama Papers is a small player in the tax-escaping offshore racket, where big banks rule. See http://www.newsweek.com/panama-papers-big-banks-mossack-fonseca-447081.

5. See why tax cuts aren't working in a 2016 update from the oldest nonpartisan group to study taxes: https://taxfoundation.org/looking-back-bush-tax-cuts-fifteen-years-later/.

6. *The Balance* blog seeks to make money personal and gives us their long view on tax cuts about to expire in 2017: https://www.thebalance.com/president-george-bush-tax-cuts-3306331.

7. See *Forbes* on the rise of American precariat workers with contingent jobs, up to 40 percent: http://www.forbes.com/sites/elainepofeldt/2015/05/25/shocker-40-of-workers-now-have-contingent-jobs-says-u-s-government/#2db935f72532.

8. BLS does no statistic gathering on discouraged workers or of prisoners at work. This article suggests they should: http://nypost.com/2015/06/23/the-seven-weirdest-jobs-that-prisoners-do/.

9. Evelyn L. Forget of the University of Manitoba issued a 2011 report, *The Town with No Poverty*, based on a forgotten pilot project. See Duke University: https://public.econ.duke.edu/~erw/197/forget-cea%20(2).pdf.

10. The US poverty line for a family of three in 2016 was $1,680 a month, but TANF cash welfare benefits have fallen in all states since 1996, in twenty-three states by 30 percent or more. None reaches the poverty line, which most agree is unrealistic for today's families anyway. See http://www.cbpp.org/research/family-income-support/tanf-cash-benefits-have-fallen-by-more-than-20-percent-in-most-states.

11. A *CNN Money* report on 2014 OECD figures showed US workers already work in the job market more than other developed countries, an average of 34.4 hours compared to the Netherlands, lowest at 26.6 hours. See http://money.cnn.com/2015/07/09/news/economy/americans-work-bush/.

Chapter 20: The Personal Is Powerful And Plentiful

1. See Peggy McIntosh's essay, Working Paper 189, "White Privilege and Male Privilege: A Personal Account of Coming to See Correspondences through Work in Women's Studies" is available for four dollars from the Wellesley College Center for Research on Women, Wellesley, MA 02181.

2. See a short excerpt of McIntosh's essay online here if impatient: www.deanza.edu/faculty/lewisjulie/White%20Priviledge%20Unpacking%20the%20Invisible%20Knapsack.pdf.

3. See also Joshua Rothman's interview with McIntosh, "The Origins of Privilege," *New Yorker,* May 12, 2014, http://www.newyorker.com/books/page-turner/the-origins-of-privilege.

4. Articles abound on the subject of women second-guessing themselves in educational settings with mixed genders, especially in fields like math and engineering where stereotypes privilege male expressive styles. See an overview of "Gender and Gender Role Differences in Self- and Other-Estimates of Multiple Intelligences" by Agata Szymanowicz and Adrian Furnham in the *Journal of Social Psychology*, May 13, 2013, online at the NIH (National Institutes for Health) website, https://www.ncbi.nlm.nih.gov/pmc/articles/PMC4118948/#R38.

5. See effects of "stereotype threat" in http://www.nytimes.com/2012/10/07/opinion/sunday/intelligence-and-the-stereotype-threat.html.

6. The Tobin tax on Wall Street transactions, first proposed by James Tobin in 1972, aimed at slowing down reckless trading, and is supported by the National Organization for Women—though like many, NOW refers to it as the Robin Hood Tax: http://now.org/media-center/press-release/now-supports-robin-hood-tax/.

Glossary

absolute income hypothesis, the idea that people tend to base consumption on their sense of expected permanent income over their lifetime.

aggregate demand, in macroeconomics a nation's total demand for goods and services at a particular time.

aggregate supply, in macroeconomics a nation's total supply of goods and services at a particular time.

algorithms, a set of rules in calculation or problem-solving procedures, often used in computer programs in finance, called *quants*.

assets, property owned by a person or company.

audit, an official financial examination required of all US businesses.

bank run, when everyone goes to withdraw money from the bank all at once.

bankruptcy, a court-ordered declaration of inability to pay debts that places settlements in the hands of a trustee.

basic income, sometimes called *universal basic income*, or UBI, is a system of unconditional income to every citizen.

bear market, a market where prices are falling, encouraging sales.

behavioral economics, a theory that suggests that consuming patterns are not strictly logical or consistent, as some economists' mathematical formulas assert.

bottom line, the final total of an account, balance sheet, or other financial document.

bourgeoisie, Marx's name for the middle class.

bull market, a market where prices are rising, encouraging buying.

capital, wealth as assets or money used for business purposes.

capital accumulation, the acquisition of assets or of durable means of production to increase profit.

capital gains, income from investments or profits from the sale of a property.

collateral, something of value a debtor surrenders should she not repay as promised.

collateralized debt obligations (CDOs), a financial product pooling debt liabilities secured by collateral.

commodities, a raw material, or agricultural or manufactured product for sale.

compound interest, the addition of interest to the principal of a loan so that interest is paid on interest.

consumption function, a mathematical relationship between consumption and disposable income.

corporation, a group of people legally authorized to function as a single entity.

demurrage, a small carrying charge for shipping space or for money not in use, an incentive to keep vehicles circulating without inflation of prices.

deregulation, government's lifting rules to create a "free market."

derivatives, financial contracts derived from the value of underlying assets, essentially bets on future prices called by many names, including credit default swaps, collateralized debt obligations, etc.

double-entry bookkeeping, a financial system in which each transaction is entered as a debit in one account, and a credit in another, resulting in a balance sheet.

dual spheres, a popular nineteenth-century idea that the nature of activities at home and work were gendered and separate yet supposedly working in concert.

due diligence, reasonable steps taken by a person to satisfy any legal requirements, especially when buying and selling.

earned income tax credit (EITC), a refundable credit toward income taxes for low- and moderate-income working people.

ecology, the branch of biology that studies organisms' relationships with each other and with their shared environment.

efficiency, as an economic principle means an organized allocation of resources for productive output.

Enclosure Acts, in Britain the Parliament's series of laws over three hundred years that transferred public common lands to the aristocracy beginning in 1604, although smaller such transfers began in the twelfth century.

equity, your share of an asset, minus any debt.

EroNomics, as an alternative to *Screwnomics*, a system wherein humans interact with the Earth to form synergistic, self-regulating exchanges supportive of conditions for life on the planet.

externality, the results of a commercial activity that affects third parties uninvolved in the activity, and usually defined either as negative or positive.

fair market price, the amount exchanged between buyers and sellers when both have relevant knowledge.

fiat currency, a currency whose value is backed by the government that issues it, contrasted with a commodity currency backed by gold, cattle, or other resource.

fractional reserve banking, our current bank system that accepts deposits and makes loans and investments, backed by a reserve that is only a small fraction of its liabilities.

futures, financial contracts obligating buyer and seller to a future price.

Gini-coefficient, a measure of wealth distribution in a particular place and time.

globalization, commerce operating at an international scale.

graduated income tax, sometimes called a *progressive tax*, increases rate of tax for people with higher incomes, originally intended to avoid a money aristocracy.

Gross Domestic Product (GDP), the sum of all currency income within a nation's borders.

Gross National Happiness (GNH), a measure that expands currency-only national accounts to include environmental and human well-being.

Gross National Product (GNP), the sum of all currency income of a nation's citizens regardless of where they made that income.

hedge, to add protections or limit losses in financial transactions, usually by taking an additional offsetting position. You hedge your bets, just in case.

HNWI, acronym for High Net Worth Individuals.

housework, a word that only appeared when economic production was separated from home by industrialization.

income, money received on a regular basis.

inflation, a decrease in the purchasing power of a currency.

interest, the rental fee for borrowed money.

investment, using money for a material result in the future.

investment bank, a private company that provides financial services to HNWI individuals, corporations, and governments, specializing in raising and underwriting large amounts of capital. It may purchase large holdings of newly issued shares and resell them.

labrys, a double-headed axe originating in Crete, which may have been used in ceremony, but was said by the Greeks to be the battle-axe of the Amazons.

laissez-faire economics, letting money matters happen "naturally," without government interference.

mansplaining, a word that Rebecca Solnit never used in her essay, "Men Explain Things to Me," but her twenty-first-century women readers coined it to describe a man's patronizing a woman, an experience apparently quite common.

micro-businesses, often part of the informal economy, these are very small operations, often a source of self-employment.

monopoly, the exclusive possession or control of the supply or trade of a commodity or service.

mortgage, a legal contract between a borrower and a creditor for purchase of a property that entitles the creditor to reclaim the property should the debtor not pay as agreed, without return of any borrower's investment.

mortgage securities, a type of asset-backed security secured by a collection of mortgages, packaged and sold by an investment bank to investors.

mutual credit associations, member-based groups that agree to interest-free credit exchanges, tracked electronically and valued at agreed upon rates.

nanny government, a conservative put-down for social programs that assist people.

national accounts, a global system of accounting that produces the GDP.

national dividend, a concept similar to the universal basic income, but its amount would be tied to national economic data and might vary from year to year. C. H. Douglas proposed it as part of the Social Credit movement in Britain.

neoconservative, a politically conservative person, also called a *neocon*, who most often is also a neoliberal or libertarian when talking about economics.

note, any paper designating an amount owed, a debit, a paper also called *bills*.

on margin, a term for purchasing securities using money borrowed from the same broker who sold the securities; a *margin call* is a term for the broker demanding payment.

opportunity cost, the value of a road not taken in order to do something else. Eating your cake means the opportunity cost of your not having it for later.

panic, when everyone in the stock market seeks to sell their stocks all at once.

Pareto efficiency says an improvement happens when one person is better off and no one is worse off.

pin money, a term for the expected household allowance provided to a wife by her husband, in a time when clothing was still made at home.

postal savings bank, a banking system that deposits savings directly to national treasuries, begun in England in 1861 to encourage people to save for a rainy day.

principal, the amount of money borrowed by a debtor and lent by a creditor.

production, the fabrication or construction of a product.

proletariat, Marx's term for the working class.

quants, jargon for a financial analyst whose specialty is mathematical or statistical quantitative methods, especially algorithms.

salary, an employee's income from work, usually paid biweekly but expressed as an annual sum.

securities, a tradable financial asset, broadly defined as *debt securities* (bonds), and *equity securities*, or stocks and shares, a part of an enterprise.

sharecropping, a form of agriculture developed after the Civil War ended slavery. A tenant produced crops for a landlord, who controlled prices, rents, and markets, receiving the share that the landlord determined. Its system exploited the poorest.

solvency, the state of being able to pay debts.

sovereign bonds, loans to national governments around the world.

stocks, a certified share of ownership in a corporation that raises collective capital based on perceived value.

subprime mortgage, a property loan that charges higher interest rates for a borrower who would not qualify for a conventional mortgage because of low income or poor credit rating.

supply and demand, the amount of a product, commodity, or service and the desire of buyers for it, both factors that free market economists say regulates its price.

TARP, acronym for the Troubled Asset Relief Program signed into law to bail out banks and aid homeowners in October 2008.

tax credit, an amount of money that offsets a tax liability, reducing a tax bill.

tax deductions, a reduction in tax liability through items that lower taxable income, depending on a tax code's rules, which vary from year to year and from state to state. Common federal income tax deductions include charitable donations and mortgage interest.

time use surveys, data gathered on time spending, whether on paid or unpaid activities including housework, volunteering, childcare, etc., sorted by demographics and used around the world to guide policy decisions.

usury, the name for the crime of charging interest from ancient through Renaissance times.

voodoo economics, a put-down for Reaganomics, also known as *trickle-down economics* or *supply-side economics*, from ideas promoted by Milton Friedman.

wages, a payment for employment, paid by an hourly rate on a daily or weekly basis.

Washington consensus, a set of free market prescriptions agreed to and widely applied by Washington, Europe, the International Monetary Fund, and the World Bank to economic crises.

Unpacked Definitions:

(In order of appearance)

Recommended Reading

Bair, Sheila. *Bull by the Horns: Fighting to Save Main Street from Wall Street and Wall Street from Itself.* 2013.

————. *The Bullies of Wall Street: This Is How Greed Messed Up Our Economy.* 2015.

Barber, Elizabeth Wayland. *Women's Work: The First 20,000 Years.* 1994.

Bhatt, Ela R. *We Are Poor But So Many: The Story of Self-Employed Women in India.* 2006.

Brown, Ellen Hodgson. *The Web of Debt: The Shocking Truth about Our Money System and How We Can Break Free.* 2008.

————. *The Public Bank Solution: From Austerity to Prosperity.* 2013.

Canterbery, E. Ray. *A Brief History of Economics: Artful Approaches to the Dismal Science.* 2005.

Cowan, Ruth Schwartz. *More Work for Mother: The Ironies of Household Technology from the Open Hearth to the Microwave.* 1995.

De Graff, John and David K. Batker. *What's the Economy For, Anyway?* 2011.

Eisler, Riane. *The Chalice and the Blade.* 1987.

————. *The Real Wealth of Nations: Creating a Caring Economics.* 2007.

Gleeson-White, Jane. *Double Entry: How the Merchants of Venice Created Modern Finance.* 2012.

Goodwin, Michael. *Economix: How Our Economy Works (And Doesn't Work).* Illustrated by Dan E. Burr. 2012.

Greco, Thomas H., Jr. *Money: Understanding and Creating Alternatives to Legal Tender.* 2001.

Hallsmith, Gwendolyn. *The Key to Sustainable Cities.* 2003.

———— and Bernard Lietaer. *Creating Wealth: Growing Local Economies with Local Currencies.*

———— and Michael H. Shuman. *Vermont Dollars, Vermont Sense: A Handbook for Investors, Businesses, Finance Professionals, and Everybody Else.* 2015.

Henderson, Hazel. *Creating Alternative Futures: The End of Economics.* 1978.

Jayaraman, Saru. *Behind the Kitchen Door.* 2016.

Kelly, Marjorie. *The Divine Right of Capital: Dethroning the Corporate Aristocracy.* 2003.

————. *Owning Our Future: The Emerging Ownership Revolution.* 2012.

Kennedy, Margrit. *Occupy Money: Creating an Economy Where Everybody Wins.* 2012.

Kivel, Paul. *You Call This A Democracy? Who Benefits, Who Pays, and Who Really Decides.* 2004.

Klein, Naomi. *The Shock Doctrine: The Rise of Disaster Capitalism.* 2007.

————. *No is Not Enough; Resisting Trump's Shock Politics and Winning the World We Need.* 2017.

Kunin, Madeleine M. *The New Feminist Agenda: Defining the Next Revolution for Women, Work, and Family.* 2012.

Lakey, George. *Viking Economics: How the Scandinavians Got It Right—and How We Can, Too.* 2016.

Leopold, Les. *Runaway Inequality: An Activist's Guide to Economic Justice.* 2015.

Lorde, Audre. "Uses of the Erotic: The Erotic as Power" in *Sister Outsider: Essays and Speeches.* 1984.

Malveaux, Julianne. *Sex, Lies, and Stereotypes: Perspectives of a Mad Economist.* 1994.

————. *Surviving and Thriving: 365 Facts in Black Economic History.* 2010.

Marçal, Katrine. *Who Cooked Adam Smith's Dinner? A Story about Women and Economics.* 2015.

May, Rollo. *Love and Will.* 1969.

McElvaine, Robert S. *Eve's Seed: Biology, the Sexes, and the Course of History.* 2001.

Nembhard, Jessica Gordon. *Collective Courage: A History of African American Cooperative Economic Thought and Practice.* 2014.

Peet, Richard. *Unholy Trinity: The IMF, World Bank and WTO.* 2009.

Prins, Nomi. *All the Presidents' Bankers: The Hidden Alliances that Drive American Power.* 2014.

————. *It Takes a Pillage: An Epic Tale of Power, Deceit, and Untold Trillions.* 2009.

Rudahl, Sharon. *A Dangerous Woman: The Graphic Biography of Emma Goldman.* 2007.

Solnit, Rebecca. *Men Explain Things to Me.* 2014.

Taibbi, Matt. *Griftopia: A Story of Bankers, Politicians, and the Most Audacious Power Grab in American History.* 2011.

Warren, Elizabeth. *A Fighting Chance.* 2014.

———— and Amelia Warren Tyagi. *The Two-Income Trap: Why Middle-Class Parents Are Going Broke.* 2004.

Weatherford, Jack. *The History of Money.* 1997.

Whyte, William Foote and Kathleen King Whyte. *Making Mondragon: The Growth and Dynamics of the Worker Cooperative Complex.* 1991.

About the Author

Rickey Gard Diamond began writing in the midst of big political change and growing American differences. In 1985, she became founding editor of *Vermont Woman*, where she continues today as a contributing editor. She taught writing and literature, feminist and media studies at Vermont College of Norwich University for over 20 years, while publishing articles and short fiction. In 1999, Calyx Books published her novel, *Second Sight*, which was reissued by HarperCollins in 2000. In 2011 she was awarded a National Newspaper Association award for her article series, "An Economy of Our Own," and in 2014 she won a Hedgebrook fellowship for her work on *Screwnomics*. Meanwhile, her short fiction, published in literary journals, was issued as a collection, *Whole Worlds Could Pass Away,* in 2017. A mother and grandmother, Rickey lives in Montpelier with her husband and their beautiful cat, blogging and connecting with EconoGirlfriends around the world, while continuing to read and write fiction. Contact her at www.screwnomics.org.

About the Illustrator

Peaco Todd is a syndicated cartoonist and author/illustrator of several books and numerous articles; she has worked as a journalist, and as professor of liberal studies for Lesley University and the Union Institute and University. Current projects include a graphic memoir about depression, *Table for One*, and Earth Comix, a non-profit to raise awareness of the fight to save elephants, rhinos, and other endangered animals. See her work at screwnomics.org, earth-comix.com, and www.peacotoons.com.

Selected Titles from She Writes Press

She Writes Press is an independent publishing company founded to serve women writers everywhere. Visit us at www.shewritespress.com.

Love Her, Love Her Not: The Hillary Paradox edited by Joanne Bamberger. $16.95, 978-1-63152-806-4. A collection of personal essays by noted women essayists and emerging women writers that explores the question of why Americans have a love/hate "relationship" with Hillary Clinton.

Transforming Knowledge: Public Talks on Women's Studies, 1976-2011 by Jean Fox O'Barr. $19.95, 978-1-938314-48-3. A collection of essays addressing one woman's challenges faced and lessons learned on the path to reframing—and effecting—feminist change.

100 Under $100: One Hundred Tools for Empowering Global Women by Betsy Teutsch. $29.95, 978-1-63152-934-4. An inspiring, comprehensive look at the many tools being employed today to empower women in the developing world and help them raise themselves out of poverty.

Stop Giving it Away: How to Stop Self-Sacrificing and Start Claiming Your Space, Power, and Happiness by Cherilynn Veland. $16.95, 978-1-63152-958-0. An empowering guide designed to help women break free from the trappings of the needs, wants, and whims of other people—and the self-imposed limitations that are keeping them from happiness.

Drop In: Lead with Deeper Presence and Courage by Sara Harvey Yao. $14.95, 978-1-63152-161-4. A compelling explanation about why being present is so challenging and how leaders can access clarity, connection, and courage in the midst of their chaotic lives, inside and outside of work.

The Thriver's Edge: Seven Keys to Transform the Way You Live, Love, and Lead by Donna Stoneham. $16.95, 978-1-63152-980-1. A "coach in a book" from master executive coach and leadership expert Dr. Donna Stoneham, *The Thriver's Edge* outlines a practical road map to breaking free of the barriers keeping you from being everything you're capable of being.

The Self-Care Solution: A Modern Mother's Must-Have Guide to Health and Well-Being by Julie Burton. $16.95, 978-1-63152-068-6. Full of essential physical, emotional and relational self-care tools—and based on research by the author that includes a survey of hundreds of moms—this book is a life raft for moms who often feel like they are drowning in the sea of motherhood.